Heinrich Bedford-Strohm, Pascal Bataringaya,
Traugott Jähnichen (Eds.)

Reconciliation and Just Peace

Theologie in der Öffentlichkeit
Theology in the Public Square

herausgegeben von / edited by

Band/Volume 9

LIT

Reconciliation and Just Peace

Impulses of the Theology of Dietrich Bonhoeffer for the European and African Context

edited by

Heinrich Bedford-Strohm, Pascal Bataringaya, Traugott Jähnichen

LIT

Bibliographic information published by the Deutsche Nationalbibliothek
The Deutsche Nationalbibliothek lists this publication in the Deutsche Nationalbibliografie; detailed bibliographic data are available on the Internet at http://dnb.d-nb.de.

ISBN 978-3-643-90557-4

A catalogue record for this book is available from the British Library

Klosbachstr. 107
CH-8032 Zürich
Tel. +41 (0) 44-251 75 05 Fax +41 (0) 44-251 75 06
E-Mail: zuerich@lit-verlag.ch http://www.lit-verlag.ch

Distribution:

In the UK: Global Book Marketing, e-mail: mo@centralbooks.com
In North America: International Specialized Book Services, e-mail: orders@isbs.com
In Germany: LIT Verlag Fresnostr. 2, D-48159 Münster
Tel. +49 (0) 2 51-620 32 22, Fax +49 (0) 2 51-922 60 99, E-mail: vertrieb@lit-verlag.de
In Austria: Medienlogistik Pichler-ÖBZ, e-mail: mlo@medien-logistik.at
e-books are available at www.litwebshop.de

TABLE OF CONTENTS

2. Reconciliation and just peace in the perspective of Dietrich Bonhoeffer

3. The ethics of responsibility and its representatives

Preface

This volume is a documentation of the lectures, discussions and devotions which together formed the international conference on Dietrich Bonhoeffer and the impulses of his theology for a just peace and reconciliation, held in February 2014 in Karongi, Rwanda, at the »Bethanie« guesthouse of the Presbyterian Church in Rwanda (EPR). In a year which marked the 20th anniversary of the genocide in Rwanda, the theme of reconciliation formed the central focus of the conference, the first in a whole series of commemorative events to be held in the country. Discussions also dealt with the concept of a just and lasting peace, an issue which, given the ongoing violence in the Great Lakes region of Eastern Congo, continues to pose a central challenge.

The point of departure for the lectures and discussions was the question of what impulses can be gained from Dietrich Bonhoeffer's theology for both African and European contexts. The stimuli he has left us in his works lend themselves ideally to being assimilated and further developed. Of all theologians of the 20th century, Bonhoeffer is arguably the most globally influential and charismatic. His writings enjoy wide circulation and have been translated into more than twenty languages, with a total of around one million copies published. This is all the more remarkable, given that Bonhoeffer was murdered by the National Socialists at the early age of 39. In spite of his youth and his many vocational duties in church parishes, at the university, and as leader of a Confessing Church theological seminary – and the fact that he was then imprisoned in the spring of 1943 for assisting Jews flee to Switzerland – his written legacy is quite remarkable, even if parts of it, such as his »Ethics«, survive only as fragments. His writings continue to exercise enormous fascination worldwide, and their topicality is unchanged. One of the major reasons for this is the admirable coherence between his theological reflections and his actions. Bonhoeffer always put his Christian convictions into practice and, to that extent, his own life – and, to an even greater degree, his death – authenticate his writings. He constituted a prime example of what the churches consistently aim to achieve: a high level of credibility, in which there is unity of word and deed.

Finally, Dietrich Bonhoeffer is nothing less than avant-garde in the way he describes the future duties of Christianity and of the churches, especially with regard to their public responsibility. In that respect, Bonhoeffer played his part in the development of a new ethics of peace and of ethical principles for the reconciliation of social groups in the public political arena. With an ethics of responsibility as his basis, he himself took an active part in putting these duties into practice in the German context of his day. In his Ph.D. thesis, revealing the relevance of Bonhoeffer's theological ethics for the process of reconciliation in Rwanda, Pascal Bataringaya has demonstrated how these impulses are of immense significance, even for the present day and for other contexts.

In order to pursue the thinking behind these impulses of Bonhoeffer's farther and to enlarge on them for the respective contexts in central Africa and in Europe, two lectures were given on each of the topics during the conference, and then discussed in the workshops. The conference languages were English and French, so that the contributions to this volume are presented in one or other of these languages. Only the preface, the introduction and the concluding declaration appear here in English and French, thereby enabling all readers to gain a good overall impression of the lectures, discussions and conclusions of the conference. The introduction also contains brief abstracts of all contributions.

In closing, we wish to express our thanks to all those who made significant contributions to the success of the conference and the production of this volume. The EPR undertook the organisation of the conference, whereby especial thanks are due to Emmanuel Muhozi, Bienvenu Musabyimana and Louise Nyiramana. All speakers at the conference generously made their papers available to us, and Helmut Keiner, Marie-Claire Legallet-Smesny, Angéline Djiokou and James Brown have been of great assistance in proofreading the texts and reworking them linguistically. Maximilian Schell, a student of theology and psychology, took on organisational responsibilities and prepared the text for printing. We wish to express our heartfelt thanks to them all, and to Dr. Rainer of LIT-Verlag for his customary, utterly reliable cooperation. The Protestant Church of Westphalia, the United Evangelical Mission (VEM), the Evangelical Lutheran Church in Bavaria and the German section of the International Dietrich Bonhoeffer Society all supported the conference financially. The Protestant Church of Westphalia also gave us a substantial grant for printing costs. For this, too, we are immensely grateful.

Kigali / München / Bochum, im Oktober 2015

Pascal Bataringaya / Heinrich Bedford-Strohm / Traugott Jähnichen

Avant-Propos

En Février 2014 s´est tenue au Centre »Bethanie« de l'Église Presbytérienne au Rwanda (EPR) au lieu dit Karongi / Rwanda une Conférence internationale sur Dietrich Bonhoeffer et les implications de sa théologie pour une paix juste et pour la réconciliation. Dans le présent volume, nous voulons documenter les exposés et les thèmes de discussions et de méditations issus de ladite conférence. En cette année 2014 marquant la commémoration des 20 ans du génocide au Rwanda, il était évident que la question de la réconciliation soit au cœur de la conférence, pour ainsi marquer le début d´une série d'événements commémoratifs dans ce pays. Dans la même lancée, la question d'une paix juste et durable était au centre des préoccupations dans le cadre de la poursuite des violences dans l'est du Congo et qui continue d´être un défi majeur pour la région des Grands Lacs.

L´intérêt de départ ayant motivé aussi bien les exposés que les débats, portait sur la question des implications de la théologie de Dietrich Bonhoeffer dans le contexte aussi bien africain qu´européen. Les réflexions qu'il nous a léguées à travers ses œuvres peuvent faire l´objet d´une reprise productive aujourd´hui comme par le passé. Bonhoeffer est le théologien du XXe Siècle dont la renommée atteint un niveau mondial. Ses écrits ont déjà connu une assez large diffusion et ont été traduits en une vingtaine de langues, avec un tirage total de près d´un million de productions. Ceci est très surprenant pour quelqu´un comme Bonhoeffer qui n´a vécu que 39 ans. Tant en raison de son jeune âge que de la diversité de ses responsabilités professionnelles aussi bien dans les paroisses qu´à la tête du Séminaire de Formation Pastorale, dans la période entre les deux guerres et dans le cadre du complot contre Hitler - dès le printemps 1943, et enfin en tant que prisonnier – on ne pouvait s´attendre qu´il ne laisse en réalité qu´un travail rudimentaire. Et pourtant ses écrits sont d'une fascination unique et toujours d'actualité. Ceci est en partie dû au fait que Bonhoeffer, dans sa vie, a pu concilier paroles et actes; sa pensée théologique et l'action sont admirablement cohérentes. Sans oublier que Bonhoeffer a, en toute conscience, mis en application dans sa vie ses convictions chrétiennes, et dans cette mesure, ses écrits sont attestés par sa vie, et plus encore à un degré élevé, par sa mort. Il allie par excellence ce que les eglises ont toujours réclamés de crédible dans la foi, que vouloir et faire doivent former une seule et même unité.

Par ailleurs, Dietrich Bonhoeffer a très tôt formulé des questions d'avant-garde pour le christianisme en raison de sa responsabilité publique, pour ce qui concerne le développement d'une nouvelle éthique de la paix et d'un principe de rapprochement des groupes belligérants dans la société. Tant la nouvelle éthique que ce principe de rapprochement de belligérants, il a pu en trouver un reflet de manière responsable dans le contexte de l'histoire allemande. Ces considérations sont d´autant plus d'actualité que Pascal Bataringaya a pu le reprendre dans sa thèse sur la pertinence et l'importance des impulsions de Dietrich Bonhoeffer dans le processus de réconciliation et la création d'une paix juste au Rwanda.

En vu de continuer à développer les impulsions de Bonhoeffer et de les approfondir dans les contextes aussi bien africain qu´européen, deux contributions ont été présentées pour chaque thème et discutées dans les ateliers durant le séminaire. Les langues utilisées lors de la conférence étaient l'anglais et le français, et c´est ce qui explique le fait que les contributions dans ce présent volume sont soit dans l´une soit dans l´autre des deux langues. Seules la préface, l'introduction et la conclusion de la déclaration finale du séminaire sont ici imprimées en anglais et français. Ceci a pour but de permettre à tous les lecteurs d´avoir une vue d'ensemble sur les différentes présentations, discussions et résultats de la rencontre, et ce aussi grâce aux brefs résumés de toutes les contributions compris dans l'introduction qui va suivre.

L'organisation de la rencontre était placée sous la responsabilité de l'EPR, ce qui nous permet ici de remercier en particulier Emmanuel Muhozi, Bienvenu Musabyimana et Louise Nyiramana pour leur engagement. Tous les intervenants nous ont aimablement mis à disposition leurs contributions. Helmut Keiner, Marie-Claire Legallet-Smesny, Angeline Djiokou et James Brown nous ont beaucoup aidé à la relecture et à la traduction des textes. Le travail d'organisation et la mise en page ont était fait par l´étudiant en théologie et psychologie Maximilian Schell. Nos remerciements les plus sincères vont aussi au Dr Rainer des éditions LIT pour la bonne et sincère coopération dans la publication de ce travail. Nous remercions également ceux qui nous ont financièrement généreusement soutenu pour cette conférence, notamment l'Eglise Evangélique de Westphalie, l'Eglise Evangélique Luthérienne en Bavière, la Mission Evangélique Unie, sans oublier la Bonhoeffer International Society, Section Allemagne. Une importante subvention pour l'impression nous a été apportée par l'Eglise Evangélique de Westphalie. Pour tout cela, nous disons à tous un grand merci.

Kigali / Munich / Bochum, Octobre 2015

Pascal Bataringaya / Heinrich Bedford-Strohm / Traugott Jähnichen

Introduction:
On the topicality of Dietrich Bonhoeffer's theological ethics – Impulses for the African and European contexts

Traugott Jähnichen & Clemens Wustmans

The fascination exercised by Dietrich Bonhoeffer's theology continues unbroken. Since the publication in 1999 of a critical edition of his complete works in German[1], the discussion and analysis of Bonhoeffer's work has been further intensified. A whole range of new aspects and issues has been dealt with in dissertations and academic articles. In addition, a new reception of Bonhoeffer on a global level has arisen in ecclesiastical and theological contexts in which he has not hitherto played any appreciable role. One such context is central Africa where, in contrast to South Africa, the work of Dietrich Bonhoeffer has been little known until now, and where hardly any studies exist dealing with Bonhoeffer's theology. The Rwandan theologian Pascal Bataringaya is the first theologian from his country, and one of the first in the entire central African context, to have dealt intensively with Bonhoeffer's work, doing so in the course of a dissertation at the Ruhr University Bochum in Germany.[2] It was largely thanks to him that a conference was made possible in Rwanda in the spring of 2014, looking at the question of impulses from Bonhoeffer's theology both for the African and for the European contexts. Lectures and papers from both African and European perspectives and comparative discussions in the course of the conference investigated aspects of Bonhoeffer's theology from their respective contextual starting points, seeking to find in it a fruitful source of present-day orientation in church and society.

A fundamental aspect of Dietrich Bonhoeffer's theological oeuvre, not only in the context of his time and of Nazi dictatorship but also of its present-day reception, is his commitment to justice and human rights. Ever since his groundbreaking dissertation, the Bavarian regional bishop and chairman of the Council of the EKD, **Heinrich Bedford-Strohm**, one of the leading exponents of »pub-

---

[1] Dietrich Bonhoeffer Werke (DBW), ed. by Eberhard Bethge, Ernst Feil, Christian Gremmels, Wolfgang Huber, Hans Pfeifer, Albrecht Schönherr and Heinz-Eduard Tödt, Gütersloh 1986-1998. The 17th and final volume (Register und Ergänzungen) was published in 1999. The complete English-language version of DBW (Dietrich Bonhoeffer Works, English Edition [DBWE]) was published in 2014 by Fortress Press.

[2] Cf. Pascal Bataringaya: Versöhnung nach dem Genozid. Impulse der Friedensethik Dietrich Bonhoeffers für Kirche und Gesellschaft in Ruanda, Kamen 2012.

lic theology« in Europe, has dealt intensively with questions of social justice[3], and his presentation particularly addresses the socio-ethical dimension of his understanding of justice. He begins by emphasising biographical aspects of Bonhoeffer's commitment to social justice, such as the founding of a centre for unemployed youth in Berlin, for example, or his championing of the Abyssinian Baptist Church in New York. Behind these activities lies the fundamental theological decision to view reality in the light of the Word of God, and particularly from the Christologically grounded perspective »from below«, i.e. from the perspective of the poor, the suffering and the marginalised. Accordingly, a Christian lifestyle choice always also entails political consequences. This is particularly true of the commitment to justice, as Bonhoeffer quintessentially emphasised in his lecture »The Church and the Jewish question«[4], in which he calls for public proclamation by the church, support for those who are casualties of state action and, in extreme instances, direct political action.

Bedford-Strohm then goes on to discuss four models of political ethics from a theological perspective. The model of compassion follows the Biblical command to love one's neighbour, albeit often in the curtailed form of an apolitical individual ethics without reference to the social conditions which are in part responsible for producing the casualties in need of support. The opposite model is that of a fundamental critique of the prevailing social and economic system, which aims at completely overthrowing Capitalism, although hardly able to point to an alternative concept. The third model can be characterised as a socio-ethical consulting model. In it, direct political solutions for concrete challenges are developed, essentially out of Christian motivation, but without any Biblical or explicitly theological reference. The fourth model, that of »public theology«[5], emphasises the political dimension of Christian ethics, thereby setting itself apart from the compassion model, yet without allowing itself to be reduced to a fundamental critique on the one hand, or a consulting function of a technocratic character on the other. Instead, on the basis of the option for the poor, it seeks to reflect social processes and to provide a stimulus for action aimed at improving the situation of the weakest in society. Bedford-Strohm is convinced that this model is consistent with the theology and ethics of Bonhoeffer.

In concluding, Bedford-Strohm emphasises the duty of the churches to defend the dignity of a humanity created in the image of God against the inherent logic of the markets and money in a globalised world. In concrete terms, this means tearing down the »golden curtain« between North and South and working for a better future for all people, just as Bonhoeffer did in his own day.

---

[3] Cf. Heinrich Bedford-Strohm: Vorrang für die Armen. Auf dem Weg zu einer theologischen Theorie der Gerechtigkeit, Gütersloh 1993.

[4] Cf. Dietrich Bonhoeffer: Die Kirche vor der Judenfrage (1934), in: DBW 12, 349-358.

[5] Cf. Florian Höhne: Öffentliche Theologie. Begriffsgeschichte und Grundfragen (Öffentliche Theologie Vol. 31), Leipzig 2015.

In his contribution, the Anglican Bishop of Rwanda, **Jered Kalimba**, discusses how impulses arising from Bonhoeffer can be taken up for present-day challenges in Africa. His inquiry focuses especially on the model of justice in a Christian sense, which is able to overcome the often violent consequences of human justice, such as is illustrated in his introductory example from the history of the royal family in Rwanda. His basis for this is a universally acceptable understanding of justice as respecting the rights of others, being unbiased, and especially defending the collective interests of the community. In order to lend this general understanding of justice a Christian profile, Kalimba continues by giving a synopsis of Bonhoeffer's theological development, highlighting in the process his concept of »costly grace«[6] in Christian discipleship. Biographically, this is presented with reference to pivotal life choices made by Bonhoeffer, such as his decision in 1939 to forsake the safety of the USA and return to Germany, as the good shepherd who does not abandon his flock, there becoming involved in the resistance against Hitler and, within the scope of his duties, contributing towards saving Jews, activities which ultimately led to his arrest.

In his final section, Kalimba substantiates these reflections with reference to the situation of African societies, in which the collective or community plays a central role, with the result that the community is primarily entrusted with the task of establishing justice. The Truth and Reconciliation Commission in South Africa and the Gacaca courts in Rwanda are examples of this. In both processes, the core issue is one of the community reintegrating people who have publicly acknowledged their guilt, and thereby establishing justice. Forgiveness, such as Bonhoeffer in particular constantly emphasised, is the decisive theological motive in the process, aimed at bringing about reconciliation and thereby renewed community. To that extent, the church is involved in these processes, but it must be vigilant against any instrumentalisation by politics and against getting too closely involved in the business of politics. It is far rather a question of bringing to bear in society the Jesuanic ethos of reconciliation and justice, in the sense of »costly grace«. In this sense the African churches, which Kalimba compares to a river that is wide, although lacking at parts in depth, can develop their own characteristic profile. Kalimba highlights, as an impressive African model for such a profile, the Ugandan Bishop Festo Kivengere, who did not yield to the dictator Idi Amin, but remained outspoken in his proclamation of the Biblical message of justice and reconciliation, just as Bonhoeffer did in his day. Remembering exemplary witnesses of faith such as Dietrich Bonhoeffer and Festo Kivengere is all about showing unwavering adherence to and giving full commitment to the goal of achieving more justice, in reliance on the Word of God, as an act of faith (that is, of what Paul Tillich paraphrased as »the courage to be«), and irrespective of the »cost« of discipleship, which can lead to suffering.

---

[6] Dietrich Bonhoeffer: Nachfolge, ed. by Martin Kuske and Ilse Tödt (DBW 4), Gütersloh 1989, 29-43.

In her contribution, **Christine Schließer** focuses on the importance of human rights by attesting to Bonhoeffer as the first to have laid down a strongly theological and ethical foundation for universal human rights. Although historically asynchronous – Bonhoeffer was executed in April 1945, whereas the resolution of the General Assembly of the United Nations adopting the Universal Declaration of Human Rights dates from December 1948 – Schließer discusses, with reference to aspects of their content, the astonishing coincidence between this document, which is rightly described as a historic milestone, and Bonhoeffer's own deliberations. Schließer identifies Bonhoeffer's rather unexpected talk of the ultimate and the penultimate in this context as the foundation for these deliberations, a concept which undergirds the Bonhoeffer's entire work on his ethics. Both terms, differentiated from one another, but at the same time related to each other, allow Bonhoeffer to argue socio-ethically and pragmatically, yet without renouncing the theological and spiritual dimension. In their concrete elaboration, however, his deliberations bear a striking resemblance to the wording of the Declaration of Human Rights of 1948: the right to and the freedom of bodily life, protection against exploitation and torture, the right to work and property, the right to freedom of speech and assembly, education, recreation and housing – the tabular list of parallels Schließer presents is extensive.

In conclusion, Schließer is able to demonstrate how theological and secular rationales go hand in hand in Bonhoeffer's argumentation – a »bilingual« argumentation, and certainly far from insignificant as a factor in the unbroken fascination of Bonhoeffer's oeuvre even beyond its original ecclesiastical and theological contexts.

Byaruhanga Ruokoo Archangel demonstrates the extent to which Bonhoeffer's grappling with human rights in his ethics can be made to bear fruit for African contexts. By way of introduction, Archangel emphasises that, in spite of being historically asynchronous, Bonhoeffer's argumentation can be regarded as a sound base for an ethical substantiation of human rights as we understand them now. In particular, Bonhoeffer's theological and emphatically Christocentric perspective becomes a firm foundation at a point where conscience and reason are only inadequate and unsuitable as a basis for ethical argumentation. The structural idea of ascribing rights, which is equally inherent in the Universal Declaration of Human Rights and in the argumentation structure of Christian and/or theological ethics, is made clearly apparent in this concrete comparison.

Bonhoeffer is therefore seen by Ruokoo Archangel as a strong defender of human rights, even if it is necessary to view him in his respective context of time and place, which to a degree is not yet fully equivalent to the present-day understanding of human rights. The frequently highlighted conjunction of Bonhoeffer's historical situation, biography and theology thus becomes apparent once more in this particular example. Ruokoo Archangel illustrates how, even if it cannot be explicitly interpreted as defence of human rights in the modern sense, Bonhoeffer's action should be regarded as a synonym. Besides his work on his

Ethics, this is primarily attested to by his active involvement in the resistance. In this resistance, manifested in the publication of sermons and texts as well as in concrete action, Ruokoo Archangel sees Bonhoeffer as indistinguishable from present-day resistance fighters who take active measures in opposition to persons and institutions who violate human rights.

Here in particular it becomes clear where the significance of Bonhoeffer's life and work for the present-day context of African discourses can lie. Ruokoo Archangel disagrees with the assertion that Bonhoeffer's concept bears the stamp of his western context so strongly as to be irrelevant for experiential African contexts and traditions. As one example, notwithstanding a legal understanding in Africa that is more strongly aligned to the community or collective, Ruokoo Archangel opposes the construct of immutable societies in Africa that are exclusively bound to tradition. Such considerations are of significance, especially for emergent democracies in a phase of transition, to which many African states can also be said to belong. Coupled with reference to the rapidly growing importance of Christianity in Africa and, at the same time, the significance of interreligious and intercultural dialogue, Bonhoeffer's argumentation takes on great significance for Ruokoo Archangel, not least on account of his concept of »religionless Christianity«. Examples from the present day and the recent past in Uganda offer impressive substantiation of these reflections.

At present, the key impulses offered by Bonhoeffer's theological ethics for the central African context relate to the tasks of reconciliation and of establishing a just peace. The conference documented here was the first in a series of high-profile events marking the 20th anniversary commemoration of the genocide in Rwanda. In view of the socially delicate process of reconciliation, the churches in Rwanda have an important role to play and – especially thanks to the work of Pascal Bataringaya – the theology of Bonhoeffer is being discovered in this context as a new impulse to help pave the way towards reconciliation and a perspective for a lasting peace. The question involved is mainly one of how it might be possible to heal the wounds of a dramatic past in a spirit of reconciliation and of how non-violent means can be found to resolve social or even ethnic conflicts. In this regard, how guilt and blame are dealt with and, consequently, the fundamental significance of confessions of guilt have an essential role to play along the route that leads to reconciliation. In his contribution, **Pascal Bataringaya** recalls the draft Bonhoeffer drew up right in the early years of the war of a culpability confession for the German churches for the period after the end of Nazi rule, and he compares this impulse with the admissions of guilt from the Rwandan context following the genocide. In this respect, the confession of the General Synod of the Presbyterian Church in Rwanda of 1996 plays a particularly central role, as it was the first instance of a Rwandan church admitting to its share of responsibility and blame with regard to the catastrophe of the genocide. Bataringaya emphasises that true reconciliation must always be based on true confession of guilt, since public acknowledgement of the painful truth and corresponding genuine contrition are essential prerequisites for any true reconciliation. Theologically, Bataringaya takes up the notion of Bonhoeffer's critique of cheap grace[7], that is to say, his critique of a grace that does not lead to repentance and reorientation. Grace is thus ultimately squandered and rendered worthless, as it is incapable of contributing to a genuine fresh start. By contrast, the Biblical message emphasises the path of sincere penance and the possibility of a new beginning, such as Jesus demonstrated in his proclamation and in his practice of reconciliation. It is to this path of reconciliation that Christians must correspond in their respective social contexts. According to Bataringaya, in Rwanda, impulses from Bonhoeffer can help break down the attitudes of hatred and mistrust which the genocide has caused between people and social groups, and confession of guilt can open up the path to reconciliation, thereby laying the foundation for a lasting peace.

Jannika Haupt also devotes her reflections to Bonhoeffer's culpability confession, initially underlining the extent to which this text, written directly during the period of National Socialism, offers significantly greater potential for an envisaged reconciliation process than other »official« church confessions of guilt, some of them drawn up at a later date. On the basis of three examples, Haupt points to the superior value of Bonhoeffer's confession compared to these other, prominent texts. In doing so, she characterises the Barmen Theological Declaration of 1934 as a text that does not constitute a confession in the real sense and which, above all, is silent on injustice towards the Jews beyond the narrowest of church contexts. She also gives a detailed presentation of how, even in the decades following the defeat of National Socialism, the document came to be the most important church confession of the Protestant church in Germany, albeit without any changes or additions. The Stuttgart Confession of Guilt of October 1945 is described as being more of a reaction to external pressure than a confession out of free volition in terms of the historic conditions behind it – the writing of a confession of guilt by the German Protestant Church as a condition demanded for reconciliation. A lack of differentiation between the institution Church and »the people« in Germany, the missing confession of concrete responsibility and, above all, the gap where confession of guilt vis-à-vis the Holocaust ought to be, are identified by Haupt as key omissions of the Stuttgart Confession. Finally, she demonstrates with reference to the »Word of Darmstadt«, which sparked off controversy from the moment it was published in 1947, how a persistent attitude exists in dealing with guilt, seen in a refusal to make comprehensive confession, especially in relation to the Holocaust.

In a second section, Haupt turns to Jewish voices on Bonhoeffer and the confession he produced; not only as a sign of respect, but also as a means of opening up and of sensitisation to real dialogue. Particularly in the Jewish critique of Bonhoeffer, Haupt sees an opportunity to render his work fruitful and, without

[7] Cf. Ibid., 29-43.

idealising him, to regard such an undertaking more as the starting point for a process of reconciliation than as its completion. Besides cautioning to semantic attentiveness, another important aspect of this sensitising is that, when dealing with the victims, it is only legitimate to initiate the possibility of dialogue and, ultimately, of reconciliation. This is not something that can be demanded, and an attitude of openness to all possible answers must be maintained.

With regard to the perspective of establishing a just peace as the continuation of the reconciliation process and based on stages in his biography, **Clemens Wustmans** traces Bonhoeffer's genesis as a pacifist, highlighting the significance of this development in concrete terms for a modern Protestant ethics of peace following in the tradition of Bonhoeffer's theology. As so often, a remarkable conjunction can be detected between Bonhoeffer's biography and his theology, an aspect which also applies to the evolution of his attitude to the question of war and peace. The young Bonhoeffer comes across in his sermons of the late 1920 s as a traditional neo-Lutheran through and through, for whom it is self-explanatory to talk of »just war«, bedded as this is in the concept of an ordered and hierarchical world coupled with a negative anthropology. The period from 1930, when he studied at Union Theological Seminary in New York, and his encounter with Reinhold Niebuhr and Jean Lasserre, triggered Bonhoeffer's metamorphosis into a pacifist, an attitude he most clearly expressed at the Fanoe Conference of 1934. His argument was based, in a manner similar to that he had encountered in his friend Lasserre, on a rigorous concentration on the text of the Sermon on the Mount, with no relativism being tolerated. However, Bonhoeffer's pacifist position in the public debate of his church was that of an outsider. Similarly, in present-day contexts and discussions, church and theological statements on the subject of war and peace are faced with the dilemma that it is, in many cases, hardly possible to end the horror of war and violence without military intervention. In this respect, a close alliance of peace with law and justice is of prime importance, providing the tight framework –in the same sense as in Bonhoeffer's ethics – for responsible action.

The contribution by **Abednego Keshomshahara** also emphasises peace as a central task and challenge for Christian action in the world in the tradition of Bonhoeffer's ethics. He likewise highlights how Bonhoeffer reflected and lived an ethics of responsibility oriented to each respective concrete situation and combining a radical pacifism based on the Sermon on the Mount with active resistance. Keshomshahara shows how Christians and the institution Church can commit themselves to peace in the concrete situation of present-day Tanzania, emphasising in this connection the central importance of interreligious dialogue, especially between Moslems and Christians, whose coexistence in Tanzania is increasingly determined by conflicts, particularly as propagated by radical Moslem forces. At the same time, he sees the task of the church as being to speak with a prophetic voice against injustice and oppression and to break the cycle of vengeance and retribution. Keshomshahara emphasises the comprehensive manner in which the task of bringing about peace must be understood. It is just as necessary to appreciate the reality of interreligious coexistence and of poverty as it is, for example, to combat the problem of immense debt amongst the poor and the poorest of the poor as sources of conflict. For a Christian to recognise peace as a challenge must involve rising to this challenge at all the various levels as it relates to each individual, to family and community, to church and mosque, and to national and international perspectives.

A further focus in the content of contributions to the conference deals with Bonhoeffer's ethics of responsibility and raises the question of the agents capable of putting these ethical impulses into practice. In his contribution, **Traugott Jähnichen** traces the terms responsibility and civil courage, which took on groundbreaking significance for Bonhoeffer, and shows how a mutual inference exists between Bonhoeffer's concrete involvement as part of the military resistance against Hitler and his theological reflections. According to Bonhoeffer, responsibility and civil courage involve constant readiness to move beyond the immediate realm of one's specific professional responsibilities, insofar as fundamental ground elements of justice and human rights are violated. Bonhoeffer saw the National Socialist dictatorship with its crimes of racism and genocide as a manifestation of evil in his time, which it is the duty of Christians to resist with all their might. However, he frequently noted the absence in his church and in his own social milieu of the commensurate civil courage necessary to be effectively set against this same evil. A particular challenge lay in the fact that, in borderline cases, participation in such resistance against evil could also involve the need to consider actions which, on the one hand, entailed a high risk of failure and, on the other, involved breaching divine precepts – in concrete terms, thc prohibition of killing and hence an assumption of guilt. Bonhoeffer reflects on these extreme cases in remarkable logical conformity with his own practice at the time, and he attempts to outline the perspective that, in reliance upon God's forgiveness and with the objective of re-establishing the enforcement of the commandments, even a breach of these very commandments, such as an assassination attempt on the dictator, can be deemed legitimate in such extreme cases.

Bonhoeffer's questions as to who resists evil or might even be prepared to actively oppose evil[8] were initially directed towards perceptions of individual civil courage. Besides the commitment of individual Christians, the churches were, for Bonhoeffer, called to be advocates of justice, diaconal helpers for the victims of political measures and, in extreme cases, direct political agents[9], and he hoped that major support in overcoming evil would arise out of the joint action

---

[8] Cf. Dietrich Bonhoeffer: Nach zehn Jahren, in: Widerstand und Ergebung, ed. by Christian Gremmels, Eberhard Bethge, Renate Bethge in cooperation with Ilse Tödt (DBW 8), Gütersloh 1998, 17-40.

[9] Cf. Dietrich Bonhoeffer: Die Kirche vor der Judenfrage.

of the churches together. In this respect, his theological reflections – especially those formulated during his imprisonment in Berlin Tegel – concentrated heavily on the future shape of the church. In this, two aspects were particularly decisive for Bonhoeffer: on the one hand, the realisation of an ecumenical fellowship of churches and, on the other, the profile of a new ecclesiastical identity as church for others.

The practical theologian **Kai Horstmann** traces the identity of the church, specifically with regard to its pastoral identity and tasks in the context of present-day church reform efforts in Germany. With reference to the term »church for others«[10], Horstmann points out parallels between current developments in the global ecumenical debate and aspects of Bonhoeffer's Christocentric theology. Ecclesiologically, a core concept of Bonhoeffer's can be thus described: Church must always be church for others and church for the world. This concept is equally as opposed to the substitution of mere moral principles for the life of faith as it is to a privatisation of religion and piety. According to Bonhoeffer, the church's role is not so much that of a political agent shaping the world, as of qualifying individual human beings for such a world-shaping task by its proclamation of the Biblical message. Horstmann sees confession and a readiness to repent in constant and exclusive orientation on the Word of God as a central aspect of Bonhoeffer's homiletics and church action. Fully applied to concrete action, he sees the necessity for a minimum of church coupled with a maximum effect of its action for others. However, it is crucial for present-day ecclesiological thinking that Bonhoeffer's ideas are neither ignored nor de-contextualised. Especially given an awareness of changing social realities, differing perceptions and experience and concrete individualism open up the church as a sphere of freedom in people's lives; diversity for others and with others is made possible through unity in Christ.

Ulrich Möller addresses the question of the ecumenical future of the church based on Bonhoeffer's thinking. He links this to the substantially and institutionally distinct ecumenical profile of his church, the Protestant Church of Westphalia. His lecture in Karongi was delivered in the context of a trip by the leadership of the Church of Westphalia to Eastern Congo and Rwanda, which included participation in the international Bonhoeffer conference. In his contribution, Möller points out how far-reaching stimuli have arisen from Bonhoeffer's visions, not only in Fanö, in the founding of the World Council of Churches in 1948, and in the ecumenical movements of the 1970 s and 80 s, but also down to our own day. He sees the current emphasis on questions of justice in all their facets as an important input for ecumenical discourses in the churches of the global South. With reference to the Biblical approach in Chapter 4 of the Letter to the Ephesians, Möller identifies a correspondence to the conflicts, crises and challenges of the present, from climate change to global financial crises.

---

[10] Cf. Eberhard Hauschildt / Uta Pohl-Patalong: Kirche, Gütersloh 2013.

Given this, the particular relevance of the 2013 declaration of the World Council of Churches in Busan becomes clear, which recognises the call to unity in Christ as an obligation for Christian commitment for a just peace and the integrity of creation.

Taking John 17:21 as his starting point – Jesus' prayer that the faithful may all be one in accordance with the unity of the Father and the Son through the Spirit – **Vincent M. Barhatulirwa** reflects in his contribution on questions of the theological foundation and consequences of a growing ecumenicity for the future of the churches. In Barhatulirwa's view, an ecumenical stance is rooted at the heart of all Christian churches, a point he substantiates with reference to ecumenical developments within Protestantism and to the unity decree of the Second Vatican Council. This is a particularly Biblically founded attitude, as references to the Pauline and Johannine writings of the New Testament in particular make clear. The unity of the faithful is a gift of the Spirit, not one that means uniformity, but one which brings about unity in the diversity of gifts and manifestations of the Spirit. To this extent, differences within the churches are not levelled off, but are far rather welcomed and serve as means to a more fully perfected unity, such as exists between the Father and the Son. In this respect, ecumenical unity is ultimately rooted in the Trinity, out of which the unity of Jesus with all his followers is nourished. This unity has as its goal that the world might believe, meaning the reconciliation of the world with God as its Creator and of the people with their neighbour and with their environment. The task of the ecumenical church is to carry this message of reconciliation into the world, just as Dietrich Bonhoeffer himself did, as an exemplary ecumenical figure, upheld by his obedience to Scripture.

The discussion of Dietrich Bonhoeffer's theology for the respective African and European contexts essentially depends on what relevance it can generate for one's own ecclesial practice and for one's own understanding of faith. This perspective was enriched by a variety of further theological impulses, by the activities in the workshops and, to no small extent, in the context of devotions.

Albert Henz, Vice President of the Protestant Church of Westphalia, who headed the delegation of his regional church already mentioned, reported on experiences of reconciliation and peacemaking responsibilities in the German context. Henz gave a critical analysis of the ultimately very reluctant development of a commemorative culture in Germany and within the Protestant church after 1945, although emphasising new insights gained from Christian-Jewish dialogue as a very special and theologically relevant benefit won from this reorientation. There is a partly biographical background to the process of reconciliation and establishing lasting peace for Henz, for he is a native of the Palatinate, a region at the border between France and Germany where not only enmity between French and Germans, as propagated in the two world wars of the twentieth century, but also personal relations between both peoples were experienced with greater immediacy than in other parts of Germany. Henz recalled how the journey towards Franco-German reconciliation began gradually, step by step, and how it came alive particularly thanks to education policy measures – especially in the form of exchange programmes – and as a result of the involvement of the churches. In this sense, the churches revised their traditional theological and ethical assessment after 1945, and evolved the perspective of a just peace as the sole Christian model for international relations. This model, which does not narrow peace down to the absence of military action, but aims to create the conditions for a lasting peace, currently determines the commitment to peace in the churches. The particular concrete forms this takes in Germany often involve support for civil crisis prevention and humanitarian aid.

A further important element in the Karongi conference, in addition to plenary discussions of the lectures documented in this volume, was the small group workshop, allowing participants to enter into discussion with each other and further explore questions raised. **Katharina Peetz** undertakes an examination in her contribution of the differences and similarities between commemorative cultures in Rwanda and Germany which were discussed there. The commemorative culture developed in Germany following the Holocaust could serve as a reference point for the lived practice in Ruanda after the genocide of 1994. The various functions of such a practice, which includes remembrance of the victims as well as the resultant »Never again!« mandate for shaping both present and future, made abundantly clear how important a culture of reconciliation and dialogue is, to no small degree inspired and shaped by Bonhoeffer's approach.

In their report, **Christine Jürgens** and **Maximilian Schell** not only document the discussion and the question of the opportunities and risks of collective confessions, but also the question of blame and responsibility for the young generation, as was discussed in a workshop amongst student participants at the conference. It is absolutely clear from this that discussing the question of guilt is far from obsolete for the respective later-born generations. It also becomes clear that the guilt and suffering of their ancestors places a concrete responsibility on the participants of the workshop. It is necessary to take a brave stand for one's own position vis-à-vis what happened, to guard against all forms of forgetting and suppression of memories, and to enable dialogue between victims and perpetrators to take place. To this extent, the considerable interest shown by students for the conference in February 2014 and for exploring Bonhoeffer and his writings and the questions of peace, reconciliation and dialogue – in Germany, in Rwanda and in Congo – gives reason to hope for a future of reconciliation and peace. A continuation of the dialogues already begun by the participants is therefore highly desirable.

Finally, devotions played a very special role during the conference, with a great deal of music and song, especially from vocal groups from Rwanda and the Congo, with meditative elements and with prayers. Pastor **Samuel Mutabazi** opened his devotions by expressing his thanks for the opportunity to draw inspiration from the life and work of the committed theologian and Christian Dietrich Bonhoeffer in the context of an international exchange. His reflection was based on Joshua 1:6-9, a text which looks at the transition of leadership from Moses to Joshua. Joshua initially considers himself inadequate for the task, anticipating how difficult the assignment that lies before him would be. He had every reason to be fearful, when the emboldening Word of God raised him up and gave him orientation: »Be strong and very courageous. Be careful to obey all the law my servant Moses gave you.« (Joshua 1:7, NIV) Just as Joshua receives a special commission, so too all Christians have a mandate to promote peace: »Blessed are the peacemakers, for they will be called sons of God.« (Matthew 5:9) Under the conditions of Nazism, Bonhoeffer attempted this in his commitment to the Confessing Church and today, according to Mutabazi, Christians are challenged, by proclaiming the validity of the divine commands, to advocate peace and justice, and especially to fight to improve the lot of the poor and the weak. In his reflection, Pastor Mutabazi passionately called all Christians to this responsibility, encouraging them – in line with God's commissioning of Joshua – to fight today against all principalities and powers which alienate and enslave. Peace and justice must be practised in everyday life, whereby the church, as Dietrich Bonhoeffer forcefully emphasised, must be especially present for the victims of social systems. Only so, as hearers of the Word of God and in the discipleship of Christ, is it possible to bring about peace and reconciliation in our societies. In all of this, the encouragement given to Joshua by God also applies to all who show a similar commitment today: »Have I not commanded you? Be strong and courageous. … for the LORD your God will be with you wherever you go.« (Joshua 1:9)

Pastor **Helmut Keiner** opened his reflection by quoting the German proverb »Blood is thicker than water«, which probably has an equivalent in almost every language, including Kinyarwanda. Most people identify themselves primarily on the basis of their extraction, their family, or their genes. However, this identity reflex results time and again in catastrophes, such as in Rwanda during the genocide. Everything that the Rwandans had previously learned, in one of the most strongly Christianised countries in Africa with 70% Christians, was forgotten.

The Gospels also tell how this relation to our »own blood« is a typically human trait that surfaces time and again. Helmut Keiner recalled two short episodes that illustrate this. In Matthew 15:21-28 it is Jesus himself who learns something new, when he finally helps a foreign woman from the Northern border of Israel. At first, he turns down her request to heal her daughter but, thanks to the tenacity of the woman, who recognises the primacy of Jesus' having been sent for the Jewish people, but who requests a small part of this for herself – just as the dogs eat the crumbs that fall from their masters' table (cf. Matthew 15:27) – he acknowledges her great faith and helps »beyond all boundaries.« A further narrative adds greater depth to this teaching, which is now passed on to the disciples (cf. Luke 9:51-57). It is evident that the teaching of Jesus always triumphs over the spirit of demarcation and enmity vis-à-vis the respective other or stranger, the identity reflex, which only acknowledges one's »own«. Such an experience also featured in Bonhoeffer's life, according to Keiner, when, as a young student in New York, he got to know a fellow French student. Together, they overcame the enmity between their peoples, which had its roots in the 19th century and had taken on a dramatic intensity during the First World War, and they came to appreciate and stimulate each other in their theological work. Keiner ended his devotions with reference to a Rwandan pastor friend of his, who felt no longer able to permit the much loved and frequently sung Rwanda song »Jye nd' Umukristo« to be sung after the genocide, and who dreamed of being able to sing this song once more someday, joyfully, candidly and from the heart: »Jye nd'Umukristo, nzahora ndi we. Mu bintu byose ngeze ku gupfa…«.

In her devotions, Superintendent **Therese Mukamakuza** made reference to Matthew 5:13-16. Following on from this injunction to Christians to be salt and light of the world, she emphasised that justice corresponds to the nature of God, for He has revealed himself as the God of justice. Accordingly, Christians and the church must practice God's justice in terms of their commissioning as salt and light of the world, overcoming oppression and injustice with love and forgiveness. As a concrete example, she recalled Bonhoeffer's lecture »The Church and the Jewish question«, where he describes establishing law and order for all members of society as an essential duty of the state. The church can only legitimise a state which does this, otherwise she must protest against its actions and, on all accounts, stand alongside the victims of state activities. This is a task which the church has frequently failed to fulfil, falling short not only in the Nazi era, but also in Rwanda during the genocide, when state power was abused for evil ends. Christians and churches were unable to either prevent or stop the genocide. More than that, some clergy and priests even went so far as to legitimise the genocide, resulting in certain parishioners murdering their Tutsi pastors. By way of contrast, Bonhoeffer's admonition that Christians and the churches must always champion the cause of the weak and the victims should be called to mind. Christians resist hatred and violence, even when this might cost them their lives. In was in this sense that Bonhoeffer spoke these words before his execution: »This is the end – for me, the beginning of life.«

The devotions led by **Jan Habinshuti van Schaardenburgh** had a markedly liturgical character: As is customary in the Rwandan church, worship began with everyone greeting each other with the word »Bavandimwe«, a term which includes both brothers and sisters and means that all take their origin from the same root. After the prayer: »Lord, make me an instrument of your peace«, van Schaardenburgh recalled a biographical turning point in the life of Dietrich Bonhoeffer, whose attitude was always one of fundamental trust in God. This trust, rooted in the motherly and fatherly love of God, finds particular expression in Psalm 131, which was prayed in unison in Kinyarwnada and English, and which formed the basis of his address, together with thoughts from the

Sermon on the Mount. Love of one's neighbour – for he is like you are, as Martin Buber's interpretative translation puts it – and love of one's enemy – for he is like you – vanquish all fear and open up paths to peace in personal and public life. A fundamental value for our personal lives is friendship, such as the paradigmatic friendship shared by Dietrich Bonhoeffer and Eberhard Bethge and to which we owe the continuing influence of impulses given by Bonhoeffer – especially in his often still random and unsorted reflections while in prison.

For his devotions, Pastor **Jörg Zimmermann** chose the Biblical watchword for the day from the Moravian Daily Texts. The *Unitas Fratrum* or Unity of the Brethren in Herrnhut, Saxony, set up the tradition of issuing a verse each from the Old and New Testaments for every day as »watchwords« or daily texts. The Old Testament text for 25th February 2014 was: »I am the Lord, and beside me there is no saviour.« (Isaiah 43:11). At first sight, this message might not seem to be fitting for an age of dialogue and tolerance. Why is the singularity of the Biblical God as a saving god emphasised to this extent? The point is to mediate to the Israelites, who have been led into Babylonian captivity, the hope of a future in which they are free. The message preached by Deutero-Isaiah is one of consolation for those who are despairing and suffering, opening up a new future for them. With this in mind, it is well worth remembering Dietrich Bonhoeffer. The power and grandiloquence of the National Socialists have perished, but the murder victim Bonhoeffer is present still, his theology and his life providing fresh inspiration, even at the heart of Africa.

Jörg Zimmermann went on to draw a line from the oppressed Israelites and Bonhoeffer's destiny to the Rwandan tragedy of the genocide. He cautiously asked whether Israel's perspective of hope in Babylon and the overthrow of National Socialism in Germany might not also offer hope for being able to cope with this tragedy Rwanda, even although this catastrophe is impossible to grasp and, for us, the God question can hardly be answered in this context. Nevertheless, the watchword is able to offer a perspective and facilitate perseverance: God is the saviour. This message can be further developed with reference to the daily text from the New Testament for 25th February 2014: »The God of our Lord Jesus Christ, the glorious Father, may give you the Spirit of wisdom and revelation, so that you may know him better.« (Ephesians 1:17). The Bible invites us to trust in God to guide the people by his Spirit to a deeper knowledge of himself.

In his inspiring closing remarks, **Elisée Musemakweli**, at the time of the conference President of the Presbyterian Church in Rwanda, and now Director of the Protestant Institute of Arts and Social Sciences in Huye (Rwanda), emphasised that, twenty years after the genocide, Rwandan society, the Rwandan churches, and the entire Great Lakes region are still in need of healing. Dietrich Bonhoeffer's theology can be of help in many respects, just as he inspired the German churches to engage in renewal after the destruction of the Nazi period. For this to happen, however, an analysis must first be made of the root causes of the tragedy in the region, the most fundamental of which – even if it is not the sole ground – Musemakweli identifies as the loss of all sense of community. If we have nothing in common, says Paul Tillich, then there is also no community and each person becomes the enemy of his neighbour. The loss of all human, social and cultural values, wherever it occurs, results in a catastrophe, such as happened in Germany and in Rwanda. Nevertheless, there are still forces and mediums of goodness and healing in all nations, a point also emphasised by Tillich, on whose work Musemakweli wrote his doctoral thesis[11]. This is why Rwanda has found the strength to rebuild and is seeking ways to renew and strengthen its social cohesion.

What role can churches and Christian faith play, both of which were incapable of preventing the catastrophe of the genocide? Musemakweli suggests two strategies. In the struggle against evil, which we are no more able to explain than the silence of God in the face of unfettered human hatred, Bonhoeffer is a prominent example for Christians of one who followed the path of suffering. He also knew what true community is, a community of sisters and brothers with Christ at its centre. It is only in the practice of living together and with a sense of universal human solidarity that the churches can serve the cause of reconciliation and lasting peace.

The second strategy is that of establishing a commemorative culture and renouncing vengeance. Remembrance is particularly able to engender the moral and spiritual strength with which to shape a new future for generations yet to come, to build a society in which the fate of every individual matters.

Musemakweli concluded by quoting Julius Nyere, the former president of Tanzania, who called for the active participation of the churches in the struggle against poverty and the marginalisation of people and peoples, without which they would be of no significance. With this in mind, according to Musemakweli, one of the outcomes of this conference must be a commitment to the cause of a lasting peace in Rwanda, in the Great Lakes region and throughout Africa.

[11] Elisée Musemakweli: Dynamique de la prédication en Afrique. Essai à partir de Paul Tillich, Yaoundé 2003.

Introduction:
De l´actualité de l´éthique théologique de Dietrich Bonhoeffer. Une impulsion pour le contexte africain et européen.

Traugott Jähnichen & Clemens Wustmans

La fascination pour la théologie de Dietrich Bonhoeffer demeure un processus ininterrompu. Depuis la publication critique de ses œuvres complètes[1] en langue allemande en 1999, la discussion autour des travaux de Bonhoeffer s´est en effet intensifiée. De nouveaux aspects et questionnements ont ensuite été relevés et discutés dans nombre de dissertations et travaux scientifiques. En plus de cela, on constate une large acceptation de Bonhoeffer au plan global dans le contexte aussi bien ecclésiastique que théologique tel que cela n´a jamais été auparavant. C´est le cas de l´Afrique centrale, où, contrairement à l´Afrique du Sud, la théologie de Bonhoeffer est demeurée peu connue et très peu de travaux s´y sont intéressés.

Le théologien rwandais Pascal Bataringaya est le tout premier théologien de son pays et même de toute l´Afrique centrale (à notre connaissance!) qui, dans le cadre de sa dissertation à l´université de Bochum en Allemagne, a travaillé entre autre sur la pensée théologique de Bonhoeffer[2]. C´est grâce à ce travail qu´en Automne 2014, un séminaire a pu avoir lieu au Rwanda, portant sur la théologie de Bonhoeffer vue sur le plan contextuel africain et européen. A travers les différents exposés selon les perspectives aussi bien africaines qu´européennes, ainsi que les débats allant dans le même sens, plusieurs aspects de cette théologie ont fait l´objet de discussions fructueuses, ce qui devait servir d´orientation et autant d´enrichissements pour l´église et la société aujourd´hui.

Un aspect fondamental des travaux théologiques de Bonhoeffer vu de son temps sous la domination de la dictature, aussi bien que dans la réception qui en est faite aujourd´hui, c´est son engagement pour la justice et les droits de l´homme.

---

[1] Dietrich Bonhoeffer Werke (DBW), édité par Eberhard Bethge, Ernst Feil, Christian Gremmels, Wolfgang Huber, Hans Pfeifer, Albrecht Schönherr et Heinz-Eduard Tödt, Gütersloh 1986-1998. 1999 parition ensuite du 17e tome: Inscriptions et ajouts. La version complète en anglais de DBW (Dietrich Bonhoeffer Works, English Edition [DBWE] parue en 2014 chez Fortress Press.

[2] Cf. Pascal Bataringaya: Versöhnung nach dem Genozid. Impulse der Friedensethik Dietrich Bonhoeffers für Kirche und Gesellschaft in Ruanda, Kamen 2012 (Réconciliation après le génocide. Vue à partir de l´éthique de paix de Dietrich Bonhoeffers au profit de l´église et de la société au Rwanda).

L´Evêque de l´Eglise Evangélique de la région de Bavière en Allemagne et membre du Conseil de l´EKD[3] **Heinrich Bedford- Strohm**, un des hauts représentants de la »théologie publique« en Europe et qui, depuis son intense dissertation révolutionnaire sur des questions de la justice sociale[4], a, dans son exposé sur l'éthique sociale, essentiellement thématisé la dimension de la compréhension de la justice sociale justement. Il met sur pied dans un premier temps l´aspect biographique de Bonhoeffer concernant l´pratique de la justice sociale, qui aura en quelque sorte abouti à la création d´un centre social pour des jeunes chômeurs à Berllin ou aussi sa participation engagée aux activités de l'Abyssian Baptist Church à New York. A l´arrière fond de ces activités se trouve la décision fondamentale de lire la réalité à la lumière de la parole de Dieu et particulièrement dans sa motivation christologique »vue d´en bas«, c´est à dire en prenant en compte les pauvres, les victimes de la souffrance et les marginalisés. Par conséquent, le mode de vie chrétien ne va pas sans avoir des conséquences politiques. Ceci est aussi vrai de l´engagement pour la justice comme l´a clairement fait Bonhoeffer, par exemple dans son exposé »L´Eglise face à la question juive« [5], dans lequel il fait appel au rôle social de l´Eglise dans son engagement d´aide aux victimes des exactions étatiques et au besoin dans le cas extrême, de faire appel à des actions politiques immédiates.

Bedford-Strohm expose dans un second temps quatre modèles de l´éthique politique vus dans la perspective théologique: Le model de la bonté du cœur suivant le commandement biblique de l´amour du prochain, malheureusement souvent réduit en une forme apolitique et individuelle, sans aucune référence aux conditions sociales, qui seraient elles aussi responsables face à des victimes qui attendent d´être protégées. Ceci a en face le modèle de la critique fondamentale du système social et économique dominant qui espère à une victoire fondamentale sur le capitalisme, sans pouvoir se référer à une contre-proposition alternative. Le troisième modèle peut se définir comme un modèle de conseil social. Ici, aux défis concrets correspondent des solutions politiques immédiates, imprégnées de motivation chrétienne, même sans un lien biblique ou théologique explicite. Le quatrième model, qui est celui du model dit de »théologie publique«[6] exprime, à la limite du model dit de Miséricorde, la dimension politique de l´éthique chrétienne, sans pour autant se laisser réduire ni à la critique fondamentale d´une part, ni à une technocratie imprégnée d´une fonction consultative d´autre part. Bien plus, elle cherchera, par contre, sur la base de l´option pour les pauvres, à mettre en exergue des processus sociaux, ainsi que

[3] L´EKD, Evangelische Kirche von Deutschland est le Conseil des Eglises Evangéliques d´Allemagne.

[4] Cf. Heinrich Bedford-Strohm: Vorrang für die Armen. Auf dem Weg zu einer theologischen Theorie der Gerechtigkeit, Gütersloh 1993.

[5] Cf. Dietrich Bonhoeffer: Die Kirche vor der Judenfrage (1934), in: DBW 12, 349-358.

[6] Cf. Florian Höhne: Öffentliche Theologie. Begriffsgeschichte und Grundfragen (Öffentliche Theologie Bd. 31), Leipzig 2015.

des impulsions pour des actions devant améliorer la situation des plus faibles dans la société. Bedford- Strohm est convaincu que ce model théologico-éthique répond bien au model Bonhoefferien.

Enfin il met en exergue le devoir de l´Eglise qui consisterait à défendre l´homme fait à l´image de Dieu dans un monde dans lequel la globalisation impose sa propre logique des marchés et des biens. Ceci signifie concrètement qu´il faut briser le rideau en or qui sépare le Nord du Sud et travailler pour un avenir meilleur de toute l´humanité, comme Bonhoeffer l´a fait en son temps.

L´évêque anglican **Jered Kalimba** du Ruanda montre dans son intervention combien les idées bonhoefferiennes aideraient dans les défis contemporains à relever en Afrique aujourd´hui. Il s´interroge spécifiquement sur le modèle de la justice dans un sens chrétien, qui soit capable de surmonter les conséquences souvent violentes de la justice humaine, comme il l´esquisse dans son introduction avec un exemple tiré de l'histoire de la famille royale au Rwanda. Il se base alors sur une compréhension générale claire de la justice dans le respect des droits des autres, de manière impartiale et qui défend en particulier les intérêts de la Communauté. Pour saisir le fond de cette justice chrétienne, Kalimba donne dans la suite un aperçu du développement de la théologie de Bonhoeffer dans lequel il conçoit sa notion de »la grâce qui coûte«[7] comme étant à la suite de celle même du Christ. Biographiquement parlant, ceci est illustré par d´importantes décisions fondamentales dans la vie de Bonhoeffer dans la mesure où, pendant les années 1939, il abandonne la sécurité qui lui avait été offerte aux Etats-Unis , et comme un bon berger qui ne laisse jamais le troupeau seul, retourne en Allemagne pour non seulement résister contre le régime d´Hitler mais aussi et surtout pour sauver les Juifs, ce qui lui aura enfin de compte valu son arrestation.

Dans une dernière étape, il cherchera à voir comment ces considérations pourraient être concrétisées dans les sociétés africaines. Dans les sociétés africaines, l´esprit de communauté joue un rôle central, ce qui explique son rôle pour le règne de la justice. Les exemples sont ici la Commission Vérité et Réconciliation en Afrique du Sud et les tribunaux »Gacaca« au Ruanda. Dans les deux cas, l´idée de base consiste en ceci que les accusées reconnaissent publiquement leurs fautes, sont de nouveau intégrés dans la société et bénéficient ainsi des bienfaits de la justice.

Ici le pardon constitue, comme Bonhoeffer le faisait si bien savoir, le motif théologique décisif pour la réconciliation et ainsi pour le fondement d´une société nouvelle. C´est dans cette mesure que l´église est impliquée dans un tel processus, mais doit aussi se protéger contre l´instrumentalisation du politique et éviter toute proximité avec les affaires politiques. Il s´agira au contraire d´aller dans le sens »de la grâce chère« pour porter l´ »Ethos christique« de la

[7] Dietrich Bonhoeffer: Nachfolge, édité par Martin Kuske et Ilse Tödt (DBW 4), Gütersloh 1989, 29-43.

réconciliation et de la justice au bénéfice de la société. Dans ce sens, les églises africaines, que Kalimba compare à une vaste rivière, bien que de temps en temps en manque de profondeur, en profitent pour développer leurs caractéristiques propres. Kalimba présente à ce propos l´évêque ougandais Festo Kivengere comme un modèle africain important, qui n´aura pas cédé au dictateur Idi Amin, et qui aura plutôt annoncé avec courage la justice biblique et la réconciliation, tout comme l´avait fait Bonhoeffer en son temps. En faisant appel à ce genre de model témoin de la foi à l´instar de D. Bonhoeffer et de Festo Kivengere, il est question d´avoir confiance en la parole de Dieu comme étant un acte de la foi, c´est à dire de courage d´être, comme Paul Tillich le réécrit si bien, quel qu´en soit le prix à payer par les suivants, et qui par ailleurs peut impliquer la souffrance, de garder inébranlablement le but à atteindre, qui conduit à plus de justice.

Dans sa contribution **Christine Schließer** se concentre sur la signification des droits de l'homme. Elle identifie Bonhoeffer comme un des premiers ayant posé des fondements solides d´une théologique éthique des droits humains universels. Malgré l´injustice de l´histoire, - Bonhoeffer est exécuté en avril 1945, alors que la déclaration universelle des droits de l´homme fait l´objet d´une résolution en Assemblée plénière des Nations Unies en décembre 1948 - Schließer s´appuie sur des éléments de contenu pour relever cette incroyable coïncidence comme étant une étape de base dans l´histoire balisée par les réalisations de Bonhoeffer. Comme fondement de ces réalisations Schließer identifie Bonhoeffer dans ce contexte à partir d´un discours plutôt inattendu portant sur des choses avant-dernières et dernière; un concept qui balise l´ensemble des œuvres éthiques de Bonhoeffer.

Les deux termes se distinguent l´un de l´autre, en même temps qu´ils sont liés l´un à l´autre, permettant à Bonhoeffer de faire valoir leur réalité sociale et éthique de manière pragmatique, sans pour autant délaisser leur dimension théologico-spirituelle. Dans ses expressions, ses remarques sont similaires aux formulations de la Déclaration des droits de l'homme de 1948, de manière frappante: le droit et la liberté à la vie physique, la protection contre l'exploitation et la torture, le droit au travail et à la propriété, le droit à la liberté d'expression et au rassemblement, l'éducation, les loisirs et le logement - Schließer en fera une liste comprise dans un tableau qui en dit long sur les parallèles en question.

En fin de compte, Schließer peut montrer comment l´argumentation théologique de Bonhoeffer iront ainsi de pair avec les argumentations séculaires de ses explications - une argumentation »bifaciale« non moins importante dans la fascination dont bénéficient les œuvres de Bonhoeffer même à l´extérieur de son lieu d´origine que constitue le contexte ecclésiastique et théologique.

Byaruhanga Ruokoo Archangel montre combien cette lutte pour les droits de l´homme dans l´éthique de Bonhoeffer peut porter des fruits dans le contexte africain. Dans l´introduction de Ruokoo Archangel, il en sort que malgré l´injustice historique, l´argumentation de Bonhoeffer peut être considérée comme la base éthique du fondement des droits de l´homme tel que nous le comprenons et l´approchons dans le contexte actuel. Actuellement la perspective théologique christocentrique de Bonhoeffer aura pour ainsi dire un fondement solide, à partir de là où la conscience et la raison se donnent à suffisance comme bases d´une argumentation éthique ferme. Les idées structurelles de l´attribution des droits incluses dans la Déclaration des Droits de l´homme ainsi que l´argumentation structurelle de l´éthique chrétienne de la théologie se laissent voir de façon concrète dans cette comparaison. Ainsi, Bonhoeffer sera, pour Ruokoo Archangel, un fervent défenseur des droits de l´homme, même si on devra prendre en considération le contexte historique vu aussi bien au plan temporel qu´au plan spatial, ce qui n´est pas forcément à assimiler, à bien d´égards, à la compréhension actuelle des droits de l'homme. Les divers lieux ayant marqués la situation historique, biographique et théologique de Bonhoeffer seront aussi cités en exemple. Ruokoo Archangel montre comment les actions de Bonhoeffer, même si elles ne sont pas explicitement interprétables dans le sens moderne de la défense des droits humains, sont à considérer comme forcément proches. Puisqu´à côté de son travail éthique, il s´est surtout activement occupé à faire œuvre de résistance. En ce qui concerne cette résistance, qui se manifeste aussi bien dans la publication des prédications et des textes ainsi que dans les actions concrètes, on ne peut soustraire Bonhoeffer, selon Ruokoo Archangel, de la lutte actuelle pour la résistance contre toutes personnes ou institutions s´érigeant contre les droits humains.

A ce niveau, on peut voir clairement à quel point la vie et les actes de Bonhoeffer ont une portée significative dans les discours contextuels des sociétés africaines. Ruokoo Archangel conteste la thèse que les idées de Bonhoeffer seraient trop imprégnées du contexte occidentale et par conséquence non adaptées aux expériences contextuelles et traditionnelles africaines. Malgré qu´en Afrique le droit par exemple est essentiellement communautaire, Ruokoo Archangel s´oppose à la considération que la société ici serait immuable et prisonnière de ses traditions. Ces considérations sont fort significatives, justement pour celles des sociétés qui se trouvent dans la phase de transition vers la démocratie, comme le sont beaucoup d´états africains. Ceci est complété par la croissance significative du christianisme en Afrique, ainsi que par la place significative du dialogue interreligieux et interculturel à partir desquels, selon Ruokoo Archangel, les arguments de Bonhoeffer prennent toute leur signification, même en prenant en compte son concept d´un »christianisme irréligieux«. Des exemples tirés aussi bien du présent que du passé récent de l´Uganda rendent ces considérations plus concrètes encore et de manière impressionnante.

Pour ce qui est du contexte de l'Afrique centrale à l'heure actuelle, l´impulsion de l'éthique théologique de Bonhoeffer est essentiellement relative aux tâches de réconciliation et d'établissement d'une paix juste. La documentation de ce séminaire dans les présentes lignes constitue une première phase d´une série de rencontres marquant le souvenir des 20 ans du génocide rwandais. Dans le cadre d´un processus de réconciliation sociale plutôt difficile, les églises au Rwanda jouent un rôle important et ceci est mis à découvert – essentiellement à travers le travail de Pascal Bataringaya sur la théologie de Bonhoeffer – comme étant une nouvelle impulsion aux étapes de la réconciliation et de développement durable de la paix. Il s´agit de poser des questions significatives comme: comment peut-on travailler à transformer un passé dramatique d´un peuple en un esprit de réconciliation, et comment résoudre de manière non violente les conflits sociaux et/ou éthiques qui s´imposent. Dans ce contexte, la manière d´aborder la question de la culpabilité et dans une large mesure, la reconnaissance de la faute, devront jouer un rôle significatif vers le chemin de la réconciliation.

Pascal Bataringaya rappelle dans sa contribution l´exemple de Bonhoeffer qui, pendant la guerre, a préparé un avant-projet de reconnaissance des culpabilités des églises allemandes après la dictature nazie, qu´il compare ensuite à la reconnaissance de la culpabilité de la société ruandaise après le génocide. Dans ce contexte, l´aveu de la culpabilité au synode générale de l´Eglise Presbytérienne au Rwanda en 1996 a joué un rôle central. Car pour la première fois, une église ruandaise a reconnu sa responsabilité face au génocide. Bataringaya appuie ce point de vue en disant que la vraie réconciliation doit passer par une reconnaissance sincère des fautes. Ainsi une reconnaissance publique de la triste vérité et une repentance sincère correspondante sont un antécédent d´une sincère réconciliation. Théologiquement Bataringaya va construire avec la critique de Bonhoeffer de la »grâce à bon marché«, c´est à dire la critique portant sur une Grâce qui ne conduit pas à une conversion ou à une nouvelle orientation. Sinon de cette manière, la grâce sera amoindrie et rendue sans valeur, puisqu´elle n´aura aucunement contribué à un vrai recommencement.

En revanche, le message biblique insiste sur la façon de procéder à une repentance sincère et ainsi de permettre un nouveau recommencement, comme Jésus l´a illustré dans son enseignement et dans sa pratique de la réconciliation. Les chrétiens sont appelés à répondre à ce processus de réconciliation dans leur contexte social respectif. Selon Bataringaya, les impulsions issues des idées de Bonhoeffer peuvent contribuer dans le cas rwandais à déconstruire les comportements haineux et de méfiance entre les gens et entre les groupes sociaux issues des affres du génocide; ce n´est qu´à travers la reconnaissance des fautes que le chemin de la réconciliation peut s´ouvrir et poser ainsi la fondation solide d´une paix durable.

Jannika Haupt consacre également ses réflexions sur les plaidoyers de culpabilité de Bonhoeffer et souligne à quel degré ces pensées de Bonhoeffer, écrites dans le contexte du national socialisme, offrent encore plus de potentialités en terme de processus de réconciliation que n´importe quel autre, comme cette confession »officielle« de péché de l´église allemande partiellement écrit plus tard. A travers trois exemples, Haupt cite les confessions de Bonhoeffer comme ayant de la valeur ajoutée contrairement aux grands textes connus jusque-là. Elle caractérise la déclaration théologique de Barmen de 1934 comme un texte qui n´est pas un aveu de culpabilité au vrai sens du terme, et souligne surtout son silence à propos de l´injustice contre les Juifs en dehors du plus proche contexte de l´Eglise.

En même temps, elle travaille à voir comment dans les décennies suivantes, depuis la fin du national socialisme, le fameux document sur les aveux de l´église évangélique en Allemagne a pris de l´importance, sans pour autant connaître aucun ajout complémentaire. La déclaration de culpabilité de Stuttgart en octobre 1945 sera considérée, dans son contexte historique – condition préalable obligatoire des églises évangéliques en Allemagne pour la réconciliation – plutôt comme une réaction en réponse à une pression extérieure plutôt que comme une libre confession volontaire. Le manque de différentiation entre l´institut qu´est l´Eglise et les »êtres humains« en Allemagne, le manque de reconnaissance d´une responsabilité concrète et surtout le manque d´aveu de culpabilité à l´égard de l´Holocauste sont compris par Haupt comme une défaillance décisive de la déclaration de culpabilité de Stuttgart. En fin, elle montre, en rapport avec la publication controversée de 1947 de la déclaration de Darmstadt que, du fait d´un refus d´aveu complet de responsabilité, surtout à l´égard de l´Holocauste, une attitude responsable dans le traitement de la reconnaissance du péché continue de faire défaut.

Dans un second temps, Haupt thématise les positions juives à l'égard de Bonhoeffer avec la reconnaissance des fautes issue de ses réflexions. Elle voit ceci non seulement comme un signe de respect, mais aussi et surtout comme une ouverture et une sensibilisation à un vrai dialogue. Et même dans la critique juive adressée à Bonhoeffer, Haupt y voit une chance qui, loin d´une possible transfiguration consistant simplement à fructifier l´œuvre de Bonhoeffer, est plutôt à considérer comme le commencement d´une entreprise vers le processus de la réconciliation et non simple fait de perfection textuelle. En plus de l´attention portée sur les questions sémantiques, un aspect important de cette sensibilisation se fait voir, notamment cette prise de conscience de la possibilité d´ouverture de dialogue avec les victimes et par ricochet l´aboutissement à la réconciliation. Ceci ne peut être considéré comme clos, d´autant que les réponses possibles à y apporter restent, elles, ouvertes.

En ce qui concerne la création d´une paix juste comme suite du processus de réconciliation, **Clement Wustmans** fournit en annexe les étapes biographiques, montrant comment Bonhoeffer est devenu pacifiste ainsi que ce que cela signifie concrètement dans le développement actuel d´une éthique évangélique de paix en lien avec la théologie de Bonhoeffer. On trouve en de nombreux endroits de remarquables connexions entre la biographie et la théologie de Bonhoeffer, comme aussi pour le développement de sa position sur la question de la guerre et de la paix. Le jeune Bonhoeffer apparaitra dans les sermons à la fin des années 1920 progressivement proche de la nouvelle théologie luthérienne ; le discours sur l´idée d´une »guerre juste« est pour lui un acquis, compris dans l´ordre et de la hiérarchie du monde, en lien avec le développement d´une anthropologie négative.

Avec son séjour d´étudiant à Union Theological Seminary à New York à partir de 1930 et la rencontre avec Reinhold Niebuhr et Jean Lasserre, commence la transformation de Bonhoeffer vers le pacifisme, une attitude qui l´a impressionné surtout lors de la conférence de Fanoe en 1934. La base de ses déclarations était une rigoureuse concentration sur le texte du Sermon de la Montagne, comme il l´en avait pris connaissance de son ami Lasserre, dont il devait s´opposer par la suite à la relativisation. Dans la discussion publique de son église, le pacifiste Bonhoeffer était marginalisé: Même dans les contextes et discussions actuels, les prises de position ecclésiastiques et théologiques sur le thème de la guerre et de la paix comportent un dilemme : l´horreur de la guerre et de la violence en plusieurs endroits ne peut presque jamais terminer sans une intervention militaire. A cet égard, il serait significatif qu´il y ait un lien étroit entre la paix, le droit et la justice – dans le sens de l´éthique de Bonhoeffer – en lien étroit avec une pratique responsable.

La contribution d´**Abednego Keshomshahara** a également souligné à la suite de l´éthique de Bonhoeffer que la paix est le devoir et le défi à relever dans l´action chrétienne dans le monde. En même temps, il souligne comment Bonhoeffer dans le Sermon de la Montagne effectue la combinaison entre le pacifisme radical et la participation à la résistance active en lien avec chaque situation concrète de la responsabilité éthique. Keshomshahara montre comment les chrétiens et l´église en tant qu´institution dans la situation concrète de la Tanzanie peuvent travailler pour la paix et insiste dans ce cas concret sur la signification centrale du dialogue interreligieux et en particulier entre musulmans et chrétiens, dont la vie commune en Tanzanie est de plus en plus conflictuelle, et particulièrement aggravée par des musulmans radicaux. Il y voit à la fois dans le devoir de l´Eglise une voix prophétique contre l´injustice et l´absence de liberté d´expression, et en même de briser le cycle de la vengeance et du châtiment. Keshomshahara insiste sur l´importance de comprendre comment le travail de pacification doit se faire. Il s´agit de prendre au sérieux la vérité de la vie interreligieuse commune ainsi que le problème de la pauvreté et lutter contre les sources de conflits que constitue par exemple le problème du surendettement des pauvres et des misérables de la société. Tout chrétien qui saisit le défi lié à la conquête de la Paix, devra pouvoir s´engager à ce devoir dans ses différents niveaux, notamment au niveau individuel comme sur le plan familial, communautaire, Eglise ou Mosquée, ainsi qu´au plan national et international.

Un autre point important de la conférence porte sur l´éthique de responsabilité de Bonhoeffer qui s´interroge sur les acteurs potentiels qui traduisent dans la pratique ces impulsions éthiques. **Traugott Jähnichen** reconstruit dans sa contribution les termes du courage civil et de la responsabilité qui, pour Bonhoeffer, sont devenus des termes d´orientation, montrant comment l´engagement concret de Bonhoeffer dans le cadre de la résistance militaire contre Hitler, ainsi que ses considérations théologiques se complètent réciproquement. Selon Bonhoeffer, responsabilité et courage civil signifient être toujours prêt à aller au delà de la zone de la responsabilité professionnelle stricte, à condition que les fondements de la justice et des droits de l´hommes ne soient pas violés.

Bonhoeffer a, à son temps, compris la dictature nazie et ses crimes racistes et génocidaires comme l´expression même du mal dont les chrétiens devaient s´opposer de toutes leurs forces. Malheureusement, il lui a souvent manqué, aussi bien dans son Église que dans son environnement social immédiat, le courage civil nécessaire pour tenir contre l'effet du mal. Un défi particulier dans une telle résistance contre le mal se situait dans le fait que, dans les cas limites, on courrait d'une part un risque élevé d'échec, et de l'autre, une violation des commandements de Dieu - en particulier l'interdiction de tuer - et donc l´acceptation de porter sur soi la faute. Bonhoeffer mène alors une réflexion remarquablement cohérente sur la justification de la mise en pratique des cas extrêmes par ces temps, et essaie de dessiner les contours d´une perspective basée sur la confiance au pardon de Dieu, avec pour but de revaloriser, dans le cas extrême, un dépassement même de ces commandements, tel qu´on a pu le voir avec la tentative d'attentat contre le dictateur.

Bonhoeffer pose alors les paramètres suivants: qui résiste au mal et s´y oppose de façon active[8] doit d'abord se mettre à l'exercice du courage civil. A côté de l'engagement des chrétiens individuellement, les églises, selon Bonhoeffer devaient se constituer en défenseurs de la justice, une aide diaconale pour les victimes de la politique et à la limite devenir elles-mêmes actrices directes de la politique[9]; il espérait par là des aides essentielles pour surmonter le mal à travers l'action commune des églises. C´est dans ce contexte - en particulier dans les conditions de détention dans la prison de Berlin-Tegel – qu'il s´est consacré dans ses réflexions théologiques à mettre un accent particulier sur la forme future de l'Eglise. Deux aspects essentiels de ces réflexions ont été décisifs pour Bonhoeffer: d´une part, la mise sur pied d'une communauté œcuménique d'Eglises et d'autre part, le profil d'une nouvelle identité ecclésiale comme Eglise pour les autres.

Les questions relatives à l'identité de l'Église ont constituées la préoccupation du théologien pratique **Kai Horstmann**, en raison de l'identité pastorale et les tâches opérées dans le cadre des efforts de réformes ecclésiastiques contemporaines en Allemagne. Sous le terme »l´église pour les autres«[10] Horstmann montre des parallèles entre les développements actuels dans les débats du mouvement œcuménique mondial et des aspects de la théologie christocentrique de Bonhoeffer. Vue sur le plan ecclésiologique, une idée de base de Bonhoeffer

---

[8] Cf. Dietrich Bonhoeffer: Nach zehn Jahren, in: Widerstand und Ergebung, publ. par Christian Gremmels, Eberhard Bethge, Renate Bethge en commun avec Ilse Tödt, (DBW 8), Gütersloh 1998, P. 17-40.

[9] Cf. Bedford-Strohm: Vorrang für die Armen.

[10] Cf. Eberhard Hauschildt / Uta Pohl-Patalong: Kirche, Gütersloh 2013.

peut se réécrire de la manière suivante: l'Eglise ne peut être qu´une Eglise pour les autres et aussi une Eglise pour le monde. Cette pensée se produit en remplacement aussi bien de la foi vécue à travers de simples représentations morales qu´à l'encontre d´une privatisation de la religion et de la piété.

D´après Bonhoeffer, l´Eglise doit ainsi se présenter moins comme simple actrice politique mondiale, que comme porteuse de la proclamation du message biblique à des personnes individuelles dans le contexte d´une telle ouverture au monde. L´engagement et la volonté de se repentir dans l'orientation continue et exclusive vers la Parole de Dieu constituent, selon Horstmann, les aspects centraux de l'homilétique et de l'action de l'Église vues par Bonhoeffer. C´est lorsqu´elle s´oriente essentiellement vers l´action concrète que la nécessité d'un minimum de travail de l'Eglise produit simultanément un effet maximum de son action au profit des autres. Cependant, ce qui est décisif pour des considérations ecclésiologiques actuelles, c´est d´éviter aussi bien d'ignorer les idées de Bonhoeffer que de les sortir de leur contexte. Justement, la perception de l'évolution des réalités sociales, y compris les différentes autres perceptions et expériences ainsi que des individualités concrètes font que l'Eglise s´ouvre comme un espace de liberté dans la vie des gens. La diversité avec et pour les autres est ainsi rendue possible par l'unité dans le Christ.

Ulrich Möller aura également consacré son intervention à la question de l'avenir œcuménique de l'Eglise sur la base de considérations faites par Bonhoeffer, qu´il combine avec le contenu et le profil œcuménique institutionnel original de son église, l'Eglise évangélique de Westphalie. Son intervention à Karongi s´est fait dans le cadre d´un voyage de la direction de l'Église de Westphalie à l'est du Congo et au Rwanda, qu´il a dû ainsi combiner avec sa participation à la conférence internationale sur Bonhoeffer. Möller montre ainsi dans sa contribution comment la vision de Bonhoeffer a contribué à un élan de grande envergure non seulement dans les réflexions de base ayant portées à la création du Conseil œcuménique des Eglises en 1948 et le mouvement œcuménique des années 1970 et 80, mais aussi restent à l´origine d´impulsions nouvelles au plan mondial, et ce, jusqu'à nos jours.

Ceci se trouve être un important défi des églises chrétiennes de l'hémisphère Sud à partir duquel il voit la nécessité, dans le discours œcuménique, de mettre à présent l'accent sur les questions de justice dans toutes ses facettes. En se référant aux versets bibliques issus du quatrième chapitre de l´épitre aux Ephésiens, Möller identifie des correspondances se référant aux questions de conflits, de crises diverses et ses défis de notre temps, en passant par les questions du changement climatique aux crises financières mondiales. Dans ce contexte, l'intérêt particulier de la Déclaration du Conseil œcuménique des Eglises en 2013 à Busan est mis en exergue dans l'appel à l'unité dans le Christ comme une obligation de l'engagement chrétien pour une paix juste et pour l'intégrité de la création.

En partant de Jean 17, 21 – portant sur la prière de Jésus pour l'unité de tous les croyants en concordance avec l'unité du Père et du Fils par l'Esprit - **Vincent M. Barhatulirwa** dans son exposé mène une réflexion sur les questions de fondement théologique et les conséquences d´une œcuménicité croissante pour l'avenir des églises. Selon Barhatulirwa, la vision œcuménique se trouve ancrée au cœur même de toutes les églises chrétiennes et il en veut pour preuve le développement du mouvement œcuménique dans le protestantisme dont fait aussi clairement allusion le décret sur l´unité du Concile Vatican II. Cette attitude est particulièrement justifiée dans la Bible.

On le voit clairement lorsque l´on se réfère principalement aux écrits pauliniens et johanniques dans le Nouveau Testament. L'unité des croyants est un don de l'Esprit, ce qui ne signifie pas uniformité, mais plutôt l'unité dans la diversité des dons et manifestations de l'Esprit. À cet égard, les différences dans l'église ne seront pas nivelées, elles seront au contraire les bienvenues et serviront de chemin vers une unité plus parfaite, à l´image de celle qui se vit entre le Père et le Fils. Par ailleurs, l'unité œcuménique est en fin de compte trinitaire et nourrit l'unité de Jésus avec tous ses disciples. L'objectif de l'unité est que le monde croie, ce qui signifie concrètement la réconciliation du monde avec Dieu comme Créateur, ainsi que de l'homme avec son prochain et avec tout autre être du monde. La responsabilité de l'église œcuménique est de porter ce message de réconciliation au monde, comme Dietrich Bonhoeffer l´a fait, en tant qu´exemple de figure œcuménique, en partant de l'écoute de l'Écriture.

La discussion autour de la théologie de Dietrich Bonhoeffer dans le contexte africain comme dans celui européen vit essentiellement de la portée qu´elle peut avoir dans le développement de la pratique ecclésiologique propre à chacun des contextes, ainsi dans leur propre compréhension de la foi. Cette perspective a été enrichie par un certain nombre d´impulsions théologiques, aussi bien en ateliers que dans les différentes séances de méditations matinales.

Albert Henz, vice-président de l'Eglise Evangélique de Westphalie, qui a dirigé la délégation de son église au cours de la visite su-mentionnée, a exposé sur l'expérience de la réconciliation et de la responsabilité pour la paix dans le contexte allemand. Le développement finalement très hésitant d'une culture de commémoration en Allemagne et aussi dans l'Eglise protestante après 1945 a été décrit de façon critique par Henz. C'était surtout par le dialogue judéo-chrétien que de nouvelles connaissances et orientations pouvaient être acquises.

Le processus de réconciliation et de l'établissement d'une paix durable ont selon lui un arrière plan biographique. Henz vient du Palatinat, une région frontalière franco-allemande qui a connu la propagation des hostilités entre les deux peuples jusque dans les relations interpersonnelles pendant les deux guerres mondiales du XXe siècle, plus encore que dans beaucoup d´autres régions d´Allemagne. Henz a rappelé comment le chemin de la réconciliation franco-allemande a commencé en allant pas à pas et en particulier à travers les politiques éducatives, - notamment les programmes d'échange –. Ledit processus n´a en fin de compte été maintenu actif que grâce à l'implication des églises. C´est en ce sens que les églises se sont engagées dès après 1945 dans une révision des jugements théologico-éthiques traditionnelles dans la perspective d'une paix juste comme seule vision chrétienne pour les relations internationales. Cet énoncé de la mission prône que la paix ne se limite pas uniquement à l'absence de la force militaire, mais cherche à mettre en place des conditions d'une paix durable, qui témoignent de la responsabilité de l´Eglise pour la paix telle qu´elle veut se concrétiser en Allemagne, et en particulier dans l'appui à la prévention civile des crises et dans l'aide humanitaire.

Un élément important de la rencontre de Karongi, à côté des discussions plénières dont les différentes interventions sont documentées dans la présente recension aura été le travail en petits groupes pour approfondir les questions en présence. **Katharina Peetz** entreprend dans sa contribution en groupe des réflexions portant sur les différences et les similitudes des pratiques commémoratives au Rwanda et en Allemagne, telles que discutées au cours du séminaire. Le développement de la culture commémorative après l´Holocauste en Allemagne pourrait bien constituer un point de rencontre avec le génocide vécu au Rwanda en 1994, dont les différentes fonctions d'une telle pratique, impliquant aussi le souvenir des victimes tout comme le mot d'ordre qui en ressort: »plus jamais ça!«, permettent de façonner le présent et l'avenir: ce qui laisse clairement voir ce qu´est une culture de la réconciliation et du dialogue, qui en définitive s´inspire des approches de Bonhoeffer.

Christine Jürgens et **Maximilian Schell** font part de leurs expériences portant sur des questions en rapport aux chances et aux risques que comporterait une reconnaissance collective de la faute et la responsabilité de la jeune génération. Ceci est discuté dans un atelier de travail constitué d´étudiants. Il en ressort que c´est un fait clair, que la discussion sur la question de la culpabilité n´est pas une question obsolète, même pour la génération à venir. Il sera clairement démontré pendant cet atelier de travail des étudiants que les fautes et les souffrances commises par des ancêtres imposent une responsabilité concrète pour la nouvelle génération. Il en ressort la nécessité du courage à se lever pour se tenir devant sa propre responsabilité face à ces événements, pour ne donner aucun espace ni à l´oublie ni à la répression, au contraire, ouvrir des espaces de dialogues entre les victimes et leurs oppresseurs. Enfin, on souligne ici l'intérêt des étudiants pour cette rencontre de Février 2014, portant sur l'étude des écrits de Dietrich Bonhoeffer sur les questions de paix, de réconciliation et de dialogue – dans le cas concret de l´Allemagne, du Rwanda et du Congo –, qui laisse entrevoir l´espoir d´une réconciliation et d´une paix durable pour l´avenir, d´où le souhait émis par les étudiants d´une suite à cette importante rencontre.

Les moments méditatifs ont joué un rôle important au cours de ce séminaire, avec beaucoup de musique et des chants des groupes venus aussi bien du Congo que du Rwanda. Le pasteur **Samuel Mutabazi** ouvre sa méditation avec un remerciement pour la chance donnée à ce programme d´échange internationale de s´inspirer de la vie et des œuvres du célèbre théologien et chrétien Dietrich Bonhoeffer. Sa méditation se réfère à Jos.1, 6-9 qui parle de la transition de leadership de Moïse à Josué. Au début, Josué pense dans un premier temps qu´il n´est pas assez mûr pour cette mission dont il voyait déjà la portée difficile. Il devait avoir de bonnes raisons d´avoir peur, lorsque la Parole encourageante de Dieu lui fut adressée, lui offrant une orientation en ces termes: »Fortifie-toi seulement et prend courage, que tu tiennes et agisses en chaque chose selon la loi que Moïse, mon serviteur t´a prescrite« (Jos.1:7). Ainsi, tout comme Josué reçut une mission spéciale, il est de même de la mission de tous les chrétiens, celle de promouvoir la paix: »Heureux les artisans de paix, car ils seront appelés fils de Dieu« (Mt. 5,9). Pour sa part, Bonhoeffer l´a essayé dans les conditions de l'époque nazie, en s´engageant en faveur de l'Eglise confessante. Aujourd´hui, selon Mutabazi, les chrétiens sont au défi de mettre en œuvre les commandements de Dieu, en s´engageant eux-aussi pour la paix et la justice, en particulier à œuvrer pour l´amélioration de la situation des pauvres, des faibles et des plus vulnérables. Le pasteur Mutabazi, dans sa méditation, appelle avec force tous les chrétiens à cette responsabilité, similaire à celle que Dieu confia à Josué. Il s´agit aujourd'hui, d´encourager la lutte contre toutes les puissances qui asservissent et qui aliènent les gens. La paix et la justice doivent être pratiquées au quotidien, et l'Eglise, comme Dietrich Bonhoeffer l´a souligné avec force, doit être là en particulier pour les victimes des systèmes sociaux. C´est seulement de cette façon, dans l'écoute de la Parole de Dieu, et à la suite des disciples du Christ, qu´il est possible d'apporter la paix et la réconciliation dans nos sociétés. C´est ainsi que s´applique l'assurance de Dieu à Josué à tous ceux qui aujourd´hui s´engagent en ce sens : »Voici, je te l'ai commandé que tu sois fort et courageux, ... car, le Seigneur ton Dieu est avec toi dans tout ce que tu feras« (Jos 1,9).

Pasteur **Helmut Keiner** introduit sa méditation par le proverbe allemand qui dit que »le sang est plus épais que l´eau«, proverbe qui doit avoir sans doute une corrélation dans toutes les autres langues, y compris le kinyarwanda. La plupart des gens définissent leur identité par leur origine, leur famille, ou par leurs gènes. Cependant, ce reflexe identitaire conduit toujours inéluctablement aux catastrophes, comme ce fut le cas au Rwanda pendant le génocide. Tout l´enseignement chrétien, appris par les Rwandais à 80% chrétiens et ainsi un des pays les plus christianisé d´Afrique, fut alors oublié. Même dans les Evangiles, on voit que la référence à »l'appel du sang« est typiquement humaine et se décompose à plusieurs reprises. Helmut Keiner rappelle deux courtes épisodes qui illustrent ceci: En Mt.15, 21-28 où on voit Jésus lui-même arguant dans le même sens, avant de finir par venir en aide à la femme étrangère venue de la frontière nord d'Israël. Tout d'abord, elle le prie de guérir sa fille malade, et c´est seulement compte tenu de la persistance de la femme, qui de fait reconnaît la primauté de la mission de Jésus au peuple juif, mais désire aussi en bénéficier un peu - tout comme les chiens qui mangent les restes de pain qui tombent de la table de leurs maîtres (cf. Mth.15, 27), quc Jésus reconnaît la forte foi de la femme et lui vient en aide par delà les frontières.

Une autre histoire approfondit cet enseignement, qui va maintenant être transmise aux disciples, c´est celle de Luc 9: 51-57. Il sera désormais clair que l'esprit de la séparation et de l'hostilité vis-à-vis de l'étranger, entretenu par le réflexe identitaire qui veut qu´on ne reconnaisse que les siens, sera en permanence dépassé par les enseignements de Jésus. Même dans la vie de Bonhoeffer il y a eu une telle expérience, lorsqu´il fit la connaissance en tant que jeune étudiant à New York d´un camarade français. Tous les deux, ancrés dans l'histoire d'hostilité de leurs peuples ont pu surmonter l'antagonisme considérablement aiguisé durant la première Guerre mondiale entre leurs peuples respectifs. Ils ont pu s´apprécier mutuellement et devenir amis par leur travail théologique commun. La méditation termine avec l´exemple d´un ami pasteur rwandais, qui a composé un chant qui a beaucoup été aimé et chanté au Rwanda »Jye nd'Umukristo« et qui n'a plus pu être chanté après le génocide, mais dont il a rêvé de le chanter à nouveau avec cœur joie: »Jye nd'Umukristo, nzahora ndi we. Mu bintu byose Ngeze ku gupfa...«.

La méditation de la présidente de région synodale **Thérèse Mukamakuza** se réfère à Matthieu 5: 13-16. En réponse à cette invitation aux chrétiens d´être sel de la terre et lumière du monde, elle pose la justice comme correspondant à l'essence même de Dieu, parce que Dieu se révèle lui-même comme le Dieu de la justice. En conséquence, les chrétiens et l'Eglise dans leur mission de sel et de lumière sont appelés à la pratique de la justice de Dieu dans le monde, à surmonter l´oppression et l'injustice à travers l´acte d'amour et de pardon. Pour rendre ceci plus concret, elle rappelle la conférence de Bonhoeffer sur »l'Eglise et la question juive«, où Bonhoeffer le décrit comme une tâche essentielle de l'Etat pour créer le droit et l'ordre pour tous les membres de la société. L'Église ne peut légitimer un État qui n´agit pas ainsi, sinon elle se sentira obliger de protester contre ses actions, et dans tous les cas, se mettre du côté des victimes de l'action inconséquente de l'Etat.

L'Église a malheureusement souvent échoué dans sa responsabilité; elle n'a pas seulement eu des manquements pendant la période nazie, on le voit aussi durant le génocide au Rwanda devant un pouvoir d'Etat entretenant le mal. Les chrétiens et les églises n´ont pu ni prévenir le génocide encore moins chercher à l´arrêter. Oui, certains membres du clergé et des prêtres ont même légitimé le génocide au point même de demander aux membres de l'église de tuer leurs pasteurs tutsis. En revanche, il faut garder à l´esprit l'exhortation de Bonhoeffer qui veut que chrétiens et églises doivent toujours être du côté des faibles, et prendre le parti des victimes. Les chrétiens doivent résister à la haine et la violence, même si cela devra leur coûter la vie. C´est dans ce sens que Bonhoeffer a prononcé ces mots avant son exécution: »C´est ici la fin, mais pour moi, c´est le commencement de la vie«.

La Méditation faite par **Jan van Habinshuti Schaardenburg** est fortement appuyée sur des éléments liturgiques: Au début il a, comme c´est le cas dans la tradition de l´église rwandaise, accueilli l´assemblée avec le mot »Bavandimwe«, mot qui unit les frères et les sœurs et signifie que tous descendent d'une même racine. Après la prière: »Seigneur, fais de moi un instrument de ta paix«, van Schaardenburg rappelle des tournants biographiques dans la vie de Dietrich Bonhoeffer, qui l´ont toujours amené à une confiance fondamentale en Dieu.

Cette confiance qui prend sa racine dans l'amour maternel et paternel de Dieu, et exprimée en particulier dans le 131e Psaume, a été dite ensemble dans la langue Kinyarwnada et en anglais, en relation avec des paroles ayant leur essence dans le sermon sur la Montagne. L'amour du prochain, – parce qu´il est semblable à toi, d´après l´interprétation de Martin Buber, et l'amour pour l'ennemi – parce qu'il est tout aussi semblable à toi -, surmonte toute peur et ouvre des voies de la paix à la fois dans la vie personnelle et dans la vie publique. Une valeur essentielle de la vie personnelle est l'amitié dont Dietrich Bonhoeffer et Eberhard Bethge ont eu la grâce d´expérimenter de façon paradigmatique et dont nous bénéficions de la perpétuation, – pensées bien que souvent désordonnées, du fait même de son emprisonnement.

Le pasteur **Jörg Zimmermann** a tiré pour sa méditation, des paroles bibliques du jour issues du calendrier morave. La communauté des frères moraves dans sa tradition a mis en place un calendrier de versets bibliques pour chaque jour, issus de l'Ancien et du Nouveau Testament. Le texte de l´AT pour le 25.02.2014 dit ceci: »Je suis l´Eternel, et en dehors de moi il n'y a point d´autre sauveur« (Isaïe 43, 11.). Ce message ne semble pas à première vue entrer dans une ère de dialogue et de tolérance. Mais pourquoi l'unicité du Dieu biblique comme Dieu sauveur est-elle ainsi unilatéralement déclarée? Il s´agissait pour des Israélites en captivité à Babylon de passer un message d´espérance pour un avenir dans la liberté. Le message du prophète Deutero-Esaïe est un message de consolation pour les désespérés et les souffrants, afin de leur ouvrir un nouvel avenir. En ce sens, on se souviens également de Dietrich Bonhoeffer. La puissance et la suffisance des nazis sont anéanties, mais le Bonhoeffer assassiné demeure présent, grâce à sa théologie et sa vie, et continue de transmettre de nouvelles impulsions, jusqu'au cœur même de l'Afrique.

Jörg Zimmermann présente ensuite la situation des Israélites opprimés et le lien nécessaire de Bonhoeffer à la tragédie du génocide rwandais. Il s´interroge non sans précaution, de savoir si la perspective d'espérance d'Israël à Babylone et la victoire sur le national-socialisme en Allemagne ne constituent pas un espoir pour le Rwanda en vue de surmonter cette tragédie, même si une telle catastrophe est incompréhensible et la question de Dieu dans ce contexte précis reste, pour ce qui nous concerne, difficile à répondre. Après tout, le verset du jour peut donner un nouvel espoir qui nous soulagera enfin: Dieu est le sauveur. La suite message permet, en se référant au verset du jour issu du Nouveau Testament pour ce 25.2.2014 : »Le Dieu de notre Seigneur Jésus-Christ, le Père de gloire, vous accorde l'esprit de sagesse et de la révélation pour le connaître«

(Eph.1,17). Ainsi, conclut-il dans sa méditation, la bible nous invite à la confiance en Dieu, qui dirige les humains par son Esprit et par une profonde connaissance de lui-même.

Dans son impressionnante allocution de clôture, **Elisée Musemakweli**, alors président de l´Eglise Presbytérienne au Rwanda et actuellement directeur du collège protestant des arts et des sciences humaines de Huye (Rwanda), constate que la société rwandaise comme les églises rwandaises, ainsi que toute la région des grands Lacs, vingt ans après le génocide, ont encore à bien des égards besoin de guérison. La théologie de Dietrich Bonhoeffer peut être à plusieurs égards, une aide, de même qu´elle a inspiré les églises allemandes dans leur processus de renouvellement après la dictature nazis. A condition de procéder avant tout à l´analyse des causes de la tragédie dans la région, comme l´un des fondements – si ce n´est l´unique – cause de ce que Musemakweli appelle perte du sens de la communauté. Si on n'a rien en commun, comme dit Paul Tillich, alors il n'y a pas de communauté et chacun devient ennemi de l'autre. Là où toutes les valeurs humaines, sociales et culturelles sont perdues, la catastrophe s´installe, comme ce fut le cas en Allemagne et au Rwanda. Cependant, il ya toujours des forces et les transporteurs du salut dans toutes les nations en dépit des catastrophes, comme l´a mentionné Tillich ainsi que Musemakweli dans sa thèse de doctorat[11]. Grâce à tous ces exemples, le Ruanda a retrouvé la force d´un nouveau recommencement et cherche maintenant les voies de renouvellement de sa cohésion sociale.

Quels rôles pourraient jouer les églises et la foi chrétienne qui n´ont pas pu empêcher la perte de la communauté et arrêter la catastrophe du génocide ? Musemakweli propose deux stratégies : Dans la lutte contre le Mal, qui reste, comme le silence de Dieu face au déchainement de la haine humaine, difficile à expliquer, Bonhoeffer est dans ce cas un exemple remarquable pour les chrétiens, lui qui a choisi le chemin de la souffrance. En outre, il a connu ce qu´est la vraie communauté, une communauté des sœurs et des frères, avec Christ comme élément du milieu. C´est seulement dans la pratique de la vie communautaire et avec une solidarité humaine générale que les églises pourraient être au service de la réconciliation et de la paix durable.

La deuxième stratégie est la création d'une culture de la mémoire et de l'abandon de la vengeance. D´autant que la mémoire peut produire des forces morales et spirituelle afin de préparer un nouvel avenir pour les générations futures, pour développer une société dans laquelle le sort de chacun est pris en compte.

Enfin, Musemakweli cite Julius Nyerere, ancien président de Tanzanie, qui a appelé à la participation active des églises dans la lutte contre la pauvreté et la marginalisation des peuples, sans quoi elles seraient elles-mêmes vides de sens.

---

[11] Elisée Musemakweli: Dynamique de la prédication en Afrique. Essai à partir de Paul Tillich, Yaoundé 2003.

Selon Musemakweli concluant ses propos, cet exemple doit aussi être le résultat de cette conférence, pour une paix durable au Rwanda, dans la région des Grands Lacs ainsi que dans toute l'Afrique.

Justice comme guide d'orientation de l'éthique théologique

Heinrich Bedford-Strohm

1. Introduction

Parler de la justice est appropriée, voire même nécessaire dans une telle conférence internationale sur Dietrich Bonhoeffer. Je vais expliquer le pourquoi tout en vous donnant d'abord un mot introductif sur la relation qui existe entre Bonhoeffer et le thème de la justice, ensuite je vais tracer le contexte biblique en rapport avec ce thème et développer la pensée de Bonhoeffer en rapport avec ce sujet avant de réfléchir sur les conséquences concernant l'éthique politique d'aujourd'hui et enfin jeter un regard sur l'avenir.

Je vais commencer à parler de l'aspect biographique. Il existe un lien biographique spécial de Bonhoeffer et le thème de la justice sociale. Comme il était fortement influencé par son milieu social bourgeois, Bonhoeffer avait une sensibilité exceptionnelle pour les contextes de vie différents de la sienne. Cela est illustré par de nombreux aspects de sa vie, comme le travail qu'il a fait avec une classe de préparation pour la confirmation à la Zionskirche dans un district de travailleurs au centre de Berlin et sa fondation d'un club de jeunes chômeurs à Berlin-Charlottenburg en 1932. Cette fonction de la personnalité de Bonhoeffer peut également être mise en évidence en se référant à son temps qu'il a passé à Union Seminary à New York en 1930. Ce n'est pas par hasard que l'un de ses meilleurs amis pendant cette période était Frank Fisher, un étudiant afro-américain. En outre, la paroisse dans laquelle il a vécu et prêché et travaillé était celle de l'Abyssinian Baptist Church sur la rue West 138th à Harlem. Une citation d'un discours à la radio que Paul Lehmann a donné à la BBC souligne la capacité étonnante de Bonhoeffer à traverser les frontières sociales: »Ce qui était impressionnant, c'était la façon dont il (Bonhoeffer) a poursuivi la compréhension du problème à ses moindres détails à travers les livres et d'innombrables visites qu'il a faites à Harlem, à travers la participation au travail avec des jeunes Noirs, mais plus encore il s'identifiait facilement avec la communauté noire de sorte qu'il y fut reçu comme l'un des leurs.«[1]. Si l'on considère le fait que les amitiés interraciales proches étaient rares dans ce temps-là, et si nous nous rendons compte combien il est interdit aux étudiants de la Colombia University encore aujourd'hui de fouler leurs pieds sur le sol de Harlem qui n'est pas si loin, ainsi nous avons une idée claire sur la nécessité actuelle de briser les barrières sociales. Geffrey Kelly avait bien raison de comparer Bonhoeffer à l'évêque martyr Oscar Romero de l'Amérique latine dans sa »sensibilité rare

[1] Eberhard Bethge: Dietrich Bonhoeffer. Eine Biographie, 6. Édition, München 1986, 192; Voir aussi Dietrich Bonhoeffer: Vie, Pensée, Témoignage, Genève 1969, 129.

aux problèmes qui frappent une sous-classe de personnes«, puis de conclure que »les deux sont considérés comme une source d'inspiration dans les luttes actuelles pour la libération et la justice sociale«.

Il apparait clair que cette sensibilité de Bonhoeffer fait de lui encore un modèle pour nous aujourd'hui. Le regard jeté au-delà de notre propre contexte limité, non seulement avec notre esprit mais aussi avec notre cœur, constitue également une condition préalable pour nous ouvrir aux problèmes de la justice. Voilà son aspect biographique.

Le deuxième aspect concerne le domaine d'application de l'éthique chrétienne. L'une des raisons pour lesquelles les questions morales sérieuses que l'injustice pose surtout au niveau international sont minimisées, est que souvent l'on préfère de se restreindre au domaine privé lorsqu'il s'agit de notre responsabilité morale. La vie et la théologie de Bonhoeffer étaient marquées par une protestation continue contre de telles priorités. Dans un passage de son éthique, qui fait également partie de son célèbre traité dans ses lettres et documents écrits après dix ans en prison, il écrit: »En fuyant le débat public, tel ou tel peut se réfugier à l'abri de la vertu personnelle. Il ne commet ni vol, ni assassinat, ni adultère, il fait le bien selon son pouvoir. En renonçant spontanément à agir en public, il parvient à rester en deçà des limites qui le préservent du conflit. Mais ainsi, il doit fermer les yeux et les oreilles devant l'injustice qui l'entoure; ce qu'il fait ne le rassurera jamais sur ce qu'il ne fait pas. Ou il succombera à cette inquiétude, ou il deviendra le plus hyocrite des pharisiens«.[2]

On ne pourrait pas plaider plus explicitement pour la priorité aux problèmes de la justice dans nos réflexions sur une bonne vie chrétienne. En raison du caractère apparemment éloigné de ces problèmes et le fait qu'ils n'ont pas de solution, on est tenté particulièrement de les éloigner de nos vies et poursuivre la vertu privée. Bonhoeffer nous encourage à consacrer une partie importante de notre temps sur ce qui se passe autour de nous tant au niveau national qu'international. Il nous encourage à lire la Bible *et* les journaux, tel que Karl Barth l'a bien dit. C'est ainsi que les questions de justice feront partie de nos vies.

Le fait que Bonhoeffer insiste tant sur la sphère publique et politique comme thème de l'éthique chrétienne, m'amène à mon troisième aspect. Cette insistance est fondée sur une compréhension théologique très précise de la réalité. Les réflexions de Bonhoeffer sur ce sujet[3] sont si fascinantes, car elles montrent la

---

[2] Dietrich Bonhoeffer: Ethique Traduction francaise de Lore Jeanneret, Genève 1965, 45. Voir aussi Dietrich Bonhoeffer: Résistance et soumission, nouvelle édition traduite de l'allemand par Bernhard Lauret avec la collaboration de Henvry Mottu, Genève 2006, 26-28; Dietrich Bonhoeffer: Ethics, New York et al. 1995, 69 (Translation changed into inclusive language). German Original: Ethik (édité par Ilse Tödt et al.), München 1992, 66.

[3] Bonhoeffer: Ethique, chapitre »Le Christ, la réalité et le bien«, 151-172 (Ethics, 186-

pertinence de la dogmatique théologique pour des questions très concrètes de la vie. Bonhoeffer comprend la réalité du monde strictement à la lumière de la réalité de Dieu: Bonhoeffer, dans ses fragments d'éthique, écrits quelques années seulement avant son exécution par les nazis, affirme sa compréhension christologique de la réalité et souligne la nécessité de s'engager pleinement dans la réalité du monde sans simplement répéter ce que le monde dit: »Dans le Christ il nous est offert la possibilité d'avoir part à la réalité de Dieu et à la réalité du monde, mais pas l'un sans l'autre. La réalité de Dieu se révèle elle-même car elle me met entièrement dans la réalité du monde, et quand je rencontre la réalité du monde, elle est toujours déjà soutenue, acceptée et réconciliée dans la réalité de Dieu. Il s'agit d'un sens profond de la révélation de Dieu dans l'homme Jésus-Christ«.[4]

Parler de l'incarnation du Christ, pour lui, signifie parler de la réalité du monde, et la réalité du monde est que chaque moindre élément de ce monde brisé est réconcilié avec Dieu, ce qui signifie: chaque moindre élément de ce monde doit être vu à la lumière du royaume de Dieu, à la lumière de l'amour de Dieu pour le monde entier. Il n'existe aucun domaine qui est en dehors de cette réalité. Quiconque tente de diviser la réalité entre un domaine chrétien avec des lois chrétiennes et un domaine mondain avec les lois de ce monde se trompe. Bonhoeffer, se référant à certaines interprétations de la doctrine luthérienne du double royaume, critique explicitement toute approche qui propose une autonomie normative de certaines sections de la vie sociale telle que l'économie.[5]

Pour des questions de justice, cela signifie que le traitement de ces questions ne peut jamais être séparé de la foi chrétienne. Voila donc un changement de perception: quand on regarde par exemple les relations Nord-Sud, nous ne regardons pas simplement les différents acteurs heureux ou moins heureux sur le marché mondial, mais nous nous basons principalement sur une communauté humaine de frères et sœurs dans des contextes culturels et politiques différents qui ont tous un droit égal à mener une vie décente. De ce point de vue, le fait que certains vivent dans l'opulence et d'autres vivent dans la pauvreté, cela est anormal. Il s'agit d'une »possibilité impossible« (K. Barth). Ainsi, la façon dont la réalité est définie influence fortement la façon dont les problèmes très concrets sont traités.

La compréhension christologique spécifique de la réalité, pour Bonhoeffer , ne peut pas être séparée de sa réflexion souvent apellée »le point de vue d'en bas«. Cette réflexion est une conséquence directe de son expérience personnelle dans la résistance contre Hitler. Mais il interprète cette expérience à la lumière de sa

---

204).

[4] Bonhoeffer: Ethique, 157 (Ethics, 55).

[5] Cf. Wolfgang Huber: Bonhoeffer and Modernity, USQR 46 (1992), 5-19, 11-13; Ulrich Duchrow: Global Economy. A Confessional Issue for the Churches, Geneva 1987, 44-46.

compréhension christologique de la réalité.

En regardant l'histoire »d'en bas, du point de vue des exclus, des suspects , des maltraités , des sans pouvoir, des opprimés, des vilipendés – en un mot, du point de vue de ceux qui souffrent« – cette perspective combine les trois aspects de la théologie de Bonhoeffer dont j'ai parlé : c'est une conséquence de sa capacité à franchir les barrières de sa couche sociale de riches, et une dimension de sa critique de la vertu privée comme objectif principal de l'éthique chrétienne qui découle de sa compréhension christologique de la réalité. [6]

Bonhoeffer ne connaissait pas encore l'expression »option préférentielle pour les pauvres«. Cette expression vient de la Théologie de libération de l'Amérique latine des années 1970 et 1980. Mais son concept de justice est profondément façonné par elle. Je vais le montrer en donnant d'abord un bref aperçu de la raison pour laquelle le concept biblique de la justice est façonné par l'option pour les pauvres, puis je donne quelques exemples de la façon dont Bonhoeffer a été inspiré par elle.

2. Perspectives bibliques

L'option biblique pour les pauvres est devenue la phrase clé qui caractérise l'Ancien et le Nouveau Testament qui, quant à elle a gagné un large consensus dans les églises du monde entier. Aucune distorsion idéologique du témoignage biblique n'a jamais été capable d'éteindre cette caractéristique clé de la Bible si importante dans ses différentes parties.

Nous en tant que chrétiens, nous parlons d'un Dieu qui est présenté dans la Bible, inséparablement lié à une option préférée pour les pauvres. Il s'agit d'un trait important de toutes les traditions bibliques que nous pouvons suivre dès le début du développement de la foi d'Israël jusqu'au Nouveau Testament et sa mis en pratique par Jésus. Le Dieu d'Israël qui révèle son être dans le buisson ardent se définit comme celui qui va conduire son peuple de l'oppression à la liberté. La loi donnée à Israël par Dieu protège donc particulièrement les faibles, p.e. les esclaves, »parce que vous avez vous-même été en esclavage et je vous ai conduits vers la liberté«! Les prophètes se battent avec passion pour la justice. Ils critiquent le culte religieux dénué de justice:

»Je hais, je méprise vos fêtes, et je ne puis sentir vos réunions solennelles. 22 . Quand vous m'offrez des holocaustes et oblations, je ne les agrée pas, le sacrifice de vos bêtes grasses, je ne le regarde pas ... écarte de moi le bruit de tes cantiques, que je n'entende pas la musique de tes harpes. 24. Mais que le droit

---

[6] Bonhoeffer: Résistance et soumission, 40. Voir aussi l'annotation no.37. Cf. Huber: Bonhoeffer and Modernity, 12f.: »So an incarnational christology leads to a perception of the conflicting character of history with the 'view from below', as described in Bonhoeffer's famous text 'After Ten Years'«.

coule comme de l'eau, et la justice comme un torrent qui ne tarit pas.« (Am 5,21 à 24) .

Un autre passage impressionnant avec une impulsion similaire se trouve dans Esaïe. Ce passage montre comment se mettre au côté des pauvres n'est pas un sacrifice mais la source d'une vie bien accomplie:

»N'est-ce pas plutôt ceci le jeûne que je préfère: défaire les chaînes injustes, délier les liens du joug; renvoyer libres les opprimés et briser tous les jougs? N'est-ce pas partager ton pain avec l'affamé, et héberger chez toi les pauvres sans abri; si tu vois un homme nu, le vêtir, ne pas te dérober devant celui qui est ta propre chaire? Alors ta lumière jaillira comme l'aurore, et ta blessure guérira rapidement, ta justice marchera devant toi et la gloire de l'Eternel te suivra.

Ainsi tu appelleras et l'Éternel répondra; tu demanderas secours par un cri, et il dira: Me voici! Si tu bannis de chez toi le joug, le geste menaçant et les paroles méchantes, si tu te prive pour l'affamé et si tu rassasies l'opprimé, ta lumière se lèvera dans les ténèbres et l'obscurité sera pour toi comme le milieu du jour. L'Eternel sans cesse te conduira, il te rassasiera dans les milieux arides, il donnera la vigueur à tes os et tu seras comme un jardin arrosé, comme une source d'eau jaillissante dont les eaux ne tarissent pas. On reconstruira, chez toi, les ruines antiques, tu relèvera les fondations des générations passées, on t'appellera réparateur de brèches, restaurateur des chemins pour qu'on puisse habiter« (Is 58, 6-12).

Dans le Nouveau Testament, Jésus est présenté comme celui qui est venu pour prêcher l'Évangile aux pauvres. Il peut même être identifié dans ceux qui ont faim, qui ont soif, sont nus, sont malades, sont en prison et des étrangers: »En vérité, je vous le dis, tout simplement ce que vous avez fait à l'un des plus petits de mes frères et sœurs, vous l'avez fait pour moi.« (Mt 25,40).

Nous pouvons trouver une impulsion similaire également dans la théologie de Paul. Nous devons faire un effort pour comprendre les implications éthiques sociales profondes d'un Dieu dont l'incarnation sur terre se termine en victime de torture, et nous ne pouvons que prendre au sérieux la réflexion de Paul sur la croix comme étant la clé de l'action de Dieu dans le monde (1 Cor 1).

Si nous réfléchissons sur tout cela, nous ne pouvons pas comprendre que prendre soin des pauvres et des défavorisés et tous les efforts possibles pour améliorer leur situation n'est pas d'un intérêt particulier de certains chrétiens qui sont politiquement tendancieux, influencés par des théologiens biaisés. Dieu à côté des pauvres et impuissants reste la caractéristique centrale de la compréhension de Dieu. Elle reste une dimension indispensable de la foi chrétienne et de la pratique personnelle qui en dérive dans la vie de chaque chrétien, y compris ses conséquences politiques.

3. Dietrich Bonhoeffer et la Justice

Quelle est l'importance du thème de la justice pour la biographie de Bonhoeffer? Pouvons-nous dire avec Albrecht Schönherr, l'un de ses élèves à Finkenwalde, que la »passion pour la justice a façonné toute sa vie«[7]. Eberhardt Bethge a maintes fois expliqué dans sa biographie de Bonhoeffer comment la question de la justice sociale a beaucoup préoccupé Bonhoeffer déjà à un stade précoce de sa vie. Déjà en 1928 Bethge rapporte comment Bonhoeffer est touché quand il trouve des contradictions sociales à Barcelone et il se demande pourquoi il n'y a pas plus de résistance contre elle. Dans son journal Bonhoeffer décrit, comment, dans les cafés »les personnes riches et nantis, les petits bourgeois et les indigents se regardent avec méfiance Apparemment la question sociale ne préoccupe personne. La situation terrible qui prévaut dans la vieille ville en témoigne.«[8]

C'est le thème de la justice sociale, dans les années qui suivirent, qui gagne un sens beaucoup plus formateur pour Bonhoeffer que reconnaissable à première vue. On peut le voir dans le passage d'une lettre à son frère Karl Friedrich écrite le 14 Janvier 1935 qui a souvent été citée peut-être sans vraiment respecter sa qualité radicale. »Je crois savoir« – dit Bonhoeffer dans cette lettre – »que je dois réellement être clair avec moi-même et vraiment sincère avec moi si je veux vraiment prendre au sérieux le Sermon sur la Montagne.« Et il continue plus loin: »'Enfin de compte il y a des choses pour lesquelles on peut lutter sans compromis, cela vaut vraiment la peine.' Pour moi, il semble que la paix et la justice sociale sont ces choses réelles, comme le Christ est réel«.[9] La paix et la justice sociale sont des réalités comme le Christ est réel. On peut difficilement imaginer un lien plus fort qui existe entre le thème de la justice et le Christ comme une pierre angulaire de l'existence chrétienne. Dans ces passages cités il y a une radicalité qui ne permet pas de fournir une autre interprétation des textes bibliques. Bonhoeffer y fait face. »Ce que vous avez fait à l'un de ces plus petits de mes frères et sœurs, c'est à moi que vous l'avez fait« (Mt 25,40) – c'est ce souffle biblique qui a inspiré Bonhoeffer à s'engager sans compromis dans la lutte pour la justice comme une partie intégrante de son témoignage au Christ.

Il s'agissait d'un lien inséparable entre le témoignage au Christ et la passion pour la justice qui a ouvert les yeux de Bonhoeffer et les cœurs à la réalité sociale de la discrimination des Afro-Américains pendant son séjour à Union Theological Seminary de New York en 1930.Ce que cette situation lui a fait

---

[7] Albrecht Schönherr: Horizont und Mitte. Aufsätze, Vorträge, Reden. 1953-1977, München 1979, 123.

[8] Cité par Eberhard Bethge: Dietrich Bonhoeffer. Eine Biographie, 6. Auflage, München 1986, 133; voir aussi Dietrich Bonhoeffer: Vie, Pensée, Témoignage, Genève 1969, 88.

[9] Dietrich Bonhoeffer: London 1933-1935, édité par Hans Goedeking / Martin Heimbucher / Hans-Walter Schleicher (DBW 13), Gütersloh 1994, 273. Voir aussi Bethge: Bonhoeffer, 249; Dietrich Bonhoeffer: Vie, Pensée, Témoignage, Genève 1969, 174.

comprendre est exprimé dans une prédication qu'il a donnée lors de son voyage court de New York à Cuba où il a prêché dans la congrégation allemande à La Havane en 1930. Il montre une compassion authentique par rapport à la situation du monde et un espoir également authentique en Christ. Les parties du manuscrit que nous avons encore se terminent par les mots suivants:

»Les cœurs humains sous l'arbre de Noël sont très différents. Et il est probablement vrai que cette année pour la personne qui regarde autour de lui dans le monde, il lui est peut-être particulièrement étrange de célébrer Noël. Il y a un grand nombre de chômeurs sous nos yeux, il y a des millions d'enfants dans le monde qui meurent de faim et croupissent dans la misère ... Et dans nos yeux se reflète la confusion désespérée. Et pourtant Noël vient. Que cela nous plaise ou non, nous sommes ou pas dans l'ambiance du Noël, nous devons l'entendre encore: Christ le Sauveur est venu«[10]

Les mots de Bonhoeffer pourraient provenir d'une prédication d'aujourd'hui du temps de l'Avent. Ils sont explicitement liés à la venue du Christ avec le désir de justice sociale. Bonhoeffer ne parle pas de la libération politique mais jette un regard sobre sur la situation de division dans le monde sans fausse harmonie de Noël. On reconnaît déjà la semence de son engagement pour la justice sans compromis que Bonhoeffer connectera plus tard explicitement avec le Christ.

C'est surtout dans ses prédications que nous pouvons voir combien Bonhoeffer a été touché par la question de la justice sociale. Outre son expérience à New York, le contact avec les jeunes à Berlin qui se préparaient pour la confirmation provenant principalement de familles socialement défavorisées a joué un rôle important.

Dans un sermon donné le 29 mai 1932 à Berlin, il a prêché sur la parabole de l'homme riche et le pauvre Lazare (Lc 16,19-31) . Dans ce sermon, il a mis en garde contre la spiritualisation de cette parabole : »Il faut en finir avec cette spiritualisation hypocrite sans scrupules de l'Evangile. Prenez-le comme il est ou détestez-le sincèrement«! Avec des mots radicaux, il s'adresse à ceux qui essaient de fuir la protestation sociale par une pacification religieuse en faisant de promesses vides de la vie éternelle: »N'est-ce pas déjà se moquer de ceux qui vivent dans la pauvreté et la misère ici, quand on donne une promesse vide d'une vie meilleure dans un autre monde à venir? On a l'impression que ceux qui prêche ainsi veulent seulement empêcher ces gens malheureux de résister contre leur sort ici ? C'est comme s'ils affirment qu'ils sont bénis ici-bas afin qu'ils restent tranquilles sans dérangement aucun? N'est-ce pas qu'en fait cela est cynique? Ils parlent de confort céleste parce qu'ils ne veulent pas donner aux autres un confort terrestre ?«[11]

---

[10] Dietrich Bonhoeffer: Barcelona, Berlin, Amerika 1928-1931, édité par Reinhard Staats et Hans Christoph von Hase (DBW 10), München 1991, 586f.

[11] Dietrich Bonhoeffer: Ökumene. Universität. Pfarramt 1931-1932, édité par Eberhard Amelung et Christoph Strohm (DBW 11), Gütersloh 1994, 426-435. Voir aussi Geffrey

Et déjà en 1934, dans un sermon à Londres sur 2 Cor 12,9 il lance un défi à la paroisse d'adopter »la perspective d'en bas«. Il en parlera explicitement de nouveau dans ses lettres et documents qu'il rédigea en prison. La vie sera différente – dit-il. Elle sera inséparablement liée aux pauvres et aux opprimés. Le christianisme »se lève et tombe avec sa protestation révolutionnaire contre la violence, l'arbitraire et l'arrogance du pouvoir et avec son plaidoyer pour les faibles.«[12]

Il est clair que Bonhoeffer a bien vu l'engagement public de l'Eglise dans les questions de justice comme étant une obligation de l'Eglise. En avril 1933, quelques jours seulement après le premier boycott public de magasins juifs (1er avril) et après la promulgation d'une nouvelle loi contre les Juifs dans la fonction publique (7 avril), Bonhoeffer a donné une conférence aux pasteurs à Berlin qui est apparue plus tard dans un article intitulé »Die Kirche vor der Judenfrage«. Dans cette conférence, il appelle l'Eglise à l'action pour défendre ceux dont les droits sont bafoués. Il décrit trois stratégies que l'Eglise peut utiliser pour résister à l'Etat. La première consiste à rappeler l'Etat à sa responsabilité car ses mesures sont moralement inacceptables. La deuxième stratégie est de prendre en charge les victimes, car soigner les victimes de la société est toujours une obligation de l'Eglise. La troisième stratégie est, au-delà du bandage des victimes, d'aller sous la roue et bloquer le rayon de la roue.

La première stratégie que Bonhoeffer décrit, concerne la théologie publique. Dans des situations où il ya la chance de gagner l'attention du public contre l'injustice, l'Eglise doit demander à l'Etat d'agir d'une manière moralement responsable. Dans son travail ultérieur Bonhoeffer a clairement déclaré que c'était exactement la dimension publique de questions morales qui caractérise et rend possible l'action morale dans le monde :

La deuxième façon de prendre soin des victimes, venir au secours et les prendre en charge, semble être pertinente pour toutes les situations, que ce soit celles de la dictature ou celles des sociétés démocratiques. Les institutions diaconales de l'Eglise ont été mises en place et développées pour donner un cadre institutionnel à cet appel quotidien pour chaque chrétien.

Quant à la troisième stratégie, Bonhoeffer décrit, qu'il avait déjà en 1933 anticipé la situation d'après 1939, lorsque l'injustice de l'Etat est devenue si grave et si vigoureuse au point que tout effort visant à générer une résistance publique qui pourrait arrêter Hitler s'est avérée vaine. Le complot et l'assassinat du tyran semblait être la seule possibilité d'arrêter l'injustice. Il est donc tout à fait approprié que les théologies de la libération luttant contre les dictatures ont souvent fait référence à cette possibilité que Bonhoeffer décrit.

Kelly: Dietrich Bonhoeffer on Justice for the Poor, in: Weavings XVII/6, November/December 2002, 26-34, 27-30.

[12] Kelly: Justice for the Poor, 34.

Bonhoeffer – nous le savons – n'a pas pu survivre les nazis et la guerre. Il n'a pas eu la chance de grandir comme chrétien et théologien. Et ainsi il n'a pas pu nous montrer s'il aurait été devenu un activiste social. Mais je pense qu'il y a de fortes indications que s'il avait été dans une situation d'appliquer le premier chemin de l'Eglise qui ramène l'Etat à la responsabilité morale, il aurait été à la pointe de ceux qui cherchent à être les défenseurs des pauvres et des défavorisés et présenter des cas sur le plan personnel et politique. [13]

Bonhoeffer a également eu des pensées qui sont réellement tout à fait concrètes quand il s'agit des conséquences économiques de la responsabilité sociale. Dans un court document qu'il a présenté à Union Seminary sur le problème du chômage, il critique l'absence de tout règlement par l'Etat quand il s'agit de l'aide sociale aux Etats-Unis et recommande le modèle allemand, puis il ajoute: »il est évident aussi ici qu'un soutien suffisant pour les chômeurs peut être garanti uniquement par une assurance de l'Etat «.[14]

Ce passage indique comment Bonhoeffer était disposé de s'engager très concrètement dans les propositions politiques afin de mettre l'idée de justice dans la pratique, ou bien d'appliquer le concept de la justice au moins comme une idée régulatrice pour juger les stratégies politiques. Cette approche n'est pas du tout usuelle.

C'est une question ouverte de savoir comment nous pouvons relier le concept de justice sous forme d'option biblique pour les pauvres avec l'éthique politique actuelle. Quelle réponse serait dans la ligne de la pensée de Bonhoeffer. Je veux décrire quatre modèles possibles et terminer par une conclusion.

4. Justice actuelle – Quatre modèles de l'éthique politique dans la théologie chrétienne

Le modèle »Charité«

Le modèle de charité considère l'option pour les pauvres principalement, voire exclusivement, comme un appel aux chrétiens de vivre le commandement de l'amour du prochain dans leur vie quotidienne en aidant et en assistant ceux qui sont dans le besoin. Les textes bibliques reflétant l'option pour les pauvres sont lus comme des appels personnels à l'action. Les lectures politiques sont explicitement rejetées comme détournement idéologique de la compréhension de la

[13] Voir sa critique de la réduction du concept de l'amour à ses dimensions personnels: »L'amour n'est pas non plus dans la relation immédiate de personne à personne, ni dans l'intérêt qu'on porte aux individus, par opposition à un humanisme 'objectif' et impersonnel. Non seulement le domaine personnel et le domaine 'objectif' sont séparés ici de manière abstraite et non biblique.« Bonhoeffer: Ethique, 30.

[14] Bonhoeffer: Barcelona, Berlin, Amerika, 407.

Bible et sont étrangères à l'Evangile.

Le modèle de la charité a dans de nombreux cas des résultats tout à fait impressionnants. Actuellement, il pousse beaucoup de gens partout dans le monde à faire beaucoup de bien pour les personnes dans le besoin. Il génère l'empathie humaine et chrétienne sincère qui est absolument cruciale pour la mission des chrétiens d'aujourd'hui. Néanmoins, il a des lacunes importantes dont je veux en mentionner une seulement.

Le modèle de charité néglige la relation inséparable qui existe entre l'éthique individuelle et l'éthique sociale. Presque toutes les questions morales de nos jours comportent aussi bien des dimensions personnelles qu'en même temps politiques. Tout le monde qui se soucie vraiment des personnes en détresse doit se préoccuper de chercher tous les moyens pour surmonter les causes de cette détresse, y compris les causes politiques.

Ainsi, le modèle de la charité ne peut pas être un modèle approprié de mettre l'option pour les pauvres en pratique. Le deuxième modèle que je veux décrire et discuter est le modèle critique fondamentale.

Le modèle »Critique Fondamentale«

Le modèle critique fondamental relie l'option pour les pauvres inséparablement à une option politique fondamentalement opposée au capitalisme occidental. Ce point de vue considère que la pauvreté a causé la mort de plusieurs milliers de personnes chaque jour comme une conséquence directe du capitalisme mondial. Les grandes puissances du monde avec leur puissance militaire défendent le capitalisme mondial pour protéger leurs intérêts. Si la mort de tant de personnes est causée par ce système, ce que le modèle critique fondamentale fait valoir de manière plausible, alors le point de vue que l'on doit prendre à l'égard de ce système économique n'est pas d'abord une question de débat politique public, mais une question de confession, un appel à prendre parti. La réponse à cet appel n'est pas beaucoup l'implication dans le débat politique quotidien sur les meilleures stratégies politiques contre la pauvreté, mais les actes clairs de résistance et d'opposition aux privilèges du monde riche et puissant.

Il ya de bonnes raisons d'appliquer l'approche fondamentale critique à l'éthique politique. Néanmoins, ce modèle n'est pas suffisant pour mettre l'option pour les pauvres en pratique. La faiblesse décisive est son insuffisance qui réside dans la relation qui existe entre son fondement moral solide et la théorie économique et politique. Beaucoup de bons chercheurs ont argumenté que le succès du développement économique en faveur des pauvres ne dépend pas de l'option pour ou contre l'économie du libre-échange. Le succès dépend plutôt de l'utilisation intelligente de cet instrument. Peu importe qu'on soit d'accord ou pas, il doit être reconnu que les chrétiens et tous les hommes de bonne volonté qui partagent l'engagement de l'option pour les pauvres, peuvent donner de bons arguments pour l'instrument du libre-échange se trouvant dans un ensemble de règles et de règlements comme l'un des instruments pour améliorer la situation des pauvres de manière durable. Si tel est le cas, le modèle critique fondamentale n'aide pas, parce qu'il entrave le débat nécessaire sur les moyens économiques les plus appropriées pour développer une économie qui garantit une vie dans la dignité pour chaque être humain. [15]

Le deuxième modèle de critique fondamentale n'est pas – en dépit de ses forces – une approche satisfaisante, car elle ne respecte pas suffisamment la valeur du débat politique et économique dans la recherche de la vérité. Ce débat doit être fondé sur des données empiriques et le raisonnement politique et économique. C'est ce que le troisième modèle met au centre.

Le modèle »Conseil Politique«

Le modèle de conseil politique répond à un besoin qui est régulièrement exprimé par les décideurs politiques. Ils traitent des problèmes très concrets à des moments spécifiques ayant des besoins spécifiques. Ils ne sont pas principalement intéressés à l'image globale éthique, morale ou théologique, mais ils ont besoins de trouver des solutions qui fonctionnent. Le modèle de conseil politique tente de réagir à cette situation en mettant l'accent sur l'énergie du travail du groupe de penseurs pour trouver des solutions qui ont une chance d'être choisies dans le processus politique. Si l'Eglise donne des conseils politiques de cette manière, vous n'y trouverez pas d'images bibliques ou langage théologique, mais un langage qui semble être technique même s'il vise à refléter les préoccupations qui viennent d'une approche éthique chrétienne.

Il ya beaucoup à dire sur le modèle des conseils politiques. Néanmoins, le modèle de conseil politique n'est pas satisfaisant non plus. Il sous-estime l'importance de la dimension des valeurs dans la pratique politique. Même si l'amélioration de la situation des pauvres est la véritable motivation pour des conseils politiques concrets, il y a de nombreuses questions au-delà du niveau de la politique concrète qui suscite des réflexions, par exemple: L'objectif principal de l'aide aux pauvres est-il vraiment l'amélioration de leur situation matérielle? Ou la pauvreté est-elle un phénomène ayant des dimensions qui sont bien au-delà

---

[15] Pour s'informer sur le débat oecuménique au sujet de la globalisation, il faut consulter les publications suivantes: Dirkie Smit: Globalization: An orientation?, in: Dirkie Smit: Essays in Public Theology. Collected essays 1, édité par Ernst Conradi (Publications of the Western Cape, Stellenbosch 2007), 125-135; Heinrich Bedford-Strohm: Public Theology and the Global Economy. Ecumenical Social Thinking between Fundamental Criticism and Reform, in: Ned Geref: Theologiese Tydskrif 48 (2007), 8-24. Pour comprendre comment le concept de la »théologie publique« se positionne dans le débat théologique sur la globalisation, il faut consulter: Max Stackhouse: Public Theology and Political Economy in a Globalizing Era, in: William F. Storrar / Andrew R. Morton (Eds.): Public Theology for the 21st Century. Essays in Honour of Duncan Forrester, London / New York 2004, 179-194.

du matériel? Enfin qu'est-ce que toutes ces questions ont à voir avec notre anthropologie. Nous devons donc nous référer explicitement au trésor des réponses que notre tradition biblique et théologique fournit. En d'autres termes: le conseil politique sans réflexion consciente et explicite des fondements théologiques est myope et donc inapproprié.

Il nous faut donc un quatrième modèle. C'est ce que j'appelle »le modèle de la théologie publique«, et comme je l'ai déjà indiqué, c'est ce modèle que je vais proposer pour lutter contre la pauvreté.

Le modèle »théologie publique«

Le modèle de la théologie publique va de pair avec la critique fondamentale et le modèle de conseil politique car il rejette l'exigence du modèle de charité qui dit qu'il n'y a pas de rôle de l'éthique chrétienne et de l'Eglise dans la vie politique. Il affirme clairement le rôle public de l'Église comme agent de la société civile.

A la lumière du modèle de la théologie publique, l'option pour les pauvres amène à la pratique de faire le plaidoyer et fournir des conseils. Contrairement au modèle critique fondamental, il ne lie pas l'option pour les pauvres à une option politique spécifique mais y trouve la base d'un discours politique menant à des stratégies politiques également applicables pour ceux qui sont au pouvoir. Toutefois, pour être clair: l'Eglise n'est pas neutre dans le débat politique, mais se considère comme un défenseur des pauvres. L'Eglise inclut explicitement la dimension des valeurs dans sa contribution au débat public. C'est ainsi elle diffère du modèle de conseils politiques. Les moyens de ses contributions vont des déclarations publiques, quand elles ont une chance de se faire entendre, aux manifestations et même aux actes limités de désobéissance civile lorsque c'est le seul moyen de dénoncer de graves injustices.

Cependant, ce n'est que dans le modèle critique fondamentale que de tels actes sont compris comme actes de témoignage et confession et actes de résistance contre le »système« (quel que soit ce système). Dans le quatrième modèle ils servent délibérément de stratégie de communication publique dans une société démocratique promouvant des mesures politiques pour surmonter la pauvreté.

Dans ses déclarations publiques – ceci est un autre point important – le modèle de la théologie publique est bilingue. D'une part, il rend compte de ses racines bibliques et théologiques à l'aide de textes et de métaphores bibliques, et d'autre part, il montre pourquoi ses propositions et affirmations sont plausibles et donnent un sens à toutes les personnes de bonne volonté, en utilisant le langage du discours laïque. En cela, elle respecte le fait que la foi et la raison sont complémentaires et non contradictoires.

Je suis convaincu que les idées de Bonhoeffer mènent à ce quatrième modèle. Sa caractéristique est un lien spécifique entre un fondement théologique clair et une expression tout aussi claire des faits empiriques et une lecture de ces faits à la lumière d'une compréhension théologique de la réalité. Il s'agit exactement des ingrédients de la théologie et de l'éthique de Bonhoeffer.

Je ne peux pas décrire les conséquences concrètes pour l'économie mondiale maintenant. [16] Mais il est clair que notre lecture des signes des temps est profondément façonnée par notre théologie.

5. Volonté de regard vers l'avenir

Actuellement la lutte pour la justice signifie un engagement dans un débat public mondial sur la meilleure voie pour sortir de la pauvreté dans le monde. Il n'y a pas de concept politique ou économique spécifique qui mérite d'être sanctifié – qu'il soit capitaliste ou anticapitaliste. Une chose, cependant, est claire: nous sommes les acteurs et non pas l'argent ni les marchés. Nous devons utiliser l'argent et les marchés d'une manière qu'ils servent tout le monde pas seulement quelques-uns. Accepter la dynamique interne destructrice des marchés mondiaux concurrentiels qui ne peut jamais être arrêtée ou modifiée, serait une déclaration de faillite de la communauté mondiale. Ce serait sacrifier la démocratie comme le pouvoir du peuple à être les agents de l'histoire. Ce serait sacrifier la démocratie sur l'autel de la pouvoir économique.

Cela ne peut pas être une option pour les chrétiens. Les chrétiens adorent un autel différent. La Foi chrétienne affirme que Dieu est le créateur, gouverneur et rédempteur du monde. Etre témoin de Dieu dans notre temps, signifie mener activement une vie vers un monde qui reflète la dignité de chaque être humain créé par Dieu. L'énergie et la motivation pour ce témoignage vient de l'expérience de l'amour de Dieu dans l'adoration, la prière et la communion chrétienne, comme nous la vivons dans nos églises.

En outre, ce pouvoir nous pousse à tourner le dos à l'agonie, synonyme de l'impuissance face aux catastrophes, qui néglige les signes d'espoir. Il existe de nombreux exemples dans l'histoire où l'impossible est devenu réalité. Comme un Allemand qui a été témoin du novembre 1989, j'ai été béni d'en avoir eu l'expérience dans ma propre vie. Après la levée du rideau de fer entre l'Est et l'Ouest, nous sommes devant le grand défi dans notre temps de lever le rideau de fer qui sépare nos populations dans le Nord des populations du Sud.

Permettez-moi de conclure en citant de nouveau Dietrich Bonhoeffer. Ses paroles décrivent bien la sobriété passionnée avec laquelle les chrétiens sont appelés à exprimer leur volonté de gérer l'avenir, même si les circonstances sont dif-

[16] Cf. Heinrich Bedford-Strohm: Poverty, Wealth and Ecology. A Theological Perspective, in: Len Hansen / Nico Koopman / Robert Vosloo (Eds.): Living Theology. Essays presented to Dirk J. Smit on his sixtieth birthday, Stellenbosch 2011, 585-600; et Heinrich Bedford-Strohm: Poverty and Public Theology. Advocacy of the Church in Pluralistic Society, in: International Journal of Public Theology 2 (2008), 144-162.

ficiles. Au plus profond de son engagement dans la résistance contre Hitler, Bonhoeffer écrit:

»Il y a bien sûr un autre optimisme, stupide et lâche, qui doit être évité. Mais personne ne doit rendre méprisable l'optimisme en tant que volonté d'avenir, même s'il se trompe cent fois. ... Il y a des hommes qui le tiennent pour pas sérieux, et des chrétiens comme non conforme à la spiritualité, d'espérer un avenir terrestre meilleur et de s'y préparer. Ils croient au chaos, au désordre, à la catastrophe comme étant le sens des événements présents et échappent, dans la résignation ou dans une fuite pieuse hors du monde, à la responsabilité pour la vie à poursuivre, pour une construction nouvelle, pour les générations à venir. Il se peut que le Jugement dernier survienne demain, et alors nous voudrons bien cesser le travail pour un avenir meilleur, mais pas avant.«[17]

[17] Dietrich Bonhoeffer: Résistance et soumission, 38 (Dietrich Bonhoeffer: Letters and Papers from Prison, New York 1972, 15f.).

La Justice comme guide d'orientation de l'éthique théologique

Jered Kalimba

1. Introduction:

Le roi rwandais du nom de Rwabugili, rénommé à cause de ses conquêtes apprit un jour que sa mère, la reine mère était enceinte. Il se demandait comment rendre justice et sauver l'honneur de la famille, de la communauté et sauver la tradition. Ainsi, il donna l'ordre de tuer sa mère et son concubin. Avant de l'enterrer, il demanda à des sages-femmes de voir si réellement sa mère portait un enfant. Hélas, la reine mère n'était pas enceinte, elle avait été victime de la conspiration, de la jalousie et de la haine des femmes du roi. Comment rendre justice à sa mère? Rwabugili tua toutes ses femmes et toute personne impliquée dans cette affaire. Il ne resta que sa femme préférée Kanjogera qui, après la mort du roi devint reine mère. Comme le jeune roi Rutalindwa n'était pas son fils, Kanjogera, en collaboration avec ses frères de la lignée d'Abega, conspira contre son pouvoir en faveur de son propre fils Musinga. Le jeune roi fut tué et tous les grands de la lignée royale. Le coup d'état de Rucunshu, tout près de Shyogwe, fut consommé, laissant le pays dans un bain de sang. Voilà les conséquences de la justice du roi Rwabugili: le bain de sang et les vengeances sans fin dans sa famille et dans son cher pays. Les survivants du clan nyiginya s'exilèrent dans les pays voisins. De cette histoire, nous pouvons nous demander comment rendre une justice juste. La justice la plus juste, trop juste ne culmine-t-elle pas en une justice injuste?

Selon l'éthique théologique, la tâche de l'éthique est de réaliser le bien, de donner la vie tout en évitant d'attirer la mort. Le bien et la vie se trouvent dans la relation avec Christ que la grâce de Dieu suscite en l'homme qui croit. La justice juste est un pilier de l'éthique théologique, car là où il n'y a pas de justice, la paix et la réconciliation font défaut. La justice dans la Bible est désignée par SEDAQAH en hébreu, IUSTITIA en latin et DIKAIOSYNE en grec. Le terme grec DIKAIOSYNE (Juste avec, juste ensemble) désigne toute une lutte pour la justice, le respect des droits de tous, la droiture dans la vie et tout cela pour le bien-être de la société, de la communauté toute entière. Chacun, en particulier chaque croyant en Christ, doit lutter avec tout son être pour être juste, droit envers Dieu, envers lui-même, envers la communauté ou les autres, et en fin de compte envers toute la création.

Nous allons nous appuyer sur la théologie et la vie chrétienne de Dietrich Bonhoeffer pour partager et discuter sur un modèle de justice chrétienne à suivre. Bien sûr que nous allons nous heurter à des situations ambivalentes, à des entorses juridiques et des distorsions faites par Dietrich malgré lui. Dieu fait justice en devenant justicier. L'homme de son côté, peut faire sa propre justice au détriment de la normalité et de la légalité. Il peut être justicier et parfois son propre justicier. La conscience de l'homme lui-même devient son premier arbitre.

Pour entrer dans la dynamique du sujet, nous allons étayer quelques notions de la justice puis analyser les aléas de la justice dans le contexte de Dietrich Bonhoeffer et enfin discuter sur la question 'Que doit faire' l'église actuelle pour arriver à une éthique théologique qui respecte le bien-être de l'autre. Comment l'éthique théologique de Dietrich Bonhoeffer nous interpelle aujourd'hui dans notre vie chrétienne?

2. Notions préalables sur la justice.

Selon la compréhension commune du concept, la justice est une vertu qui fait qu'on respecte le droit des autres et qu'on rend à chaque personne ce qui lui appartient. Cette approche rend compte d'une dimension relationnelle et induit la fonction de la justice comme moyen pour réparer et réhabiliter la partie lésée. Rendre justice conduit à punir mais permet aussi de rétablir l'ordre. Elle réintègre le malfaiteur et lui accorde le droit et le privilège de vivre dans la société et de se réconcilier avec elle. Elle différencie le crime du criminel, même si son crime est vraiment monstrueux, la justice intervient pour distinguer le criminel du monstre. Elle se positionne comme un principe fondamental, selon lequel le criminel est un être humain destiné à vivre son humanité. Par la justice, l'homme recouvre une dignité perdue et acquiert sa liberté, en reconnaissant sa responsabilité face à ses actions et à ses réactions.

Dans ce sens, la sanction, la réparation, éléments constitutifs de la justice, sont à son service. La sanction, prise comme moyen de retrouver sa dignité, doit être considérée favorablement et acquiert une fonction pédagogique, en ce qu'elle concourt à protéger la société contre d'éventuels troubles causés par l'infraction. Cette pédagogie touche la conscience des individus constituant la société et s'avère thérapeutique non seulement pour l'offenseur mais aussi pour l'offensé, pour son entourage et par extension pour toute la société. La justice jette un pont entre le criminel et sa victime. Elle s'intercale entre ces derniers et intervient pour prévenir, contrecarrer le suicide ou la vengeance directe. Grâce à la justice, le bourreau peut réparer son crime, se faire pardonner par la victime et le cas échéant, se réconcilier avec elle.

Dans la pratique de la justice, la société fait confiance à des personnes neutres, les juges, auxquels elle donne un mandat pour gérer un cas de conflits ou de crime. Sans ces personnes médiatrices, la vie est menacée et ladite société s'embourbe dans une situation de catastrophe. La personne qui porte le mandat doit être absolument neutre. Si la balance penche du côté de l'offensé ou de l'offenseur, le porteur du mandat perd sa crédibilité, la voie de la réconciliation est faussée et les conditions requises pour rendre la justice ne sont pas remplies.

D'autres pratiques existent en matière de justice comme la grâce présidentielle et l'amnistie. Celles-ci n'ont pas les mêmes effets, elles sont avant tout des mesures de clémence permettant de libérer les détenus malgré des forfaits commis. Ces formes de justice ne favorisent pas une vraie réconciliation. Le droit de grâce reconnu par certaines constitutions aux présidents n'efface pas le crime de la personne graciée. Celle-ci demeure en situation de culpabilité ou de frustration. Pour elle et pour toute la société, le criminel demeure un accusé qui ne peut pas justifier de son innocence éventuelle. L'amnistie laisse le criminel dans un esprit de culpabilité, et l'accusé perd l'occasion de prouver son innocence. Elle implique ainsi des conséquences néfastes tant pour la victime que pour l'offenseur. L'amnistie ne guérit pas du désir de vengeance. La victime reste derrière, privée de réparation, frustrée, alors que ses bourreaux libres continuent de jouir de leurs privilèges sans crainte de poursuite judiciaire.

L'amnistie, comme forme de justice, ne fait pas appel à la prise de conscience ni du criminel ni de la victime. Elle se présente comme une sorte de pardon unilatéral accordé sans appel à la reconnaissance de la faute commise par le coupable. Pour avancer dans la voie de la réconciliation et mener une justice juste, il est souhaitable de rechercher des moyens pacifiques de résoudre les conflits avant de recourir aux moyens judiciaires.

La Bible recommande aux croyants de régler de prime abord les conflits entre eux, dans la communauté (1 Cor 6, 1-11; Mt 18). Paul rappelle que, seule, la voie de la réconciliation honore le Seigneur. Si le coupable accepte de s'humilier et de faire acte de repentance et de réparation, la victime devra renoncer à toute poursuite judiciaire, sous peine de se convertir elle-même en bourreau. La voie judiciaire n'est pas une fin en soi, mais elle peut constituer un pont pour rétablir les relations. Pour Jean Calvin, la justice, c'est d'abord celle qui vient de Dieu. Le Christ est en effet le visage de cette justice libératrice et gratifiante de Dieu. La justice est définie par Calvin comme droiture, équité ou égalité dans le traitement des hommes ainsi que dans la répartition des biens. La justice de Dieu est toujours le fondement des droits de l'homme. La Bible lie justice et liberté. Seul Dieu peut libérer l'homme de ses fantasmes, sa justice va à la rencontre d'autrui et ne l'enferme pas dans un légalisme craintif. La justice de Dieu nous appelle à construire une humanité plus fraternelle et plus solidaire.[1]

La justice doit être neutre, impartiale et éviter d'être l'instrument des vainqueurs. Sa mission première est de défendre les intérêts de la communauté, de la nation. Pour y parvenir, pour juger correctement, il faut éviter l'interférence, la pression ou l'ingérence des autorités, des partis politiques ou d'une tierce personne. Les sanctions devraient être proportionnelles aux forfaits commis. La 'justice juste' n'utilise pas de lois conçues pour nuire à une couche sociale de la

---

[1] Cf. Erich Fuchs / Christian Grappe: Le droit de résister, le protestantisme face au pouvoir, Genève 1990, 18-22.

population. De façon générale, le mauvais fonctionnement de la justice favorise les conflits.[2]

3. Approche sur la Justice et l'Ethique Théologique selon Dietrich Bonhoeffer

L'Eglise comme communauté des croyants:

Pour Dietrich Bonhoeffer, l'Eglise est une communauté et non une somme d'individus. Elle préexiste toujours à l'individu. Il va jusqu'à considérer la piété individuelle du protestantisme comme une perversion. Celle-ci conduit à poser une telle question: qu'est- ce que je gagne à aller au culte? Pour Bonhoeffer, l'Assemblée est le miracle et l'acte de Dieu. Je me trouve en premier lieu où se trouve la Parole. Ma place est dans l'Assemblée. Je ne me pose pas non plus la question, en quoi ma mère m'est utile. Je suis lié à elle tout simplement.[3] La justice doit être faite par la communauté elle-même, les conflits se résolvent dans l'Assemblée. En dehors d'elle, il n'y a rien de bon pour l'homme.

Il distingue sécularisme et sécularisation de l'Eglise. Le Sécularisme consiste à renoncer à toute forme de propriété et à tout privilège tandis la sécularisation dissout l'Eglise et l'instrumentalise pour d'autres objectifs. Ainsi l'Eglise doit lutter contre toute mainmise, en particulier de l'Etat. Sa seule arme et sa clé de voûte doit être uniquement la Parole du Christ présent dans le monde, pour la justice.

L'Eglise et l'Etat

La vraie justice de l'Eglise consiste à s'élever contre la fausse doctrine selon laquelle l'Eglise aurait, en dehors et à côté de cette unique Parole, d'autres puissances ou d'autres vérités que l'unique Parole de Dieu. Toute décision de l'Eglise doit s'assujettir à cette affirmation: »Il vaut mieux obéir à Dieu plutôt qu'aux hommes« (Actes 5,29). Tous les domaines de notre vie doivent être soumis à Jésus Christ. Pour Luther, Dieu ne veut ni ne peut laisser régner personne en dehors de lui seul. Si le pouvoir temporel a la prétention d'imposer des lois à l'âme, il empiète sur le Royaume de Dieu et ne fait qu'égarer et corrompre les âmes.[4] La vraie justice faite à l'Eglise est que celle-ci se refuse de devenir un simple rouage de l'Etat. De là, l'Eglise confessante, Bekennende Kirche, contrairement aux Deutsche Christen, proclame la Seigneurie de Jésus

---

[2] Cf. Jean-François Obembe: La conquête de la paix, stratégie du passage de la guerre à la paix, Paris 1999, 144.

[3] Cf. Fréderic Rognon: Dietrich Bonhoeffer, un modèle de foi chrétienne incarnée et de cohérence entre les convictions et la vie, Lyon 2011, 63.

[4] Cf. Fuchs / Grappe: Le droit de résister, 37.

Christ et refuse toute emprise de l'Etat.

Justice de la non-violence.

La cause de la paix dans le monde reste plus que jamais la préoccupation de Bonhoeffer. Pour lui, les frères en Christ obéissent à sa Parole, ils gardent son commandement de paix. Ils n'ont pas honte, en défiant le monde, même de parler de paix éternelle. Le chemin de la paix n'est pas celui de la sécurité. La paix est le contraire de la sécurité. Demander des garanties, c'est douter, et ce doute à son tour, conduit à la guerre. Les combats sont gagnés non par les armes mais avec Dieu. Ils sont gagnés surtout lorsque le chemin mène à la croix. Et pour Dietrich, si la guerre éclatait, il demanderait à Dieu de lui donner la force de ne pas prendre les armes.[5] Dietrich fut même tenté de rendre visite à Mahatma Gandhi, car il était convaincu que dans les méthodes de résistance non-violente, le 'païen' Gandhi avait un rôle à jouer pour le réveil de la foi chrétienne moribonde en Europe et pouvait offrir aux Allemands une alternative au totalitarisme et à la violence.

Le prix de la grâce

Comme nous avons vu auparavant la grâce présidentielle ou l'amnistie libère le criminel malgré les fautes commises mais intérieurement, il n'est pas blanchi pour autant et la victime reste angoissée par cette liberté gratuite et imméritée de son tortionnaire. Pour les deux côtés, il y a douleurs, regrets et rancœurs.

Au niveau de l'éthique théologique, la grâce est gratuite, et d'après la Réforme, elle ne coûte rien du tout car, on est sauvé par la grâce et non pas par les œuvres. Donc, le salut est un don gratuit de Dieu qu'on peut refuser ou accepter. Cependant, Dietrich interprète cette justice théologique autrement. Il distingue la 'grâce à bon marché'et la 'grâce qui coûte'. Pour lui on a tellement surévalué le salut par la grâce, qu'on en a oublié le prix. Nous nous sommes endormis sur la grâce et nous avons oublié l'obéissance au Christ. Nous l'avons remplacé par d'autres chefs, Hitler par exemple. Au lieu d'être pris pour un séducteur, il fut appelé le conducteur, le »Führer« (»guide«)et ainsi a pris la place du Christ. Dietrich dans son contexte fait remarquer: »la grâce à bon marché est l'ennemi mortel de notre Eglise. Actuellement, dans notre combat, il en va de la grâce qui coûte. La grâce à bon marché, c'est la grâce considérée comme une machine à brader, c'est le pardon au rabais, la consolation au rabais, le sacrément au rabais…c'est la grâce sans aucun prix, sans aucun coût…«.[6]

Pour Bonhoeffer, la grâce à bon marché, c'est la grâce que nous avons-nous-mêmes, sans avoir besoin de changer en quoi que ce soit notre façon de vivre, en essayant de nous conformer le plus possible au monde. Tandis que la grâce

---

[5] Cf. Rognon: Dietrich Bonhoeffer, 23-33.

[6] Ibid., 77.

qui coûte, elle coûte parce qu'elle appelle à devenir disciple du Christ. Elle coûte parce qu'elle coûte à l'être humain le prix de sa vie. Elle est chère parce qu'elle a coûté à Dieu la vie de son fils. Elle coûte parce que le pécheur repentant fait demi-tour pour suivre le Christ. Le prix de la grâce est donc une justice qui demande introspection, réparation, changement, transformation et si nécessaire sacrifice.

Le pâtre se sauve et le loup déchiquette les brebis: fuir ou rester

Jésus affirme qu'il est le bon berger car, le bon berger donne sa vie pour ses brebis, contrairement au voleur qui les laisse entre les dents des loups (Jean 10). Bonhoeffer lutte contre sa conscience. Faut-il laisser l'Eglise être anéantie par la montée des périls, l'engrenage infernal de la guerre et fuir, s'exiler aux USA ou faut-il endurer ou mourir avec les siens s'il le faut? Au lendemain de la guerre, Dietrich se trouve aux USA, il s'interroge sérieusement et doit absolument discerner profondément l'ampleur de sa vocation. Il devient en fait justicier de lui-même. Finalement, il sent que rester aux USA est une fuite. Alors que ses amis américains lui conseillent de rester à l'abri, il fait un retour précipité vers l'Allemagne. Pour lui, quoi qu'il lui en coûte, sa place est auprès de son peuple. Après cette justice faite à lui-même, Dietrich se sent serein, souriant et libéré.

Faut-il collaborer à tuer le tyran? Résistance ou soumission?

Martin Luther distingue clairement le règne spirituel et le règne temporel. La politique ne saurait prétendre régner sur les âmes. Zwingli veut préciser la tâche de l'Eglise face aux pouvoirs en disant que la justice humaine et la justice divine doivent rester constamment en relation pour se limiter et s'interpeller réciproquement.

Bonhoeffer sépare les deux règnes. Il en vint même à conspirer pour tuer le tyran. Il a pris assez de temps pour réfléchir à l'implication éthique et théologique de sa décision: rejoindre le groupe des conjurés qui préparent un attentat visant à assassiner Hitler. Pourtant il y a tant de questions à se poser quant à l'éthique théologique: Est-ce qu'un chrétien a le droit de collaborer au tyrannicide? Celui qui prendra l'épée ne périra-t-il pas par l'épée? Pourrait-il ensuite rester pasteur et célébrer la Sainte Cène? Ces questions le hantent pendant des mois. Bonhoeffer se décide enfin à dépasser son pacifisme radical des années trente. Il entreprend une démarche sacrificielle et transgresse l'interdit du meurtre pour sauver son peuple, se plaçant ainsi sous le jugement de Dieu. Il s'en remet cependant à la grâce de Dieu et sa miséricorde. Pour lui, si un fou est au volant d'un camion et va écraser les passants, un chrétien n-a-t-il pas le devoir de tout faire pour l'en empêcher? Sa réponse: l'Eglise doit se faire justicière du tyran, elle ne doit pas seulement consoler les survivants et enterrer les victimes tombées sous les roues du pouvoir totalitaire, elle a le devoir de lui mettre les bâtons dans les roues.[7] Bonhoeffer négocie avec les chefs des églises et des gouvernements étrangers. Hélas, le plan d'assassiner Hitler avorta à quelques minutes près du but, la bombe blessa légèrement le tyran. Les conséquences de ce forfait furent lourdes: un grand nombre de personnes furent arrêtées, plus de deux cent personnes impliquées furent pendues, d'autres, par peur de la revanche de Hitler le tyran, se suicidèrent. Dietrich ainsi que certains membres de sa famille proche et des amis, après une comparution en cour martiale dans un simulacre de procès qui les condamnent à mort, furent pendus au petit matin du 9 avril 1945. Douze jours après la pendaison, le camp de Flossenbürg étaient libéré. Seulement 29 jours après le 9 avril la guerre et la terreur du régime nazi étaient finies. C'est ainsi que la justice fut faite.

Mensonge ou vérité pour protéger la vie?

Par des moyens truqués, Bonhoeffer fit fuir 13 personnes d'ascendance juive vers la Suisse mais aussi il refusa de faire son service militaire. Pour lui, on devrait combattre en suivant ses convictions, si l'on ne peut concilier le service militaire avec sa conscience, il faut refuser de servir dans l'armée. Ce geste aura des conséquences graves envers lui-même et sa famille. En outre, il se pose des questions de conscience au sujet de la vérité: comment un chrétien peut-il vivre en vérité? Que signifie la vérité? Peut-il mentir pour protéger les siens? Y-a-t-il un saint mensonge? Seule la vérité nous affranchit, pourtant un mensonge peut sauver une vie humaine. Comment un chrétien authentique peut-il se comporter devant une telle situation ambigüe?

Bonhoeffer conclut en disant que le chrétien ne doit pas dire la vérité seulement à son Dieu mais aussi à son semblable; car il n'y a pas de vérité vis-à-vis de Jésus sans vérité vis-à-vis des êtres humains. En effet, la vérité est la ruine de la fausse communion et établit la véritable fraternité. Ainsi le mensonge est proscrit et la vérité est exigée du chrétien en toute circonstance.

4. Justice et éthique théologique dans notre contexte.

La vie de Dietrich Bonhoeffer interpelle l'Eglise d'aujourd'hui. A travers son histoire, nous pouvons nous demander comment les chrétiens peuvent se positionner face aux défis, aux turbulences et aux tragédies de la société moderne. Nous ne sommes pas capables de trouver des réponses plausibles. Cependant, nous pouvons nous interroger et scruter le fonds de notre conscience pour trouver un comportement adéquat permettant la bonne marche de la communauté, tout en respectant les vertus de la justice juste et enfin de compte en honorant les valeurs de l'éthique chrétienne.

---

[7] Cf. ibid., 39.

Justice et communauté.

Dans les sociétés traditionnelles surtout africaines, la communauté a depuis des temps joué un rôle prépondérant dans la vie de la société. Dans la société rwandaise préchrétienne par exemple, le sens des intérêts de la communauté, de la famille était une évidence pour chacun. L'individu était profondément inséré dans sa communauté. Ce faisant, la règle de vie répondait à l'adage 'chacun pour tous et tous pour chacun'. C'est de là que dans la plupart des pays, surtout africains, la justice était du ressort de la communauté. L'exemple des tribunaux Gacaca au Rwanda et des TRC (Truth and Réconciliation Commission) en Afrique du Sud nous interpelle. Alors que les autorités de l'Afrique du Sud, dans leur effort de réconcilier la nation déchirée par les vicissitudes de l'apartheid, optèrent pour une justice collective basée sur la vérité, le pardon et l'aveu, les responsables de la politique rwandaise choisirent une autre voie: la justice Gacaca. Pour les Sud-Africains, il n'y a pas de réconciliation et de justice sans pardon, pour les Rwandais, il n'y a pas de réconciliation sans justice.

Le choix est bien clair pour les deux pays. Cependant, tous ces pays visent une justice restauratrice, réparatrice basée sur la tradition et la communauté y joue un grand rôle. Beaucoup de pays en conflits en particulier africains expérimentent cette justice communautaire en quête d'une réconciliation du peuple. La question pertinente pour nous est: Quelle est la position de nos églises face à cette justice restauratrice? D'après Bonhoeffer, pourquoi la vie communautaire de l'Eglise se dilue et perd son sens originale et théologique? Comment restaurer ces valeurs en perdition? Quelle est la part de l'Eglise à l' égard du crime commis par un adhèrent ou un de ses leaders? Si l'Eglise accepte de demander pardon à la place de ses adhérents criminels, accepterait-elle aussi de réparer les forfaits commis?

L'Eglise et l'Etat.

En 1998, David GITARE, l'ancien Archevêque du Kenya, dans sa prédication au Rwanda conseille aux chrétiens de ne pas s'éloigner mais de ne pas non plus s'approcher trop de la politique. Il s'explique en disant que la politique est comme un feu, tu t'approches trop et son feu te brûle; tu t'en éloignes trop et tu refroidis. Quelle sera donc la position de l'Eglise face à la politique et au pouvoir de l'Etat? A travers les siècles, l'Eglise a lutté pour ne pas être un instrument de l'état. Mais la réalité était et est encore que l'Eglise a été dominée par l'état et dans ce cas l'Eglise a été utilisée par l'état pour arriver à ses fins, les fins de l'état. Il y a eu des cas où l'Eglise a dominé l'état et l'Empereur devint une toupie, une manipulation du spirituel. Ainsi on a vu des règnes théocratiques et césaro-papistes. De nos jours les églises ont tendance à se rabattre et à s'incliner face au pouvoir du prince. Au lieu de juger, de conseiller et de jouer le rôle prophétique dans leur patrie, elles deviennent des jouets et imitent la façon d'agir du pouvoir en place. Quelle est donc notre position face au pouvoir temporel? Rendre à César ce qui lui appartient et à Dieu ce qui lui est propre?

Que pensons- nous de nos frères en Christ, leaders religieux qui participent à la politique de leur pays en devenant des membres du parlement ou du sénat? L'Eglise a-t-elle le droit de fonder un parti politique? Comment l'Eglise peut-elle pratiquement jouer son rôle prophétique sans perdre son identité et diluer sa mission?

Justice de la non-violence

Nelson Mandela, Prix Nobel de la Paix en Afrique du Sud, a cherché la paix avec les partisans de l'Apartheid. Mais à la longue, il s'est rendu compte que les moyens utilisés par les méthodes de la non-violence n'étaient pas possibles et n'amèneraient jamais son parti à la victoire. Pour lui le feu est éteint par le feu. La non-violence a toujours été une position de l'éthique chrétienne à l'exemple de Martin Luther King aux USA et de Gandhi en Inde. Cependant, il y a des fois où l'usage des armes est une obligation sine qua non pour arriver à la paix. Quelle est la position de nos églises face à l'usage des armes, doit on encourager nos fidèles à faire la guerre, à faire le service militaire et à utiliser le fusil?

Le prix de la grâce

L'Eglise en Afrique est considérée comme une rivière très large mais dépourvue de profondeur. Ce qui signifie que ses églises sont remplies à craquer mais la foi en Jésus reste superficielle, ils mélangent les vertus du sacré et du profane. N'est-ce pas la grâce à bon marché que les adhérents appliquent pour faire de leur église un lieu de vente au rabais où la foi manque tant de profondeur et produit des fruits amers. Alors que les églises africaines manquent de profondeur, celles de l'occident en particulier de l'Europe manquent de largeur. Beaucoup ont perdu l'intérêt de la communauté, l'Eglise a peu de valeur à leurs yeux, car elle ne joue aucun rôle prophétique dans leur vie. Les jeunes se sont détournés de la foi et ont embrassé n'importe comment tout l'attrait de la sécularisation. Ceux qui ont la foi profite de la grâce à bon marché. Pour eux, Dieu est plein de grâce, il pardonnera tous les êtres humains et tous hériteront de la vie éternelle.

Que faire pour que le sens de la communauté, que le sens du culte et le prix de la grâce soient compris d'une manière authentique et juste pour ne pas en faire, selon Dietrich, une marchandise au rabais? Comment faire pour que la théologie et la prédication répondent aux besoins quotidiens de nos fidèles et que la mission de l'Eglise soit accomplie d'une façon juste?

Fuir le tyran ou rester avec les brebis

Idi Amin de l'Ouganda fut un dictateur de renom. Il pourchassa les hommes d'Eglise surtout de l'Eglise anglicane. L'Archevêque LUWUM fut tué par le tyran et d'autres pasteurs et évêques s'enfuirent vers l'étranger. Certains fidèles reprochèrent à l'évêque Festo KIVENGERE évangéliste bien connu de les avoir abandonnés au loup pendant cette tragédie. Quand le dictateur fut renversé, KIVENGERE revint de l'exil et rejoignit son pays. Grâce à sa sagesse et avec son expérience, il fut l'un des grands leaders qui aidèrent le pays et l'Eglise ougandaise à se stabiliser. Sa revanche contre Idi Amin fut d'écrire un livre intitulé, »J'aime Amin Dada«. A ce sujet des questions se posent: doit-on fuir le tyran quand il menace la vie des leaders ou des membres de l'Eglise? Est-ce que, dans ce cas précis, le Pâtre a-t-il le droit de fuir, de s'exiler? Ne devrait-il pas rester avec ses brebis pour les protéger contre l'attaque du loup? Voir la mort en face et ne pas fuir, n'est-ce-pas en quelque sorte un homicide, un suicide? Dietrich Bonhoeffer connaissait le danger, mais il est revenu des USA pour être avec les siens. Est-ce qu'il a commis un suicide? Et s'il était resté en exil aux USA?

Résistance ou soumission?

Certaines autorités du monde et en particulier africaines sont victimes de corruption et de déraillements de toutes sortes. Le problème est qu'une voix d'opposition audible fait défaut. Des leaders religieux n'ont pas le courage de résister et de jouer le rôle prophétique assigné à leur vocation. Ils préfèrent se taire et se soumettre. Beaucoup font comme s'ils ne voyaient rien, comme s'ils étaient des aveugles ou des sourds-muets face à l'exploitation et à la servitude du peuple de Dieu par le tyran. Nombreux sont les leaders de nos Eglises qui emboitent leurs pas dans ceux du tyran, ils sont du côté de leur dirigeant politique parce que ils viennent du même groupe ethnique, de la même région ou bien ils sont séduit par la même idée mégalomane sur la supériorité de leur convictions que leurs dirigeants et acceptent la corruption pour arriver à leurs fins. Dietrich ne fut pas d'accord avec l'Eglise allemande qui prit Hitler pour le »Führer« (conducteur). Pour Dietrich, Hitler est un séducteur comme Satan et il préfère résister et si possible assassiner le tyran pour que la justice de Dieu règne. Quel courage et quelle leçon pour nous aujourd'hui?

Vérité ou mensonge?

La place de la vérité dans le secteur de la justice est très importante et la vérité véhicule toute une philosophie dans l'organisation de la société. En mettant en place les tribunaux Gacaca au Rwanda et de la TRC (Truth Reconciliation Committee) en Afrique du Sud, la vérité a énormément contribué à la réussite de ces systèmes judiciaires. Sans vérité, les tribunaux ne peuvent réussir leur mission. En effet, sans vérité, il y a corruption, erreur et mensonge.

Comme dans d'autres cultures, dans la culture rwandaise, la vérité et le mensonge sont inséparables. Car, ils signifient la même idée exprimée tantôt dans le sens positif, tantôt dans le sens négatif. Quelques exemples de proverbes rwandais sur ces deux termes en témoignent: *aho kuryamira ukuri waryamira ubugi bw'intorezo* (au lieu de se coucher sur la vérité, mieux vaut se coucher sur le tranchant d'une hache); *ikinyoma kica nyiracyo*(le mensonge tue son auteur);

ukuri guca mu ziko ntigushya (la vérité passe dans le feu sans se brûler); *ukuri kwimura ikinyoma ku ntebe (la* vérité chasse le mensonge de son siège). La hiérarchisation de la société induit une gamme de nuances sur le sujet de la vérité et de ses contraintes. La ruse et le mensonge permettent de se tirer d'affaire dans une société hiérarchisée. L'intérêt pervertit souvent les relations sincères, comme le traduit ce proverbe: *ukuri wavuze uraguhakishwa* (la vérité que tu as à dire, tu l'échanges, tu la transformes, pour allécher ou acquérir les faveurs du chef).

De là, nous pouvons nous demander comment, en tant que chrétiens, utiliser la vérité pour nous tirer du piège du mensonge. Comment emboiter nos pas dans ceux de Jésus pour que la vérité nous affranchisse et qu'elle ait le dernier mot? Le »mensonge saint« fait pour sauver une vie, est-il condamnable? Comment aider tous ces frères et sœurs en Christ qui ont utilisé le mensonge pour sauver des vies dans des occasions compliquées ou pendant les génocides au Rwanda et en Allemagne par exemple? Quoi qu'on fasse, sachons que Jésus reste le chemin, la VERITE et la vie, suivons le.

5. Conclusion

Dietrich Bonhoeffer a laissé à l'humanité un héritage théologique et éthique fécond. Il présente un modèle de chrétien exemplaire mis en évidence par la pertinence de sa pensée et de ses engagements. Sa pensée ne se limite pas au contexte historique et politique de l'Allemagne des années trente et quarante du siècle dernier, mais son œuvre interroge notre époque. Il nous laisse alors des questions difficiles à répondre: comment à notre époque rendre la justice juste? Une fois sous l'emprise d'autres pouvoirs ou idoles, comment nous y prenons-nous? Comment faire pour que nos Eglises ne se contentent pas d'enterrer les morts mais fassent tout leur possible pour mettre les bâtons dans les roues d'un pouvoir totalitaire? Jésus Christ est-il toujours le sens de notre vie, notre raison de vivre, notre unique espérance?

Enfin, la vie de Dietrich questionne la justice de Dieu. Si Dieu est puissant, omniscient et juste comment peut-il laisser échouer le projet d'assassiner un tyran? La mort de Dietrich juste vingt-neuf jours avant la fin de la guerre et sans avoir pu se marier avec Maria, sa fiancée, ne laissent-elle pas une douleur profonde et des doutes face à la justice de Yahvé? Pourquoi croire à ce Dieu si faible dont la justice trouve sa force dans la souffrance et le dépouillement? Ce faisant, rappelons que la justice de Dieu est basée sur les fondements du Sermon sur la Montagne et sur le paradoxe de la Croix de Jésus. C'est à la croix qu'il y a la souffrance atroce, la mort mais aussi la vie nouvelle d'un Dieu vainqueur à travers la résurrection de son Fils. L'Eglise d'aujourd'hui devrait trouver la nécessité de croiser les mémoires pour mettre sur pied une évaluation dans la mission qui lui est confiée. Elle devrait éviter d'être engloutie par les ouragans du moment mais aller plutôt de l'avant dans la ligne qui honore la Parole de Dieu. Le croisement des mémoires nous permettrait de scruter notre être intérieur, notre conscience á fin de prononcer un 'oui' originel qui ne contredirait pas notre foi et qui nous donnerait l'espérance de vaincre la mort et de donner la vie.

Nous conclurons en disant que rendre une justice plus juste est un acte de foi. La foi qui selon Paul Tillich est le courage d'être.[8] Ce courage d'être n'est pas exclusivement religieux ou chrétien; il est cette conviction quasi viscérale qui dit à tout être humain qu'il vaut la peine de toujours continuer malgré tout. C'est là un leitmotiv sur lequel insiste le prophète Esaïe: 'Si vous n'avez pas la foi, vous ne tiendrez pas (Esaie 7).[9]

[8] Cf. PaulTillich: Le courage d'être, presses de l'université, Québec, 1998.
[9] Cf. Ensemble: Journal des Eglises Protestantes de Strasbourg, No 272, nov. 2013, 13.

»The first theological-ethical doctrine of basic human rights developed by a twentieth-century German Protestant theologian« – Dietrich Bonhoeffer and Human Rights

Christine Schliesser

Introduction

Due to his early, violent death in 1945, Dietrich Bonhoeffer never witnessed the adoption of the Universal Declaration of Human Rights (UDHR) by the United Nations in 1948. This declaration – celebrated rightly as a milestone – is the first global expression of rights which belong inherently to all human beings, and it was crafted as a direct response to the horrors of World War II. Though Bonhoeffer is rarely directly associated with the precursors of this declaration, I want to argue in this paper that he might as well be. For he presents, as the editors of the German edition of *Ethics* maintain, »the first theological-ethical doctrine of basic human rights developed by a twentieth-century German Protestant theologian« (DBW 6, 218, footnote 162).[1]

In the following, I will trace the development of Bonhoeffer's concept of human rights in four subsequent steps: First, I explore the grounding of his concept of human rights within his understanding of the ultimate and the penultimate. Second, I discuss the development of concrete human rights that Bonhoeffer expounds, such as the right to bodily life. In a third part, I briefly connect the human rights Bonhoeffer develops to their equivalents in the UDHR. And finally, I offer some thoughts on the connectivity of Bonhoeffer's decidedly theological grounding of human rights with non-theological approaches.

1. The Foundation of Human Rights: The Ultimate and the Penultimate

Bonhoeffer's approach to the topic of human rights is somewhat unusual in the sense that he does not start with the individual or an individualistically understood right to freedom. He rather begins by making a fundamental distinction

---

[1] Cf. Heinz Eduard Tödt: »Soweit ich weiss, ist dies im protestantisch-deutschsprachigen Raum vor dem Ende des Zweiten Weltkriegs die einzige ethische Ausarbeitung eines Theologen zu dieser Thematik, also das einzige systematisch in Angriff genommene evangelische Menschenrechtskonzept.« Heinz Eduard Tödt: Dietrich Bonhoeffers theologische Ethik und die Menschenrechte, in: Theologische Perspektiven nach Dietrich Bonhoeffer, ed. by Ernst-Albert Scharffenorth, Gütersloh 1993, 138-145, 139.

between the ultimate and the penultimate. This distinction is of considerable importance to Bonhoeffer. Not only is this the title of one of his chapters in his *Ethics*,[2] but he thought about structuring his entire work along these lines, as he mentioned in a letter to Eberhard Bethge.[3]

The premise from which Bonhoeffer works is this: »The origin and essence of all Christian life are consummated in the one event that the Reformation has called the justification of the sinner by grace alone« (DBW 6, 146). This is what he calls the »ultimate«. It is ultimate in two ways, qualitative and temporal: The *qualitative* aspect refers to the fact that there is no word of God that goes beyond God's grace; it is the ultimate reality. Its *temporal* dimension means that there is always something penultimate preceding the ultimate, such as »some action, suffering, movement« (DBW 6, 150).

In trying to establish their mutual relationship, Bonhoeffer first points to two misapprehensions: The *radical solution* emphasises the ultimate to the utter neglect of the penultimate, while in the *compromise solution* the penultimate becomes something in its own right. Bonhoeffer gives a succinct characterisation of both radicalism and compromise: »Radicalism hates time. Compromise hates eternity. Radicalism hates patience. Compromise hates decision. Radicalism hates wisdom. Compromise hates simplicity. Radicalism hates measure. Compromise hates the immeasurable. Radicalism hates the real. Compromise hates the word« (DBW 6, 156). To Bonhoeffer, the only solution which avoids both pitfalls is Jesus Christ. We encounter here a theme that runs through most of Bonhoeffer's theology, his Christocentricity. »In Jesus Christ God's reality and human reality take the place of radicalism and compromise« (DBW 6, 155). The penultimate depends on the ultimate for its existence; there is no penultimate as such.

As Jürgen Moltmann says in his *Ethics of Hope*: »It is the ultimate that gives meaning to the penultimate.«[4] Yet to follow from this a disregard for the penultimate on Bonhoeffer's part would be misconceived. Quite the contrary is the case. For the sake of the ultimate, the penultimate is endowed with a rather high standing: For if the penultimate is wounded, so is the ultimate: »Arbitrary destruction of the penultimate seriously harms the ultimate.« (DBW 6, 160). And: »When, for example, a human life is deprived of the conditions that are part of being human, the justification of such a life by grace and faith is at least seriously hindered, if not made impossible« (DBW 6, 160). The penultimate must

---

[2] »Ultimate and Penultimate Things.« DBW 6, 137-162.

[3] Letter to Eberhard Bethge from Ettal on November 27, 1940: »Today a possible title for my book occurred to me: 'Preparing the Way and Entering In' – corresponding to the division of the book (into penultimate and ultimate things).« DBW 6, 453.

[4] »Das Letzte gibt dem Vorletzten seinen Sinn.« Jürgen Moltmann: Ethik der Hoffnung, Gütersloh 2010, 20. All translations, if not otherwise indicated, are my own.

be understood, therefore, as a preparing of the way (»*Wegbereitung*«) for the word.[5]

Though not yet clothed in the language of rights, Bonhoeffer makes it clear that hunger, poverty, slavery, injustice, etc. are concrete obstacles to the ultimate, while bringing »bread to the hungry is preparing the way for the coming of grace« (DBW 6, 163). This, one could say, contains *in nuce* the foundation of Bonhoeffer's social ethics. Preparing the way is not only understood as an inner activity, but takes place as clearly visible and concrete action.[6] »The hungry person needs bread, the homeless person needs shelter, the one deprived of rights needs justice, the lonely person needs community, the undisciplined one needs order, and the slave needs freedom« (DBW 6, 163). If it were not eight years too early and with the possible exception of the reference to discipline and order, one might almost think one is reading the UDHR. Yet I believe Bonhoeffer would be misunderstood if reduced to the socio-ethical dimension of his thoughts. Clearly, he calls for concrete action such as the alleviation of very real hunger, yet »[n]evertheless, everything depends on this action being a spiritual reality, since what is finally at stake is not the reform of worldly conditions but the coming of Christ« (DBW 6, 164). Bonhoeffer manages to combine being as socio-ethical as any humanist advocate for human rights, yet still being thoroughly theological by embedding his call for human rights profoundly in a spiritual dimension, without, however, lessening its very worldly and very real appeal. As he writes in one of his prison letters to Bethge: »We are living in the penultimate and believe the ultimate, isn't that so?« (DBW 8, 213).

2. Concrete Human Rights

Based on this framework, Bonhoeffer proceeds to elaborating the concrete consequences in terms of human rights. Some 35 years later, Wolfgang Huber and Heinz Eduard Tödt would take up Bonhoeffer's grounding of human rights in the penultimate in their book on human rights (*Menschenrechte*), when they

[5] In a similar vein, Karl Barth writes that the state »could administer justice and protect the law. [...] In so doing, voluntarily or involuntarily, very indirectly yet none the less certainly, it would be granting the gospel of justification free and assured course.« Karl Barth: Church and State, in: Karl Barth: Community, State, and Church, edited by Will Herberg, Gloucester, Mass. 1968, 101-148, 119. Bonhoeffer, understanding »justification« as ultimate and »justice« as penultimate, agreed with Barth. Cf. the discussion by Andreas Pangritz on Bonhoeffer and Barth's essay in: Andreas Pangritz: Karl Barth in the Theology of Dietrich Bonhoeffer: A Clarification Whose Time Has Come, Grand Rapids 1999, 63ff.

[6] Bonhoeffer bases his ideas on a socio-ethical interpretation of biblical scripture speaking of the coming of the Lord. When it says in Isaiah 40:4 »Every valley shall be lifted up«, Bonhoeffer understands the valley to mean the »depth of human misery, [...] of human bondage, of human poverty« (DBW 6, 161).

speak of the fight for human rights as a fight for something penultimate, yet for the sake of the ultimate.[7]

The first »systematic attempt at a Protestant concept of human rights«[8] as Tödt calls it is found in the manuscript »The natural«. Given its uniqueness it is quite »surprising«[9], how little attention it has received, even in Bonhoeffer scholarship. When Bonhoeffer left the monastery in Ettal in February 1941, where he had been working on both manuscripts discussed here – »Ultimate and Penultimate Things« and »Natural Life« – his draft of »Natural Life« was cut off. We do have, fortunately, in addition to this manuscript, six *Ethics* working notes that contain drafts of the intended structure. According to them, there are seven aspects in total that Bonhoeffer had meant to discuss. The manuscript we have shows that Bonhoeffer could not even finish the first one.[10]

The close relationship between Bonhoeffer's biography and his theology has been pointed out numerous times already.[11] Bonhoeffer's discussion of the »Natural Life« is a particularly striking example of how he takes contemporary events into account, such as the church's devastating failure in objecting to the forced sterilisation after 1933 and the euthanasia programme of so-called »worthless life« after 1940, a problem all the more virulent for the church as many of those deemed worthless lived in church-related institutions.[12]

Being an audacious writer, Bonhoeffer was not afraid to »courageously and strongly reach out for the old and new Catholic wisdom« (DBW 6, 419). In the German context, I have to add here, this was not customary in Protestant theology at that time – and is, perhaps, not even today. This »daring venture« (edi-

---

[7] »Der Kampf der christlichen Gemeinde um die Menschenrechte, auch um die Religionsfreiheit, ist in der Tat ein Kampf um Vorletztes – um des Letzten willen.« Wolfgang Huber / Heinz Eduard Tödt: Menschenrechte. Perspektiven für eine menschliche Welt, Stuttgart / Berlin 1977, 215.

[8] Tödt: Bonhoeffers theologische Ethik, 139.

[9] Ibid.

[10] Cf. Ethics working notes 52, 47, 49. The drafts differ from one another. Each of the six drafts contains, however, the right to happiness (»Recht auf Glück«). Other rights include: the right to work, the right to community, the right to piety, [protection from] intellectual violation.

[11] This holds true especially for his *Ethics* which shows according to their editors how »contemporary events – along with ecclesiastical, theological, and ethical failures when faced by these events – have been taken into account more intensely and more consciously than in perhaps any other previous Protestant ethic« (DBW 6, 428).

[12] See also Bonhoeffer's church confession, DBW 6, 139: »The church confesses that it has witnessed the arbitrary use of brutal force, the suffering in body and soul of countless innocent people, that it has witnessed oppression, hatred, and murder without raising its voice for the victims and without finding ways of rushing to help them. It has become guilty of the lives of the weakest and most defenceless brothers and sisters of Jesus Christ.«

tors DBW 6, 419) included notably Bonhoeffer's attempt to regain the concept of the natural from the perspective of the gospel.

In regaining the concept of the natural, Bonhoeffer begins by first refuting two common misunderstandings, namely either regarding the natural as completely contaminated by general sinfulness or as reflecting the original, immaculate creation. These misunderstandings along with the fear of letting anything diminish grace had led to the abandonment of the natural from Protestant thought. A great loss, indeed, for now the church had lost a valuable resource for giving orientation in concrete questions of natural life.

Bonhoeffer differentiates between the natural, which is part of the fallen world, and the created. Again, his characteristic Christocentricity shows. »Only by Christ's becoming human does natural life become the penultimate that is directed toward the ultimate. Only through Christ's becoming human do we have the right to call people to natural life and to live it ourselves« (DBW 6, 174). From this christological foundation, Bonhoeffer moves on to define the natural from two perspectives, form and content. With regard to *form*, the natural is determined by its orientation towards Christ and God's will to preservation and can only be recognised by looking at Christ. Its *content*, however, is recognised by reason.[13] Reason recognises the natural as given, not set.

With regard to the two extremes of viewing the natural life as either exclusively an end in itself or as mere means to an end, he emphasises their connectedness, again in Christ. »In Jesus Christ life as an end in itself expresses its createdness, and life as a means to an end expresses its participation in the kingdom of God« (DBW 6, 179). It is here that we find the origin of life's rights and duties. *Rights* are the expression of life as an end in itself, while *duties* arise from life as means to an end. Against Kant, Bonhoeffer sets rights before duties, because God gives before God demands. Accordingly, Bonhoeffer first expounds basic human rights, before he had wanted to turn to life's duties, which he, however, could not carry out.

Bonhoeffer begins by discussing the well-known *suum cuique*, going back to Roman law and before,[14] and the *ius nativum*, before coming to »[t]he most

---

[13] Bonhoeffer distances himself in two ways from the Catholic understanding of the natural. *First*, while the Catholic tradition regards reason as having retained an essential integrity, Bonhoeffer views it as being completely immersed in the fall. Second, the Catholic doctrine allows reason to comprehend the formal dimension of the natural. Bonhoeffer differs from the Enlightenment in that he bases the natural in the »objectively given« and not in the »subjective spontaneity of reason« (DBW 6, 175, annotation 1).

[14] »Honeste vivere, alterum non laede, suum cuique tribuere« (»live honestly, do not harm others, give to each his own«) are the three basic guidelines for human conduct given by the Roman lawyer Ulpian. The origin of these commonplaces goes back even further. Plato points to fifth century B. C. E. Simonides who already defined justice as suum cuique. Cf. DBW 6, 181, footnote 39.

primordial right of natural life [namely] the protection of the body from intentional injury, violation, and killing« (DBW 6, 186).

I would like to use his discussion of this right as an example to demonstrate Bonhoeffer's way of reasoning here, which is two-dimensional. He strives to always give a *theological* as well as a *non-theological* grounding for the right he discusses. In this case, the *theological* argument claims that »[s]ince by God's will human life on earth exists only as bodily life, the body has a right to be preserved for the sake of the whole person. [...] [T]he preservation of bodily life is the very foundation of all natural rights« (DBW 6, 185). The *non-theological* argument points to the *ius nativum*, deducing from the fact of the body the right to its preservation which is »born with us« (DBW 6, 185). We will encounter Bonhoeffer's attempt to provide a double base for his argument – theological and non-theological – as a red thread running throughout his discussion of human rights, even though he does not make this intent explicit. His non-theological arguments refer to nature and reason, including Kantian reasoning or pragmatic arguments such as the slippery-slope argument. Quite contrary to a theological tradition which tends to disregard the body, the right to bodily life leads Bonhoeffer to rather astounding ensuing rights, the first one being the »right to bodily joys« (DBW 6, 186),[15] which not only includes »shelter«, »food«, and »clothing«, but also the rights to »recreation« and »play« as well as »sexuality«.

While explicating the »first right of natural life [, namely] the protection of bodily life from arbitrary killing« (DBW 6, 189), he tackles the very concrete problem of euthanasia. This was an urgent topic of his time, for until 1941 about 100,000 people, deemed »unworthy« of life, were killed by the Nazi euthanasia programme.[16] Bonhoeffer defines arbitrary killing as the deliberate killing of the innocent and firmly rejects the idea of a utilitarian, relative right to life. Bonhoeffer's discussion of euthanasia reveals the difference between his own concept of human rights and other Western concepts. Many Western concepts start with the individual as the bearer of all rights. Social contract theory has the individual surrender certain *alienable* rights to the community he or she joins, in order to have their *inalienable* rights protected, among them human rights. Bonhoeffer, in contrast, understands »the natural life« *itself* as primary bearer of the rights. Tödt rightly emphasises the social aspect of this approach, for whoever understands him- or herself as bearer of the gift of natural life, sees the ensuing fundamental connection to the other, who is bearer of the same gift.[17]

---

[15] The editors of his *Ethics* are right in pointing out that »[p]roviding a theological basis for 'a right to bodily joys' was rare in German Protestant preaching and ethics during the first half of the twentieth century« (DBW 6, 187, footnote 57).

[16] According to the editors of DBW 6, Bonhoeffer wrote the manuscripts »Ultimate and Penultimate Things« and »Natural Life« between November 17, 1940 and February 22, 1941. DBW 6, 16.

[17] »Geht man, wie Bonhoeffer, von den Rechten des natürlichen Lebens aus, so ist es

Natural life itself may at times even confront the individual's will, such as in Bonhoeffer's example of an incurably ill patient who demands his or her life to be ended. Bonhoeffer sees the doctor not only obligated to the will of the patient, but to the patient's natural life itself (DBW 6, 192). The same holds true for suicide and abortion, which he calls »murder« (DBW 6, 206).[18]

Further rights that spring from the basic right to bodily life include the »right to reproduction«, the »right to personal choice of a marriage partner« (DBW 6, 203) and the »right of life that will come into being« (DBW 6, 206). Bonhoeffer discusses a »right of birth control« (DBW 6, 208)[19] before dealing with sterilisation, an urgent issue of his time when the Nazi regime sterilised about 400,000 people against their will.[20] Bonhoeffer bases this discussion as well on the human body's »right to inviolability« (DBW 6, 212). It is the right to bodily life that leads Bonhoeffer to the right of »protection against arbitrary encroachment on the freedom of the body« (DBW 6, 214). Concretely, Bonhoeffer establishes »the right of a person freely to give or withhold her or his own body, especially its sexuality« (DBW 6, 214). The likes of »rape«, »exploitation«, »slavery«, »torture« and »arbitrary imprisonment« violate this right to freedom of the body.

After the discussion of the »right to bodily life« Bonhoeffer had planned but could not finish a section on »The natural rights of the life of the spirit«, spirit meaning here, as Clifford Green clarifies, »all aspects of the conscious person – such as mind, intellect, imagination, feeling, judgment, and will« (DBW 6, 217, footnote 159.).

With these different human rights – and their possible violations – in mind, the question arises, if it is permissible to fight for one's rights. Bonhoeffer answers this question by first emphasising that it is »God who stands up for these rights« (DBW 6, 184), frequently by using life itself: »In the end, it is life itself that

---

unmöglich, zum Beispiel die Freiheitsrechte isoliert individualistisch, also egozentrisch zu interpretieren, wie es stets eine Gefahr in liberal-kapitalistischen Verhältnissen gewesen ist; denn wer sich als Träger der Gabe natürlichen Lebens versteht, der weiss sich fundamental mit anderen verbunden, denen die gleiche Gabe zuteil geworden ist, und sieht sich veranlasst, das Recht anderer Träger natürlichen Lebens zu respektieren und ihm dienlich zu sein.« Tödt: Bonhoeffers theologische Ethik, 142.

[18] It is a different matter with the fictitious scenario of the plague having broken out on a ship and the only option of everyone else surviving is the death of the sick. But even there, he leaves the decision open. This scenario could be understood as a hint towards Bonhoeffer's own motives in participating in the coup d'état against Hitler. DBW 6, 195. Cf. Glen H. Stassen: Human Rights, in: Global Dictionary of Theology, ed. by William A. Dyrness and Veli-Matti Kärkkäinen, Downers Grove 2008, 405-414, 411.

[19] Bonhoeffer questions Catholic rigorism that only allows for abstention. Instead, Bonhoeffer argues for a »right to full bodily communion.«

[20] Between 1934 and 1945 and on the basis of »Gesetz zur Verhütung erbkranken Nachwuchses (GezVeN)« from July 1933.

tends toward the natural and ever again turns against the unnatural and breaks it down« (DBW 6, 176). Contrary to the modern emphasis on the individual, Bonhoeffer employs a timeframe transcending the individual life's span, conceding that for some individuals, their rights might never be restored during their lifetime. As to the legitimacy of defending one's right, he stresses that »[u]nder all circumstances they must defend a right in such a way as to make it credible that God, not the individual, is standing up for the right« (DBW 6, 185). This cautious phrasing seems in some ways unsatisfactory. Are we not more used to phrases like »stand up and fight for your right«? Notice that Huber and Tödt use a more assertive language, too; they actually speak of a »fight« (»Kampf«) for human rights. Notice also that Bonhoeffer's own biography, especially his participation in the planned coup d'état, points to a more assertive approach as well. Yet Bonhoeffer is in good theological company here, with Martin Luther himself differentiating between asserting (»bekennen«) a right and winning (»gewinnen«) a right and recommending leaving one's rights to God.[21]

Bonhoeffer has furthermore been criticised for a general scepticism towards human rights. Katharina Kunter points to Bonhoeffer's comments on William Paton's work »The Church and the New Order in Europe« (1941).[22] There Bonhoeffer argues how freedom is »in the first place not an *individual* right but a *responsibility*; freedom is not in the first place oriented toward the individual but toward the neighbour«[23] and how »the question of individual freedoms – such as freedom of speech, freedom of the press, freedom of assembly, etc. – can be addressed only within this overarching context« (DBW 16, 532). From this, Kunter infers that »Dietrich Bonhoeffer had difficulties with human rights.«[24] She portrays Bonhoeffer as an adherent of the »radical solution«, overemphasising the ultimate to the detriment of the penultimate. She is mistaken, I think, for Bonhoeffer distances himself explicitly from this. In addition to this, Bonhoeffer had no problem in actually claiming human rights for the church and for Christianity. In »Church and World I« he writes: »In the hour of danger, the children of the church who had become independent and had run away now returned to their mother […] Reason, justice, culture, humanity and other concepts like these sought and found new meaning and new strength in their origin« (DBW 6, 341).[25] Kunter is right, however, in pointing to the fact

---

[21] Cf. Martin Luther: The Magnificat, in: The Sermon on the Mount (sermons) and the Magnificat. Luther's Works 21. St. Louis 1956, 336. If it is not possible to »win« one's right, one should leave it to God. Cf. DBW 6, 185, footnote 50.

[22] Katharina Kunter: Vor Freiheit bewahre uns, o Herr!, in: Zeitzeichen 2 (2002), 17-19, 17.

[23] DBW 16, 528-533, 532.

[24] »Deutschlands Protestanten, auch Dietrich Bonhoeffer, taten sich mit den Menschenrechten schwer.« Kunter: Vor Freiheit bewahre uns, o Herr!, 17.

[25] The explicit mentioning of human rights is found in an earlier draft: »The newly

that general Protestantism for a long time has taken a critical stance towards human rights, viewing them as a product of the unchristian French Revolution. Wrongly, for – as Glen Stassen emphasises – »The full concept of human rights was first developed and articulated during the free-church struggle for the right of religious liberty in Puritan England in the 1640s.«[26]

3. Human Rights in the UDHR and Bonhoeffer – A Comparison

Even though Bonhoeffer is not commonly thought of as one of the precursors of the UDHR, one could argue he might as well be. For a comparison of the rights Bonhoeffer discusses with the individual rights included in the UDHR yields quite astounding similarities – even though they each were developed independently. It must be left to conjecture what other rights Bonhoeffer would have included had he been able to finish.[27]

UDHR	*Dietrich Bonhoeffer*
1. All human beings are born free and equal in dignity and rights. They are endowed with reason and conscience and should act towards one another in a spirit of brotherhood.	»a right we are born with« (182)[28] »human 'reason' is the organ for recognizing the natural« (174)
3. Everyone has the right to life, liberty and security of person.	»the right to bodily life« (185) »the freedom of bodily life« (214)
4. No one shall be held in slavery or servitude; slavery and the slave trade shall be prohibited in all their forms.	»the exploitation of the human body […] we call […] human enslavement« (215)
5. No one shall be subjected to torture or to cruel, inhuman or degrading treatment or punishment.	»torture [is] the arbitrary and brute infliction of bodily pain« (216)
9. No one shall be subjected to arbitrary arrest, de-	»arbitrarily robbing […]

awakened general and passionate quest for natural law, for basic rights and for human rights, felt itself to be in very close proximity to Christianity«, DBW 6, 340, footnote 7.

[26] Stassen: Human Rights, 405.

[27] It seems quite reasonable to assume, for example, that rights such as the freedom of religion would have been included in his discussion of the »The natural rights of the life of the spirit.«

[28] If not indicated otherwise, page numbers refer to DBW 6.

tention or exile.	people of freedom by imprisonment […] or by arrest« (217)
12. No one shall be subjected to arbitrary interference with his privacy, family, home or correspondence, nor to attacks upon his honour and reputation. Everyone has the right to the protection of the law against such interference or attacks.	»forcibly and unjustly separated from their homes, their work, and their families« (217) »deprived of the honor« (216)
16. (1) Men and women of full age, without any limitation due to race, nationality or religion, have the right to marry and to found a family. They are entitled to equal rights as to marriage, during marriage and at its dissolution. (2) Marriage shall be entered into only with the free and full consent of the intending spouses.	»right to personal choice of a marriage partner« (203)
17. (1) Everyone has the right to own property alone as well as in association with others. (2) No one shall be arbitrarily deprived of his property.	»the natural right to work and property« (*Ethics* working note No. 49, *ZE* 75) »forcibly and unjustly separated from their homes« (217)
18. Everyone has the right to freedom of thought, conscience and religion; this right includes freedom to change his religion or belief, and freedom, either alone or in community with others and in public or private, to manifest his religion or belief in teaching, practice, worship and observance.	»intellectual violation [geistige Vergewaltigung]« (*Ethics* working note No. 47, *ZE* 74)[29]
19. Everyone has the right to freedom of opinion and expression; this right includes freedom to hold opinions without interference and to seek, receive and impart information and ideas through any media and regardless of frontiers.	»freedom of speech« (*DBW 16*, 532) »'intellectual' killing of inferior minds« (*Ethics* working note No. 49, *ZE* 75)
20. (1) Everyone has the right to freedom of peaceful assembly and association. (2) No one may be compelled to belong to an as-	»freedom of assembly« (*DBW 16*, 532) »right to community«

[29] ZE = DBW 6 Ergänzungsband.

sociation.	(*Ethics* working note No. 47, *ZE* 75)
22. Everyone, as a member of society, has the right to social security and is entitled to realization, through national effort and international co-operation and in accordance with the organization and resources of each State, of the economic, social and cultural rights indispensable for his dignity and the free development of his personality.	»communal order« (217) »the natural right of the life of the spirit: [...] culture« (*Ethics* working note No. 49, *ZE* 75)
23. (1) Everyone has the right to work, to free choice of employment, to just and favourable conditions of work and to protection against unemployment.	»the natural right to work« (*Ethics* working note No. 47, *ZE* 75)
24. Everyone has the right to rest and leisure, including reasonable limitation of working hours and periodic holidays with pay.	»recreation, play« (186)
25. (1) Everyone has the right to a standard of living adequate for the health and well-being of himself and of his family, including food, clothing, housing and medical care and necessary social services, and the right to security in the event of unemployment, sickness, disability, widowhood, old age or other lack of livelihood in circumstances beyond his control.	»housing, food, clothing« (186)
26. (1) Everyone has the right to education. Education shall be free, at least in the elementary and fundamental stages. Elementary education shall be compulsory. Technical and professional education shall be made generally available and higher education shall be equally accessible to all on the basis of merit. (2) Education shall be directed to the full development of the human personality and to the strengthening of respect for human rights and fundamental freedoms. It shall promote understanding, tolerance and friendship among all nations, racial or religious groups, and shall further the activities of the United Nations for the maintenance of peace.	»education [Bildung]« (*Ethics* working notes No. 51, *ZE* 76) »education [Bildung]: working reality as a whole into one's own mind and spirit« (*Ethics* working notes Nor. 51, *ZE* 76)

27. (1) Everyone has the right freely to participate in the cultural life of the community, to enjoy the arts and to share in scientific advancement and its benefits. (2) Everyone has the right to the protection of the moral and material interests resulting from any scientific, literary or artistic production of which he is the author.	»community« (*Ethics* working notes No. 47, *ZE* 75) »giftedness, genius, talent: working reality into artistic [künstlerisch] expression« (*Ethics* working notes No. 51, *ZE* 76)
28. Everyone is entitled to a social and international order in which the rights and freedoms set forth in this Declaration can be fully realized.	»communal order« (217)
29. (1) Everyone has duties to the community in which alone the free and full development of his personality is possible. (2) In the exercise of his rights and freedoms, everyone shall be subject only to such limitations as are determined by law solely for the purpose of securing due recognition and respect for the rights and freedoms of others and of meeting the just requirements of morality, public order and the general welfare in a democratic society.	»duties spring from the rights themselves« (180) »freedom is not in the first place oriented toward the individual but toward the neighbour« (*DBW 16*, 532)

I will close by briefly offering some reflections on Bonhoeffer's theological foundation of human rights in the light of other, secular foundations.

4. A Theological Foundation for Secular Human Rights?

Human rights are both in need of foundations and open to them, as the political scientist Anton Pelinka points out.[30] They belong – in the sense of the Böckenförde-Diktum[31] – to the realm of those premises that the modern constitutional state depends on yet cannot give to itself. They therefore cannot be grounded solely in the societal-political context, but rather require a different rationale. This is what Pelinka means by »in need of foundations« (»begrün-

[30] »Menschenrechte sind begründungsbedürftig und begründungsoffen.« Anton Pelinka (Ed.): Weltethos und Recht, Berlin 2011, 211.

[31] »Der freiheitliche, säkularisierte Staat lebt von Voraussetzungen, die er selbst nicht garantieren kann.« Ernst-Wolfgang Böckenförde: Staat, Gesellschaft, Freiheit. Studien zur Staatstheorie und zum Verfassungsrecht, Berlin 1976, 60.

dungsbedürftig«). The plurality of modern constitutional democracies in matters of religion and world-views resists any one absolute grounding of human rights but rather calls for a variety of approaches, thereby reflecting the neutrality of the state as well as societal pluralism. This is meant by the rights' »openness to foundations« (»begründungsoffen«). Pointing to the justified scepticism towards an optimism of reason, especially in light of the experiences of the 20th century, Pelinka argues that it is not only possible and valid to also offer a theological grounding for human rights, but even sees it as possibly providing a deeper grounding than a mere secular rationale could.[32]

While a theological grounding of human rights might therefore be deemed legitimate in principle, it is a different question if or in how far it is communicable to other, non-theological approaches. In Bonhoeffer's case, I think, such a connection is possible.

Bonhoeffer wrote from a decidedly theological stance. His ultimate foundation of human rights in the penultimate and the ultimate is explicitly theological and difficult to communicate on non-theological grounds. Yet within the course of his argument, there is a lot that seems very accessible from a non-theological point of view, especially Bonhoeffer's emphasis on reason as the organ for recognising the content of the natural. While for Bonhoeffer himself, there is always a deeper theological layer, reason often must suffice: »The suum cuique is the highest possible recognition of reason, which corresponds to reality and, within natural life, discerns the right that God (whom reason does not know) gives to the individual« (DBW 6, 184). This accounts for the fact that in his line of reasoning, Bonhoeffer always strives to provide a theological as well as a non-theological dimension of his argument. This is close to being what Christiane Tietz would call »bilingual«.[33] Theological and non-theological arguments should not be viewed as standing in opposition to each other in Bonhoeffer's grounding of human rights; rather, they are two dimensions of one argument. As Tödt argues: »Because Bonhoeffer recovered the concept of the natural from the gospel, he made it possible to relate discourse based on nature and reason to theological statements«, thereby »creating a level of discourse with all, who opposed the destructive in reality with insights of relative reason and acceptance of life«[34].

---

[32] »So ist es nicht nur möglich und zulässig, die Menschenrechte (auch) theologisch zu begründen, es kann sogar gegenüber einer rein säkularen Herleitung eine tiefere Fundierung bedeuten.« Pelinka: Weltethos und Recht, 212.

[33] For Tietz' call for bilingualness and the »translation« of religiously grounded ethical arguments into publicly understood language based on reason cf. Christiane Tietz: … mit anderen Worten … Zur Übersetzbarkeit religiöser Überzeugungen in politischen Diskursen, in: Evangelische Theologie 72 (2012), 86-100, 98.

[34] Tödt: Bonhoeffers theologische Ethik, 144f.

Dietrich Bonhoeffer and the Struggle for Human Rights in the Context of Africa

Byaruhanga Rukooko Archangel

1. Introduction

The story and meaning of Dietrich Bonhoeffer's life is as intriguing as it is predictable; it is as contemporary in transitional democracies as it is old in older democracies, but nonetheless a true blueprint life of any person who disagrees with and challenges policies of any dictatorial regime and faces dire if not fatal consequences. His opposition to Nazi ideology was very risky indeed, as it would have been today under any dictatorship like North Korea, Zimbabwe, Uganda, Sudan, Rwanda, Burma or any dictatorship and this makes it predictable. Yet, although Bonhoeffer was a Lutheran Pastor, a theologian, a deeply religious man, he was also a founding member of the Confessing Church and a robust anti-Nazi activist. Besides, not only did he fight against the violation of the rights of vulnerable people, especially the Jews, but he was also a human rights thinker. Finally, though Bonhoeffer was not essentially a philosopher, his work delved into philosophical issues of metaphysics and epistemology – as if he was responding to Martin Heidegger's ontology in his *Being and Time.*[1] For these reasons, Bonhoeffer is many things in one, but can be best reductively understood in the context of his theological views that crystallised into a Christocentric ideology, which he tried to live, work and finally, die for.

In connection with human rights, Bonhoeffer's contribution to the foundation and growth of the theory of human rights is just becoming more appreciated, the citadel of which is in his unfinished manuscript of *Ethics*[2]. As such, the work of Michael Westmoreland-White *Contributions to Human Rights in Dietrich Bonhoeffer's Ethics* is particularly worth mentioning.[3] The work of Christine Schliesser *»The First Theological-Ethical Doctrine of Basic Human Rights Developed by a Twentieth–century German Protestant Theologian« - Dietrich*

---

[1] In Being and Time, Martin Heidegger was concerned with the individual who is lost in the »they-collectivity«. Cf. Martin Heidegger: Sein und Zeit, completely revised 18th edition (orig. 1927), Tübingen 2001. Yet, Bonhoeffer was interested in the solidarity of the others and the individual.

[2] Ethics was one of the several works of Bonhoeffer in prison but unfortunately, it was left unfinished. However, much of his contribution to human rights is set out in this text. Cf. DBW 6.

[3] Michael L. Westmoreland-White: Contributions to Human Rights in Dietrich Bonhoeffer's Ethics, in: Journal of Church and State 39 (1997), 67-83.

Bonhoeffer and Human Rights is even more significant because of its specificity, relevance and comprehensiveness in the sense that she also situated it in the post-1948 Universal Declaration of Human Rights' period.[4]

Bonhoeffer's several aspects of his life provide us with a monumental challenge in terms of sizing his contribution to human rights and most especially in the context of Africa today. Do we study him purely from the viewpoint of his actions and role as an activist with a view to appreciating his strategies and tactics, or do we solely focus on his writings or do we combine both? Or do we concern ourselves purely with his ideas that underpin human rights as we understand them today? Can we legitimately treat him as a human rights defender when the concepts of »human rights« and »human rights defenders« were not yet decidedly defined and properly applied? For instance, it is currently held that a human rights defender should never use violent means, yet many human rights activists like him were supportive of violence. Should a religious leader become a human rights activist or a politician? Indeed, more theoretically, along with other theorists, Schliesser and Schaber[5] accept the derivation of human rights from a theological/religious foundation as legitimate, but Schroeder[6] has rejected this. So how do we proceed?

Since 1998, the use of the term »human rights defender« has become dominant in human rights literature, work and parlance, in spite of lack of clarity in its application. Thus, in a bid to further delineate Bonhoeffer's contribution to human rights in the African context, we confront his theoretical and practical ideas as well as his actions against the concept of a *human rights defender*. This attempt will achieve two objectives; namely, to interrogate the concept of a human rights defender which has become commonplace therefore determining its internal consistency as applied in our times, and second, to size up the image of Bonhoeffer as a human rights defender. In this paper, therefore, we posit three hypotheses: First, that, Bonhoeffer's core philosophy is a strong ethical foundation of the current understanding of human rights. Second, that Bonhoeffer is a truly human rights defender not dissimilar from the ones being defined as such today. Three, that his life and conception of human rights is relevant to Africa – Africa as part and parcel of transitional democracies. My beginning point therefore, is, in brief, what is Bonhoeffer's philosophy that underpins human rights?

---

[4] Christine Schliesser's paper »The First Theological-Ethical Doctrine of Basic Human Rights Developed by a Twentieth–century German Protestant Theologian« – Dietrich Bonhoeffer and Human Rights, is more comprehensive and tries to study the correspondence between Universal Declaration of Human rights (1948) and the rights raised in Bonhoeffer's work. Cf. her paper in this book.

[5] Cf. Peter Schaber: Human Rights and Human Dignity: A Reply to Doris Schroeder, in: Ethic Moral (2014), 155-161, Published Online, May 2013.

[6] Cf. Doris Schroeder: Human Rights and Human Dignity, in: Ethical Theory and Moral Practice 15 (2012), 323-335.

2. Bonhoeffer's epistemic-ethical Philosophy

Impotence of conscience and reason

To begin with, Bonhoeffer rejected the use of conscience and reason as formidable means to build a consistent ethical system. Accordingly, rational pursuits do not convey and support an adequate ethical system especially in the face of massive evil because they attempt to find God apart from the world and humanity that God created and to which he was reconciled. People of reason, private virtue, principles or the people of conscience, or *the fanatic* as Bonhoeffer calls them, lose sight of the totality of evil and end up fighting lonely battles against overwhelming forces of evil whose solutions cannot be found that way. The people of reason are ultimately confused as they are caught in indecision and therefore end up accomplishing nothing which may result in worse evil than the one they expected to prevent. Instead, only in Jesus Christ, who reconciled God to history, can one see the world, humanity and God.

Thus, motivated by his Christocentric interpretation of the world and reality, Bonhoeffer launches his New Testament Biblical starting point with John 19:5 and Pilate's »Ecco Homo« or »Behold the man!« as he presented Jesus Christ to the crowds as an innocent person, although we also know that the crowds reacted rather differently, i.e. they still demanded the death of Jesus. With this point at the back of his mind, Bonhoeffer was able to make his major claim about God and the fallen world as well as humanity, namely, that in Christ, the world and God were reconciled when Jesus bore the guilt of humanity by becoming guilty of our sins and accepting to die for them. In real terms, Bonhoeffer meant that human beings had become reconciled to God through the death of Jesus. In this way, then, Bonhoeffer was able to recover and restore the dignity of human beings which they had lost in, and due to, their sinfulness. As Westmoreland-White observes, Bonhoeffer offers a pragmatic view of the Christian ethic of human rights for real actual human beings with all of their dignity and all of their frailties and sins.[7] That is to say, his Christian ethic is a realistic and pragmatic view of humanity, whose dignity is accessible; it can never be seen in terms of the extremes of viewing it either fallenness (sinfulness) or as too good! It is however important to observe that Bonhoeffer's ethics is clearly based on Christian religious faith without which there is no legitimate ethics, a view that is currently very difficult to sustain.[8]

---

[7] Westmoreland-White: Contributions to Human Rights.

[8] It is very ironical indeed, that the very brand of ethics – of reason, that Bonhoeffer rejected would be exactly the type today's ethics would be defended. Cf. Chloe Schwenke: Reclaiming Value in International Development: The Moral Dimensions of Development Policy and Practice in Poor Countries, London 2009.

Ultimate versus the Penultimate

The dignity of humanity is further rejuvenated through his idea of the dynamic of the »ultimate« and »penultimate«. Thus, whereas the ultimate is the »last things«, the penultimate is »things before the last« which could either be some movement or action. The ultimate is the proclamation of the gospel of justification of the sinner by »grace alone« through faith, which was a central claim of the Protestant reformation. As noted by Schliesser, the ultimate is so in two ways: the qualitative and the temporal.[9] In the qualitative, there is no other word of God that goes beyond God's grace – God's grace is the ultimate which is also the most important task of the church. It is however, temporal in the sense that there is always something preceding the ultimate like movement, action, suffering, etc, and this is the penultimate. Nonetheless, important as it is, Bonhoeffer informs us that the ultimate is not the only duty of the church or individual Christians; penultimate things are also important because of their relationship to the ultimate and, indeed, the penultimate is a necessary logical path to the ultimate.

However, Bonhoeffer declares that the radical choice of concentrating on the ultimate only – that of God's grace – is a misapprehension as much as that of the »compromise solution« – of watering down the gospel. We cannot achieve much by either concentrating on the ultimate or trying to focus only on the penultimate – of trying to eradicate the conditions that hinder the realisation of the ultimate, which he thought would be making the gospel fit comfortably in the world. Thus, each of these solutions fails to maintain the unity of the incarnate, crucified and risen Christ. What then do we make of this ultimate–penultimate dialectic in terms of human rights?

In my view, it is not always clear and consistent what it is that we have to derive from Bonhoeffer's dialectic of the ultimate versus the penultimate. However, in relation to human rights, it seems to suggest that ultimate is the sacredness of humanity even though it is protected and mediated and delivered by God's grace, especially as delivered through the suffering and death of Jesus due to man's sinfulness. It is only through God's grace that the human being's glory is realisable and made sacrosanct; otherwise, it is in sinfulness and therefore in indignity!

In our current understanding of human rights, the concept of human dignity is a *superb bonum* – the ultimate – even though it is expressed in theological terms as Schroeder argues.[10] In other words, by God's grace, human dignity, the ultimate value, is realised. Thus, whereas the ultimate is an important pursuit of Christians, there are conditions or hindrances to get to the ultimate; such conditions include hunger, discrimination, fleeing from genocide ethnic violence,

[9] Cf. Schliesser: Dietrich Bonhoeffer and Human Rights.
[10] Cf. Schroeder: Human Rights and Human Dignity.

forced sterilisation and other challenges that make it difficult to absorb the gospel. These are the penultimate. For this reason, then, Christians must try to prepare the way for the ultimate to prevail by trying to abolish those negative conditions that hinder the realisation or access to the ultimate. However, this interpretation, in my view, remains non-committal and therefore difficult to rely on. For instance, can we equate the ultimate with human dignity simply because the ultimate is justified by God's grace? It is also not clear to me whether Bonhoeffer himself was clear on this point.

Indeed, his description of the conditions that hinder realisation of the ultimate easily fit in the category of conditions that can be defined as human rights violations – even though they are categorised as obstacles to the proclamation of the word of God's grace in Jesus Christ. Christians have got a strict obligation to remove the obstacles. In other words, the obstacles that hinder the proclamation of the word of God are also equivalent to conditions that hinder realisation of human rights. These conditions seem to reflect absence of civil and political rights as well as economic and social cultural rights as we know them today. Today, we talk of the right to food, the right to education, etc. In fact, the prevalence of these conditions undermines the dignity of human beings which Bonhoeffer like any human rights defender and theorist would wish to negate and eradicate. For instance, consider this statement: »The hungry person needs bread, the homeless person needs shelter, the one deprived of rights needs justice, the lonely needs community, the undisciplined one needs order, and the slave needs freedom« (DBW 6, 163).

Hence, the ultimate-penultimate dynamic integrates Christian culture and the environment in which the gospel takes place; something that may point to the cultural relativity of human rights. For instance, suppose Bonhoeffer was a Moslem, would the death of Jesus be of as much value as he assigned it? Nonetheless, he still informs us that those who would collapse faith into only the struggle against social injustice are equally inadequate, because such a struggle is always at the service of the ultimate whose pursuit is more than this struggle. In this way, the ethic of human rights is well laid out in the context Christianity in spite of the challenges that this position creates for itself, like the tracing the source of human dignity to the death of Jesus. Hence, from this (ultimate-penultimate) dynamic, Bonhoeffer develops an idea of the Natural and Unnatural that easily provides a better understanding of human rights as we understand them today.

The »Natural« versus »created« as sources of human rights

Once again, his reasoning was steeped in a theological context – »Christological« to be exact. His concept of human rights is derived from the *natural* as is understood in *the Catholic wisdom* (DBW 6, 419) most likely, from the Thomist sense which also extended to the Roman law, and which, according to him, had been abandoned by the Protestant reformation. He therefore tried to regain the

»natural« because he thought it was a useful concept. In order to regain the concept of the »natural«, he started by refuting two common misunderstandings. One, regarding the world as completely contaminated by general sinfulness, and two, of regarding the world as an original immaculate creation.

First, he differentiates between the natural, which is part of the fallen world, and the created world – through Christ.[11] He thus contended that although *the natural* has been abused and lost in sin and fallenness so as to defend such things as slavery and segregation, still, the natural should not be discarded altogether because it is what prepares the way for salvation. As he claimed, only by Christ's becoming human do we have the right to call people to natural life and to live it ourselves. Moreover, with Christ's becoming human, natural life becomes the penultimate that is directed toward the ultimate (DBW 6, 174).

Thereafter, Bonhoeffer attempted to define the *natural* from two standpoints of content and form. In regard to form, the natural is determined by its orientation towards Christ and God's will to preservation and can be only recognised by looking at Christ.[12] On the other hand, the content is recognised by reason, even though this reason is as a given and not otherwise. From this point, Bonhoeffer tried to reconcile the puzzle of seeing natural life as either exclusively an end or as a means to an end. Using the role of Christ, he argues that insofar as Jesus Christ's life expresses its createdness, it is an end in itself, and insofar it expresses its participation in the kingdom of God, it is a means (DBW 6, 179). Consequently, it is here that the origin of human rights must be located.

Thus, Bonhoeffer contended that rights are the expression of life as an end in itself while duties arise from life as the means to an end. Unlike Kant who emphasised duties first, Bonhoeffer argued that God gives before He demands – thus one has rights before one bears duties: rights come before duties! Skirting through Roman law and other naturalists before it, Bonhoeffer declares that the most primordial right of natural life is the protection of the body from intentional injury, violation, and killing (DBW 6, 186). This is what now is understood and encoded as the right to life – a fundamental right – without which other rights cannot be enjoyed. Indeed, he himself wrote: The foundation of bodily life is the foundation of all natural rights (DBW 6, 185).

His defence of this natural from a theological point of view is that since by God's will human life on earth exists as bodily life, the body has to be preserved for the sake of the whole person (ibid). At the same time, he also argued that the body is born with us and therefore natural to us. Out of this natural interpretation of the body (both theological and non-theological), Bonhoeffer derived other rights including the »right to bodily joys« which in turn includes, shelter, food, clothing, recreation, play as well as sexuality. He also derives oth-

[11] Cf. Schliesser: Dietrich Bonhoeffer and Human Rights.

[12] Cf. ibid.

er rights from the right to bodily life, including the right to reproduction, the right to personal choice of a marriage partner, the right of birth control, the right to inviolability, and many other rights as properly encoded in international treaties, charters and protocols (DBW 6, 185-217). Although he intended to deal with the natural rights of the life of the spirit (like mind, judgment, will, feeling, imagination), he never did. Nonetheless, although these documents were developed independently, as Schliesser confirms the astounding similarity between Bonhoeffer's list of human rights and the current bill of rights enshrined in our conventions and other relevant documents.[13] Of particular interest also, is the similarity between Bonhoeffer's conception of human rights and the general African understanding as we shall see later on.

Bonhoeffer and the defence of human rights

Bonhoeffer was faced with the question of what to do with human rights violations so as to protect the gift of life and other rights. Although he was a Protestant priest, he was aware that a totally Christian grounding of human rights would probably not be sufficient to appeal to everyone including non-Christians. Indeed, although Bonhoeffer assumed state-church relations and also accepted social inequality in society, he was nonetheless interested in reaching out to everybody – hence his idea of »religion-less Christianity«. In his collected letters, »After Ten years«, Bonhoeffer summarises his view of a true Christian as a true humanist, striving toward human solidarity and the fellowship of the spirit. Although the acceptability of this view beyond Christians is another matter, it suffices to note that he was interested in »real action« which arose from the discovered unity of man with other men and with himself. If human solidarity was his means to achieve human rights, how could this be accomplished? What, then, would be the role of individuals in fighting for their rights?

Bonhoeffer's initial response would have been that human rights are God-given and therefore, no one should violate them. This is however, left unsaid. His immediate response is generally contradictory. Initially, his answer is that it is God who fights for these rights – rather, in his own words, it is God who stands up for these rights (DBW, 6, 184). However, later on, he improves on this stance and writes that »under all circumstances, they must defend a right in such a way as to make it credible that God, not the individual, is standing up for the right« (DBW, 6, 185). Yet, when one traces the whole or major part of the role Bonhoeffer played in fighting the Nazi policies to a point of plotting the assassination of Hitler, the need for individual struggle for human rights in Bonhoeffer is betrayed.

In general therefore, Bonhoeffer's human rights ethic is originated in the epistemological view of the world – ultimate and penultimate dynamic and mediated through Christ. Second, it is also derived from the natural conception of real-

[13] Cf. ibid.

ity, which means rights are God-given. Third, the defence of human rights is fundamentally by God who stands for the rights of human beings although individuals may themselves be involved. In my view, therefore, Bonhoeffer's epistemological and metaphysical claims are pertinent to the theory of human rights as understood today. However, would this stance make Bonhoeffer a human rights defender? But first, what does the concept of human rights defender mean in our current context?

3. The Concept of a Human Rights Defender

The term »human rights defender« is a new concept and its definition is still developing, and has yet to crystallise into a clear, acceptable and effective concept. In human rights parlance, it is increasingly replacing »activist«, »professional«, »worker« or »monitor«.[14] This term is preferred because it is considered relevant and more useful because it provides for neutrality, identity and disciplinary authority and place in society – an attempt to provide for its professionalism in the world professions. However, how useful the term is is not explained. It is my view that real reasons were not given and such reasons may include an attempt to create a professional identity within this fast expanding international business and activity. Such terms as a human rights »worker« or »activist« or »monitor« remained adventitious or casual but nonetheless ineffective. The term »activist« is still widely used but its meaning remains one of a campaigner, or one who takes part in activities that are intended to achieve political or social change especially if such a person is a member of an organisation.[15]

Moreover, the framers of the UN Declaration on Human Rights Defenders (1998) did not realise the relevance of providing a working definition of such for such an important document. In this regard, therefore, its definition is elusive and perhaps likely to confuse rather assure the users[16]. For instance, does a leader of a political party who is seeking power and criticises the government of the day, accusing it of violating citizens' rights belong to the club of human rights defenders? What about those involved in offering financial support to children to attain education, something that would be described as development work? What about a priest who preaches against rigging of elections or violation of the right to vote? I have heard Pope Francis being quoted as having ad-

[14] East and Horn of Africa Human Rights Defenders Project (EHAHRDP): »Only the Brave Talk About Oil«, Kampala 2012, 5.

[15] Cf. Michael Mayor (ed.): Macmillan English Dictionary for Advanced Learners, International Student Edition, 2002.

[16] The declaration on Human Rights Defenders is an abbreviation of »The Declaration on the Right and Responsibility of Individuals, groups and organs of society to Promote and protect Universally Recognized Human Rights and Fundamental Freedoms.«

vised Europeans to accept migrants as if they were receiving Jesus himself.[17] Is he a human rights defender? Does he become a human rights defender because he has articulated the rights of migrants? What if a dictator or state agent curtails the freedom of a protester claiming that he/she is protecting the rights of those who are likely to be hurt by the protestor?

In the context of these ambiguities, the apologists (of the term) have adopted an inclusive meaning and a broad-based approach to the targeted group.[18] However, this does not solve the problems mentioned above, and the opening up of the definition creates an even bigger risk for the defenders because the perpetrators of human rights violations, usually the state, will exploit the vagueness and absence of a clear definition to exclude or include whoever they wish to target.

To provide more clarity, it is claimed that human rights defenders must be defined by the character of their actions and contexts.[19] Thus, they »must be defined according to the rights they are defending and according to their own right to do so, provided they do so by peaceful means«.[20] But how do we distinguish the character of human rights defenders and those involved in other endeavours? How do we categorise a regular human rights columnist? Besides, if we concede that human rights defenders must use peaceful means, what do we do with the so-called »liberators« or »freedom fighters« who are clearly fighting a dictatorship, or stone-throwers in the streets fighting against a repressive regime? Must violence be totally excluded from the occupation of human rights defending? What happens to the just war theory?

It is further asserted that the title or the name of the organisation he/she works for is not so important in defining a human rights defender, but rather, the human rights character of the work undertaken do define a human rights defender.[21] This is the view that is espoused by *Frontline Defenders*, except that they attempt to list various categories of human rights defenders.[22] However, if one tries to list the categories of these people, how exhaustive can this be? Besides, this »character of the work« needs to be made clear. As asked earlier, is a person sponsoring education of the girl child necessarily a human rights defender?

The European Union in its Guidelines[23] exploits the operative 1 paragraph of the UN Declaration on Human Rights Defenders that »Everyone has the right,

---

[17] BBC News, 2nd Feb. 2014.

[18] Cf. EHAHRDP: »Only the Brave Talk About Oil«, 5.

[19] Cf. ibid.

[20] Ibid.

[21] Cf. ibid.

[22] Cited from BBC News, 2nd Feb. 2014.

[23] The European Union in its Guidelines - ENSURING PROTECTION –EUROPEAN UNION GUIDELINES ON HUMAN RIGHTS DEFENDERS: http://www.consilium.europa.eu/uedocs/cmsUpload/16332-re01.en08.pdf (visited on 15th April 2014).

individually and in association with others, to promote and to strive for the protection and realisation of human rights and fundamental freedoms at the national and international levels«. Consequently, their view of human rights defenders »is those individuals, groups and organs of society that promote and protect universally recognised human rights and fundamental freedoms«. In addition, »they seek the promotion and protection of civil and political rights as well as the promotion, protection and realisation of economic, social and cultural rights« and also »promote and protect the rights of members of groups such as indigenous communities.«

However, it is not clear which legitimate way one may adopt to strive for the protection and realisation of human rights as it is being suggested above. Further, this clarification too, creates application problems for understanding the roles and activities of many people who played exactly similar roles in the past, before the current definitional references like human rights conventions were crafted. In this category the list is inexhaustible. In an attempt to overcome this gap, it is claimed that in »Africa, human rights defenders include persons who may not define themselves as such but whose operations in activism or academia or otherwise as a consequence promote respect of human rights in Africa«.[24] Then, finally, they define human rights defenders as those who individually or with others, act to promote human rights.[25] This gap refuses to go and it creates room for every person to become a human rights defender as well as possibly exclude everyone from the group of human rights defenders. In short, the concept of human rights defender is not clearly defined and therefore very difficult to universalise. Nonetheless, a number of things in these definitions are important: one, that, a human rights defender includes those people who act to promote and protect human rights; two, according to the character of the rights they are defending and according to their own right to do so; three, endeavours of human rights defenders must be devoid of violence; and four, based on the European Union Guidelines on Human Rights Defenders, the scope of human rights defenders is restricted to reference to conventional human rights.

4. Bonhoeffer as a human rights defender

As said above, a human rights defender is one who acts to promote and protect human rights as the European Guidelines for Human Rights Defenders declares and as indicated above. Bonhoeffer's actions may not have been explicitly expressed in legal human rights framework as we understand it today, and as the European Union guidelines for human rights defenders suggest, but his actions were synonymous with a human rights defender as understood today.

---

[24] EHAHRDP: »Only the Brave Talk About Oil«, 5.

[25] Cf. ibid.

To begin with, apart from his decision to write a book (Ethics) providing an ethic for human rights as alluded to in his core philosophy above, Bonhoeffer lived a life of sacrifice and love for others especially those suffering oppression and violation of human rights. He hated, and tried to fight exclusion and discriminatory policies as he saw them in the US and as they radically got concretised in Nazi Germany and other countries. As we all know, discrimination and exclusion are, by all accounts, at the heart of human rights conceptualisation. Therefore, in both thought and deed, Bonhoeffer was on the side of the vulnerable which quality provides a strong grounding for human rights defence.

It may be argued that what Bonhoeffer lived for and defended, was much more Christology than human rights. Further, as Schroeder has argued, the religious foundation of the concept of human dignity is religious yet its religious foundation is no longer tenable because its explanatory power has been diminished and rendered useless and misleading.[26] Indeed, she suggests that another justification should be looked for. After all, when Bonhoeffer underpins his concept of human rights on the »gospel of Grace alone«, how do we validate it? However, this would be a mistaken view of the role of a human rights defender like Bonhoeffer.

First of all, there is a thin line between the religious and secular way of interpreting human rights even today. If anything, in a secular sense, the idea of natural rights could be as secular as it is religious. The view that God bestows rights upon every human being and the secular view that human beings have inherent rights because they are human are hardly distinguishable from each other. Second, his dynamic of the »ultimate« and »penultimate« and »the preparation of the way« are very insightful logical structures as they relates it to human rights. The right to food, right to housing, right to life and others as ingredients of the »penultimate« are legitimate considerations of a contemporary human rights framework. The Genesis part of the Bible proclaims shared fatherhood to all people and the case of Cain and Abel raises the issue of being »a brother's keeper« which is a strong underpinning for understanding human rights. [27]

Further, even if he based his thought on Christ's life to derive human rights, it is stunning that he introduced the concept of »religionless Christianity« – an attempt to cross the Christian boundaries to accommodate those outside it. This is significant in the sense that the current understanding is based on the universal denominator of the dignity of human beings irrespective of any social characteristic like race, type of religion, ethnicity, gender and other characteristics, which Bonhoeffer sought to accommodate in his human solidarity project.

Besides, the challenge to his religious thought, Bonhoeffer could also be easily categorised as more of a politician than a human rights defender. But then, who

[26] Cf. Schroeder: Human Rights and Human Dignity.

[27] Cf. Paul Gordon Lauren: Evolution of International Human Rights. Visions Seen, Pennyslavania 1998, 6.

is a politician? Is he/she not the same as a human rights defender? Not exactly! Whereas a politician is often involved in struggles of acquisition, retention, dispensation and relinquishing of power, a human rights defender is concerned with protection and promotion of the human rights of everyone including a politician. Whereas a human rights defender is concerned with empowerment of the people, especially the vulnerable people, a politician is concerned with how to empower himself/herself and those that he chooses, but he/she also tries to disempower those competing for and for retention of power. The interest of the politician is in the dialectic of gaining and losing power since politics is historically competitive. Further, whereas a human rights defender is necessarily a universalist – that is, he/she is interested in the rights and welfare of every human being, a politician is not necessarily a universalist – he/she could easily be a relativist, only concerned with his/her constituency and concerns of the time.

However, as is well known, human rights are never obtained on a silver platter, implying that human rights are also about struggling and negotiating – this is evident in the history of evolution of human rights including the goings-on behind scenes before the Universal Declaration of Human Rights in 1948[28]. Further, a politician does not necessarily have to respect human rights unless he is a democrat. Equally, human rights defenders don't have to be politicians although they may be involved in the politics of rights. After all, as is said above, it is the nature of activities that will define a human rights defender either as a politician only, or as a politician who is also a human rights defender. But it is true, a politician can also qualify as a human rights defender if such a politician has a focus on the promotion and protection of human rights. But also, equally, a human rights defender can be a politician if he/she gets involved in activities of acquiring and of the retention of power. It may, for instance, be difficult to distinguish between a politician and a human rights defender who is focused on civil and political rights. In this regard, the two terms are neither necessarily exclusive nor necessarily inclusive but the definitive expression could be the dominant characteristic. Second, it is also worth noting that the difference is thin and, as we apply the terms, we ought to be careful about the intended meaning. Therefore, Bonhoeffer could have been a politician but it did not, and does not, strip him of the title of a human rights defender. However, being a politician creates problems for a person like Bonhoeffer because his intentions became suspect and therefore vulnerable to the politicians who may wish to scare off those threatening their hold onto power. Indeed, Bonhoeffer was killed by Hitler's agents for exactly this reason. In general therefore, a politician could be human rights defender, and a human rights defender can also, at the same time, be a politician. Bonhoeffer was both.

---

[28] See Lauren: Evolution of International Human Rights, 205-240. The level of struggle that proponents of the Universal Declaration of Human Rights went through was very intense, and obviously, issues of politics were dominant.

Regarding violence, my view is that it is always risky in terms of solving social problems through violence and more so, political problems, because violence attracts more violence. However, in a large measure, most of the human rights encoded in different documents including the Declaration of Universal Human Rights are often products of violence, the latter of which was borne out by the Second World War experience which also in turn derived from the Nazi Hitler and his supporters. In other words, we may need violence to regain human rights and indeed, in many instances, human rights are realised after violence and struggling; hardly ever are human rights obtained on a silver platter. Second, usually violations and abuses of human rights involve violence, humiliation and creation of hopeless situations for the vulnerable people who are put at the mercy of those violating their rights. This was situation of the Jews under the Nazis or black Americans in the US or blacks under apartheid. Bonhoeffer realised that the religious institutions were powerless and were doing little in the face of mass murder of the Jews. As he argued, it is not entirely correct to concentrate on the »ultimate«; rather, we should be concerned with preparing the way – remove the violations or things that hinder access of the ultimate. Otherwise, it is also absurd to look on or simply pray when a mass murderer is rolling on the heads of innocent lives or is busy chopping heads off innocent women, men and babies. In my view, that is the highest price he was prepared to pay in defence of the right to life of the poor, vulnerable Jews and others. And in my view, this is a justifiable reason for violence.

Finally, it may be argued that Bonhoeffer joined the Abwehr (German Military Intelligence) with intentions of fighting the Nazi leadership and possibly assassinating Hitler, which seems to provide grounds for excluding him from the fraternity of human rights defenders. Moreover, he was more a politician who was not simply disagreeing with the Nazis, but who was also involved in criminal activities that included blackmailing the Nazi state. In my view, this argument is particularly hard to crack or negate because the definition of human rights defenders excludes the use of violence and does not permit criminal means, the »sinister intentions« aside which Bonhoeffer advocated and also got involved in.

Indeed, the »just war theory« has been in existence for long. When a person or a group of persons are deliberately targeted and their life is in danger, is it not legitimate that human beings should use any means available including violence to protect themselves against a murderer? Is a person not in order when he/she kills in self-defence or in defending those whose life is threatened? Is a person wrong when he is protecting the rights of others as we used to hear of freedom fighters? Of course, history is replete with erstwhile freedom fighters who are now dictators but that does not mean that people cannot try to overthrow the oppressors as Locke argued in his Second Treatise of Government (1690). People must resist when their rights are not respected by the so-called leaders who would have violated a social contract between them and citizens.

As it has always been argued that we cannot talk of human rights in reference to the pre-Universal Declaration of Human Rights in 1948 (preferring to use entitlements), Bonhoeffer's status as a human rights defender may be challenged. How can he have bestowed upon him an honour of something that was not in existence when he was acting? During his time, neither the definition of human rights as we understand it today nor the definition of a human rights defender as the current instruments (like the European Union) would seem to suggest, were known or applicable. However, as is often the case, it is not easy to separate Bonhoeffer from his historical circumstances in which he wrote and acted. He reacted to the circumstances and within a limited period of his life and history, especially when we are looking for his contribution to human rights. His physical life was outside the current understanding of human rights, but what he said and did was well connected to the present circumstances. His portrait as a human rights defender does not seem different from the life of human rights defenders of today's Africa and specifically Uganda, Rwanda, Somalia, Syria and many other developing countries. He opposed the state (which is normally the primary human rights violator), for which he was persecuted, arrested and finally executed.

Therefore, three things define him as a human rights defender: first, he lived in a period of blatant violation of human rights and he tried to restore the rights. Second, although the language, structures and institutions of human rights were not yet developed as they are today, Bonhoeffer's thinking was as much steeped in the human rights discourse as it is today.[29] In other words, he is important because of his transcendent thought and palpable impact. Third, he lived a life of a human rights defender in precisely the same way any human rights defender would claim to live today.

It is noteworthy that Bonhoeffer's historical context was also his limitation. Whereas Bonhoeffer speaks to the people of Europe and other parts of the world in Christocentric language and ideology, unfortunately however, such a religious message is now diminishing in its effect and therefore hardly acceptable to the same audience as Schroeder argues.[30] The history of religion and its thrust is less attractive to make Bonheoffer attractive to the human rights discourse. To make it worse, the Christology he advocated is intensely hated and opposed by some other religious groups – the mere mention of Christ evokes threats of death in some communities.

Nonetheless, considering that the world is increasingly multi-cultural, multi-religious and multi-many other things, it would be unfair to Bonhoeffer. Hardly any ethical view becomes easily acceptable to the whole world, noting that one of the greatest challenges to human rights practice is the universalisation of hu-

[29] Cf. Schliesser: Dietrich Bonhoeffer and Human Rights.

[30] Cf. Schroeder: Human Rights and Human Dignity.

man rights. Even then, his wish to universalise the concern for all human beings is also present in his work and it is the intention that matters most.

In the context of the foregoing, therefore, it is legitimate to accept the title of a *human rights defender* for Bonhoeffer, although as said earlier, the term should be used more carefully. For instance, Bonhoeffer was more than one thing and we may miss what we want to communicate. Besides, the concept of *human rights defender* is still evolving and needs to be properly defined and customised to human rights parlance and professional application. Even as a secular actor, Bonhoeffer wins the trophy as being a human rights defender because these are truly human rights issues that should be addressed. After all, natural rights are what we have today called *prima facie* rights in the sense that although they are not so absolute and can be overridden by circumstances, nonetheless, they are fundamental rights. If it happens that they are overridden, the one who overrides them bears the burden of proof.[31] This is what we today cherish as an important aspect of human rights theory and protection, for which Bonhoeffer should be lauded as a human rights defender.

After all, his courage to speak early against Hitler's intentions was characteristically prophetic and daring because for one to become a human rights defender, it requires courage and wisdom to discern injustices and evil schemes and then not only to speak out but also to act against them. In tracking down Bonhoeffer's history, we find invaluable choices and actions that he did very well including sacrificing his own life, but unfortunately, which has its own undesirable consequences as well – including death. For instance, should a human rights defender sacrifice his life? What about the people who depend on such a person? How is the desire to sacrifice for others to be distinguished from selfishness of wanting to become a martyr or exploit the situation for one's selfishness?

5. Bonhoeffer's Relevance to Africa

To begin with, it may be argued that Bonhoeffer's conception of human rights is steeped in the Western conception and therefore irrelevant to African historical experience. Yes, indeed, Bonhoeffer view of human rights is not exactly similar to the African conception. Whereas the Western conception is originally a property or claim of individuals – so-called rights claimants – Africans believed that human rights were communal entitlements because the community was prior to the individuals.[32] As John Mbiti wrote, many traditional Africans

[31] Westmoreland-White: Contributions to Human Rights.

[32] Much as this may be true, I also know that individual rights or entitlements were recognised. As Prof. Mbiti writes, »Even though the individual exists for his society and not vice versa, the community respects his property and life«. John Mbiti: Introduction to African Religion, London 1975, 178.

believed and conducted themselves in such a way that: »Since we are, therefore I am«, or, otherwise stated, »I am because we are« and not the other way round.[33] In a general sense, life was largely communal, and it still remains largely communal, although the Western individualised concept is fast spreading amongst Africans. Otherwise as Akinosho pointed out:

»By contrast, the African concept of human rights is based on the conception of communalism, which is collectivism since rights exist because of the communality of humankind and this concept derives its power from aspects of human dignity which corresponds with communal duty«. [34]

That is why, for instance, moral rights including sexual and moral rights are communally dispensed to the extent that crowds claim authority of punishing the so-called »offenders«. This is further explained by national processes of legislating against what the community thinks may be immoral irrespective of being a right or not.[35] Equally, in Africa, children's rights like the right to health, right to food, social security, and others were a communal duty and not individualised as is the modern concept of human rights.[36]

Yet, on the contrary, Bonhoeffer contended that, rather than the individual bearing rights, »natural life« is the bearer of rights which we share with all other human beings. This point is based on the belief that if one understands himself or herself as a bearer of the gift of natural life, he or she will easily see the commonality they both have – both have the same gift of natural life. In other words, there is reciprocity between and among people who share the natural life, but nonetheless, rights are of, and for individuals. Whichever way one sees Bonhoeffer's viewpoint on human rights, it is nonetheless entirely Western, since it is of individual claims rather communal claim. In view of the foregoing,

---

[33] Mbiti: Introduction to African Religion, 175.

[34] Lekan Akinosho on http:nigeriaworld.com/articles/2009/apr/051.html (visited on 15th April 2014).

[35] In December 2013, the Ugandan Parliament passed an anti-homosexuality bill, claiming that it was not according to the Ugandan culture. Namely, that were it not for the Western efforts to spread it in Africa and Uganda, it would not have been in Uganda and Africa. Although in a survey carried out recently found out that there was nothing to suggest that foreigners were recruiting anybody or children as is being claimed by the Ugandan leadership generally. See also Sam Stewart Mutabazi, Mob Justice in Uganda: Lack of Faith in the Judicial Process: Communities taking the Law in their hands, March 28, 2012 on http://www.amazon.com/Mob-Justice-Uganda-Judicial-Communities/dp/3846592587 (visited on 28th May 2014).

[36] Cf. Mbiti: Introduction to African Religion, 176.

therefore, Bonhoeffer's position does not seem to rhyme with the African understanding.

However, these seemingly contradictory positions are obviously misleading. In the first instance, it assumes that African communities have remained traditional and immutable, besides thinking that Africans think the same way. The reality however, is that so much change in African thinking and practice has taken place, so much so that the language of human rights in the conventional sense has become the dominant form of describing our political, social and economic life of Africans. And this thinking has underpinned human rights practice as well.

Also, Bonhoeffer's human rights relevance to Africa could be demonstrated from the fundamental and existential context of the dire conditions this continent finds itself in. For instance, if any argument were to be made as to which society needs human rights most today (trite as it is), there is no doubt that transitional democracies (including African states) would form the majority of such a category. This is not because others do not need rights; but rather, Africans seem to fit the experience and conditions that Bonhoeffer described in his penultimate. This is the case because it is the human rights of the vulnerable that are at risk and are easily violated – in poverty, armed conflict, political unrest, ethnic and religious disagreements, fragile governance structures and processes and many other challenges specific to Africa and other transitional democracies. All these undermine the realisation and enjoyment of human rights. Therefore, the articulation and provision of such a strong ethic to human rights is not lost to those concerned with problems facing Africa.

In general terms, compared to other continents, Africa's commitment to Christianity and general religious adherence is said to be fast growing.[37] If this is the case, then it is not difficult to see the relevance of Bonhoeffer's Christocentric justification of human rights. This is because the reception of such a message and frame of mind corresponds with Christian Africa, and indeed, is arguably the most convenient methodology through which to talk to Africa. In this regard, Bonhoeffer is relevant.

However, this claim assumes that Africa is uniformly Christian and also united in outlook as if Africans are one immutable, monolithic entity. Yet, we know that Africa is not only variegated but is also defiant to general categorisation. Africans are both in the world of Africa but they are transcendent; Arab Africa

---

[37] There is a general admission that Christianity is the fastest spreading religion in the world and specifically in Africa. As an observer in the region, I also see many Christian formations especially those non-denominational ones increasing in number and variety. See Georg Conger, Conversions Propelling growth of Christianity around the world, Newspaper, July 5th 2013. However, there is a widening space of non-religiosity especially with the liberal policy framework encouraged and implemented by both international and national forces.

is quite different from sub-Saharan Africa, much as time and different human experiences produce different people – with different attitudes and outlooks. West Africans are different from East Africans in a number of ways. In fact, although there is a claim that Africa is Christianising fast, it is also possibly true that it is becoming nominalistic in terms of Christianity; it is also fast Islamising. Evidence of this nominalism is that churches are often occupied by children on Sundays, the official day of worshiping God. The older Christians seem to attend churches only on special occasions like Easter and Christmas celebrations, beyond which attendance drastically plummets.[38] Nonetheless, even if it can be said that there is a degree of cynicism, there is a still a significant number of Christians that are receptive of Bonhoeffer's philosophy.[39] This number that is still receptive to this kind of philosophy is still African and can appropriately appreciate Bonhoeffer's justification of human rights.

A closely related point of Bonhoeffer's relevance to Christian Africa is his effort and desire to create solidarity amongst all people – thus recommending »religionless Christianity« and calling for respecting cultural and religious themes that promote the human. Addressing the West for instance, he pointed out that it should recognise the contributions of both ethnic and religious minorities as well as secular forces in harming or making a better human society. In the view of Westmoreland-White, Bonhoeffer provided a strong ethic for human rights grounding because he rejected two negative attitudes of then and now. While one attitude romanticises and idolises some group of human beings, another despises some other or the same group of human beings. This has been one of the major human rights concerns of our time, which has led to unimaginable suffering, exclusion, oppression, impoverishing, humiliation and comprehensive loss of life – as it did in Rwanda in 1994, in Uganda from 1986 to 2009, in the Central African Republic in 2014, in south Sudan in 2013-14 – and of which many other transitional democracies are relevant examples. In short, he was striving to make Christianity appeal to a pluralistic society in a manner comparable to international human rights today; Christianity was expected to be as objective as any public policy just as we understand and implement human rights today. Moreover, his »rescuing« of »the natural« re-emphasised the equality and humanity we share as human beings and God's creation. As such, his claim that every human being has a gift of life made his ethic of human rights more appealing to a number of people including those inside and outside

[38] Bonhoeffer himself made a difference between religion and faith in his Letters from Prison, and called the former (religion) a garment of faith, based on the Protestant church's failure to restrain the Nazis from causing mayhem to the world.

[39] In fact, it is also claimed that more people are abandoning Islam than are abandoning Christianity. Cf. http://www.faithfreedom.org/oped/sina31103.htm (visited on 24th November 2014).

(especially the Protestant) churches which for a long time had taken a critical stance towards human rights.[40]

Further, it should be appreciated that Bonhoeffer lived at a time when social, political and economic challenges were as bad as they are in most of Africa today. His theological and social views were greatly influenced by what type of life he lived and saw around him. His autobiography would probably not read differently from that of Desmond Tutu of South Africa during and after apartheid; and closer to Uganda, Bonhoeffer would be in company of Christian leaders who have courageously spoken against violation of human rights by governments of the day and ended up being killed or reviled.[41]

Like what is happening today, Bonhoeffer argued that the church had become indifferent or separated from the existential world of human suffering; and that, instead, it seemed to be satisfied with simply the admiration of the universe or nature as such. This view resulted from the conduct of the church at the time – allying with the oppressor and alienating other members of the community[42]. In Africa, examples of state-church (Islam-state) alliance which resulted in the violation of human rights are present. The case of the Uganda People's Congress (UPC) in alliance with the Church of Uganda was always a concern for many Ugandans because the discrimination against those outside that alliance is well documented in Uganda.[43] Consequently, Bonhoeffer's realisation is worthwhile, because the church's increasingly ineffective and negative image contributed to religious scepticism and cynicism in the world today.

Yet, it is not entirely true that the church is quite distant from human suffering and problems facing mankind. The church is a human institution, and as such, it can still be used for doing »good« because of its intended purpose, structure and resources it has at its disposal. The Pope and other religious leaders like Archbishops Desmond Tutu (in South Africa),[44] Bishop Robinson (of Canada), Car-

---

[40] Cf. Schliesser: Dietrich Bonhoeffer and Human Rights.

[41] In Uganda, during Amin's regime, Archbishop Janan Luwum of the Anglican Church was killed in 1977, Archbishop Nsubuga of the Catholic Church in Uganda was always reviled by the Obote regime and in current times, Bishop Niringiye, a retired Anglican bishop has been condemned and reviled by the current regime of President Museveni.

[42] At the time, the German Christian Movement was trying to amalgamate Nazi nationalism with the Christian messages/gospel, something that was utterly wrong in the eyes of Bonhoeffer. To his surprise, Bishop Theoder Heckel, the government official in charge of evangelical Church foreign affairs travelled to London to warn him against any ecumenical activity not authorised by Berlin. In a characteristic principled style, Bonhoeffer refused to take heed.

[43] Cf. Rubaraza Samwiri Karugire: A Political History of Uganda, London / Nairobi 1980.

[44] In February 2014, when President Museveni was about to sign the Anti-Homosexuality Bill into an Act, Bishop Desmond Tutu appealed to the former, urging him not to sign the Bill. Although President Museveni ignored Bishop Tutu, he still has

dinal Wamala and Archbishop Ntagali (of Uganda), are still looked up to for moral guidance, and indeed, their voices and deeds on many moral issues and their work in communities are still relevant; and in fact, their leadership also contributes to the realisation of human rights.

After all, we now know that Bonhoeffer's views had a great impact on liberation theology and the acceleration of its development in North as well as South America, apartheid South Africa and other oppressed societies. It emboldened the oppressed to exploit religion and churches for the betterment of their lives and to regain their rights. These prophetic voices of the church and religious leaders are still relevant and can be called upon to intervene, especially in situations of repression, armed conflict or political instability. The opposition leader in Uganda, the retired Colonel Besigye recently expressed his frustration at the religious leaders and institutions for doing little to reduce human rights violations caused by the NRM government.[45] Doing so also means they are keeping ignoring their responsibility. As we know, Bonhoeffer's criticism of ecclesiasticism and his prophetic call upon the churches to give up their concern for privileges, status and join the ranks of the poor resonates with the recent message of Pope Francis[46]. In other words, church leaders should do much more in defending the rights of the citizens, which apparently they are not doing.

Even more importantly, Bonhoeffer's theoretical and practical life displays magnificence and sacrifice for others, a life of virtue, and is a model for human rights defenders especially in transitional democracies. He lived a life of conviction and tried to communicate it; but he participated in the struggle to liberate the vulnerable people as well. In Uganda, leaders often change their views at a time when their followers expect them to demonstrate integrity in the decisions they make. As already alluded to, our members of Parliament voted to remove term limits after receiving a bribe of five million from the president who was the potential beneficiary because his time was almost over. Only recently, some of the MPs from the ruling party stampede the rest of the MPs to retain Museveni as the sole candidate for the 2016 general elections, although there is a general wish that there should be a regime change after nearly 30 years in power.[47] In short, Bonhoeffer's principled life is worth emulating by Africans.

---

to consider and judge himself in regard to Tutu's word.

[45] VOA, »Uganda Opposition Leader Fighting for Equality not Presidency«, January 31, 2014 (visited on 20th May 2014).

[46] »Pope says 'no privileges' for bishops on abuse« http://news.yahoo.com/pope-says-no-privileges-bishops-abuse-224636197.html (visited on 28th May 2014).

[47] The incident occurred on 11th February 2014, at Kyankwanzi Leadership Institute. Having sensed that one of the senior leaders wanted to compete against Museveni for the presidency, some trusted members of parliament stood up and proposed that Museveni should be the sole candidate of the party in 2016. Although it was not on the agenda, the political environment was such that no one would oppose it in the presence of an interested leader who has been President for nearly 30 years.

As earlier indicated, human rights rarely come from »heaven«; they are born of struggles and although violence has been negated by the definers of *human rights defenders*, I keep wondering what would have happened to the world and Jews (and many other people) if their oppressors had not been defeated in the war! In a couple of instances, much more than activism or human rights defence work is needed if the situation has to change for the better. We may support non-violence means, but how far do they go in changing the situation? Today, the world is able to honour Nelson Mandela, Desmond Tutu and others because of their roles in human rights work. Yet we know that they were also supportive of violence in their fight against apartheid or any other oppressive regime. So Bonhoeffer's choice of violent means is still applicable, especially when all other means have failed or when the life of many people is under threat.

It should also be appreciated that in the development of his theory of natural rights, Bonhoeffer employed the Latin motto of *suum cuique*, which means »to each, his/her own«. This stance allows Bonhoeffer to treat different people based on different needs or capacities. He also affirmed that these rights are God-given and inherent in the nature of human beings and, as we now acknowledge, that they are neither granted by the state nor by anybody else. They are applicable to everyone irrespective of race, gender or any other social categorisation. This position is particularly appealing to the oppressed or suffering people (many of whom are in Africa) because it gives them assurance that they are as worthy as anybody else, and that the implementation of their rights should be pursued and defended.

In addition, Bonhoeffer's view was, among other things, motivated by the experiences of suffering minorities, especially the Jews and Black-Americans whose life represented the fallenness of the natural. His fellow preachers (Black Americans) articulated the problem of social injustice in their evangelical work which also practically awakened him to a sensitivity to the suffering of other human beings. This thinking was also reflected in the American civil rights movement of the time. Second, but equally important, was the personal realisation that the preaching of the church alone was not competent enough to bring about integration and justice of the excluded and oppressed. He realised that if he was going to effect change in the lives of the suffering he needed to use means that went beyond the confines of the church. He therefore, started identifying himself with the oppressed as he claimed that he began to see things from below and that he turned from »phraseology to reality«. This implied that he started seeing and appreciating the vulnerable underdogs as his brothers and sisters – a universal benchmark for conceiving human rights.

Also, the life of a human rights defender has been risky and remains risky all over the world like it was for Bonhoeffer. Even in the developed world, Snowden, who is accused by the US government of having released confidential US intelligence information, is now a refugee even when we know that the right of access to information is fundamental. In transitional democracies, especially in armed conflict or civil unrest areas, the life of the human rights defender can be worse – often characterised by humiliation, physical attack and loss of life and violation of human rights of the defenders themselves, but also of their family members and friends.[48] As we do this type of work (of human rights defence), we should also be aware of the above-mentioned possibilities, including death and violation of other rights such as economic opportunities and education.

Of course, Bonhoeffer has limitations, both theoretical and practical – for instance, he did not approve of autonomous reasoning as a satisfactory tool for underpinning an ethical system because of its limited appeal to most Christians.[49] However, this is also his undoing because, at another point, he emphasises reason as the organ of recognising the content of the natural. In fact, this is a short route to chaos and setting a stage for possible extensive violation of human rights. If Jesus is the sole kingpin of his thought in the fight against evil, how does he expect Moslems or other religious groups to accept this worldview? Besides, how is it effective when it does not allow fighting back against enemies? How valid is it to rely on miracles and prayer to solve worldly problems? Yet, as Schliesser observes, there is a lot in Bonhoeffer's justification that is accessible to non-Christians,[50] in particular, his rejection of discrimination among people and courageous defence of human rights. In a nutshell, Bonhoeffer's ideas, actions and his life generally, speak volumes to Africa.

6. Conclusion

In conclusion, the philosophy and life of Bonheoffer are important to the whole project of human rights of both theorists and human rights defenders, but more importantly, to vulnerable categories largely found in transitional societies including Africa. From his entrenched ideology of Christology, Bonheoffer innovated the dynamic epistemology of ultimate and penultimate that metaphorically underpins and justifies the conceptualisation of human rights.

The concept of human rights defenders has gained usage in the human rights fraternity but there is not much to show that it has been interrogated and rid of its risky connotations. Pitted against human rights defenders' standards, Bonhoeffer clearly stands out as one of the human rights defenders in spite of supporting and using violent means to achieve the liberation of the vulnerable people.

---

[48] In this regard, we are reminded of the conspiracy to smuggle Bonhoeffer out of prison by a guard named Corporal Knobloch but Bohnhoeffer refused, fearing retribution on his family especially his brother Klaus and his brother-in-law Hans von Dohanyi who were already in prison. Similarly, this has been the case with many human rights defenders in Africa. In Uganda at least, this is common.

[49] Cf. Westmoreland-White: Contributions to Human Rights.

[50] Cf. Schliesser: Dietrich Bonhoeffer and Human Rights.

Bonhoeffer's experience of the church's behaviour and expendability left him with bitterness that forced him to found a new church – the Confessing Church. The founding of human rights on religious ground is shaky. In this regard, the church and African human rights defenders have a lot to learn from the life of Bonhoeffer because the bad times of Europe are still with us in Africa.

Nonetheless, his Christocentric thought can only serve as one of groundings of human rights. In this way, he made his contribution upon which others can add or remove. As shown above, Africa can tentatively be one of those entities to exploit Bonhoeffer to regain their dignity.

La confession de la culpabilité et le chemin vers la réconciliation

Pascal Bataringaya

Dans cette contribution la question est traitée, comment la violence peut être surmontée par la réconciliation et quel rôle l'Église doit assumer. Nous voulons démontrer, quel rôle joue l'éthique de la réconciliation de Bonhoeffer, qui est enracinée dans une confession de la culpabilité et comment la parole de la paix de Dieu aide les chrétiens à s'engager pour la réconciliation et la paix. Nous voulons analyser ces questions, en les appliquant à la situation concrète du Rwanda et nous voulons proposer des solutions.

Lorsque Dietrich Bonhoeffer parle de »Confession de la culpabilité«, il met en relation trois éléments à savoir: la culpabilité (la faute), la justification et le renouveau. Ainsi il affirme qu'en abandonnant le Christ, l'homme chute, se détruit lui-même et abandonne sa propre nature. Pour cela, le retour et le renouveau ne sont possibles que par le chemin où l'on se reconnaît coupable envers le Christ. La faute qu'il faut discerner et confesser c'est le reniement même du Christ, de la figure qui doit prendre forme en nous et nous conduire à notre »moi« véritable. Ainsi la vraie reconnaissance de la faute ou de la culpabilité ne peut provenir que de la personne du Christ. D'où, la reconnaissance de la culpabilité est toute entière fondée sur la grâce du Christ. C'est dans cette reconnaissance de la culpabilité que commence le processus qui aboutit à l'homme formé à l'image du Christ, donc qui conduit au processus de la réconciliation[1]. Pour cela Dietrich Bonhoeffer affirme que l'Eglise est le lieu, où cette confession de culpabilité devient réelle. L'Eglise est bien donc cette communauté d'hommes qui, par la grâce du Christ, ont été amenés à discerner et à reconnaître leur faute et leur culpabilité. S'il en était autrement, l'Eglise ne serait plus elle-même. L'Eglise est ainsi la communauté d'hommes et de femmes qui, saisie par cette grâce puissante du Christ, confesse son péché et le fait sien, son péché propre et celui de la chute du monde. Les auteurs de la Confession de Detmold parlent de »colmater la brèche«. C'est un signe de la présence vivante du Christ dans une communauté des hommes qui ont une conscience aigüe et constante de leur propre infidélité: on prend sur soi toute la faute.

Par cette réflexion, Bonhoeffer se demande: en quoi consiste cette faute? Qui la prend sur soi de telle sorte que puissent venir le salut et le renouveau? Pour lui, c'est à l'Eglise qu'il revient de prendre sur soi la faute, sans réserves ni conditions: n'a-t-elle pas trahi la figure du Christ? (...) L'Eglise est le lieu où chacun de ses membres est en situation de renoncer aux regards obliques, à droite et à

[1] Dietrich Bonhoeffer: Ethique, Genève 1965, 84-85.

gauche, et de confesser qu'il a fait ce qu'il ne devait pas faire, et qu'il a omis ce qu'il aurait dû faire.[2] C'est ce que Tharcisse Gatwa renforce en ces termes:

»Si le Dieu des Ecritures est connu pour son mouvement de repentance, de changement d'attitude envers son peuple rebelle, connu comme un Dieu de justice et d'amour, pourquoi l'Eglise refuserait-elle de se repentir? Si elle a la vocation d'être la conscience du peuple, elle peut œuvrer pour la justice et la paix seulement si elle se montre un modèle de renouveau par la confession et la repentance«[3].

Pour Dietrich Bonhoeffer, la communauté est donc à même de porter la faute qu'aucun de ses membres ne peut porter; elle est capable de porter davantage que tous ses membres. Elle porte la faute en ce que le pardon lui est accordé par la Parole, et en voyant sa faute effacée sur la croix. Elle peut prendre sur elle les péchés des particuliers lorsqu'elle s'édifie sur la Parole de la croix, et se sait réconciliée et justifiée par la croix de Jésus. Elle est le Christ présent lui-même; voilà pourquoi être »en Christ« et »dans la communauté« est équivalent; voilà pourquoi le Christ lui-même porte la faute des particuliers qui pèse sur la communauté.[4]

Ainsi, fixer ses regards sur cette grâce du Christ permet à l'homme de ne plus regarder la faute des autres et le fait tomber à genoux en confessant: *mea culpa, mea maxima culpa.* Dans cette confession, affirme Dietrich Bonhoeffer, toute la faute du monde retombe sur l'Eglise, sur les chrétiens. Pour autant que les chrétiens la confessent plutôt que de la contester, le pardon devient possible. Selon lui, on ne recherche pas ici le vrai coupable, on n'exige pas l'expiation comme punition du méchant et récompense du bon, et le méchant ne reste pas attaché à son mal. C'est d'abord dans son péché personnel que l'on reconnaît la source empoisonnée de la communauté. Le péché de chacun, même le plus secret, est une souillure et une destruction du corps du Christ. Je ne peux pas vivre tranquillement en me disant que ma part n'est que minuscule; on ne mesure pas: je dois reconnaitre que c'est mon péché justement qui est responsable de tout. Ici Bonhoeffer affirme que ce qui caractérise l'homme, qui a pris véritablement conscience de sa faute, c'est qu'il cesse de mesurer et de s'irriter contre les autres en reconnaissant son propre péché, sans qu'il s'agisse pour autant d'une déformation égocentrique de la réalité.

Etant donné que l'ensemble des individus composent »le moi collectif« de l'Eglise, en eux et par eux l'Eglise confesse et reconnaît sa faute. A ce sujet, Karl Jaspers[5] nous adresse l'avertissement suivant:

---

[2] Ferdinand Schlingensiepen: Dietrich Bonhoeffer 1906-1945. Biographie, Paris 2005, 316.

[3] Tharcisse Gatwa: Rwanda Eglises: Victimes ou coupables. Les Eglises et l'idéologie ethnique au Rwanda 1900-1994, Yaoundé / Lomé 2001, 258.

[4] Fréderic Rognon: Dietrich Bonhoeffer, Lyon 2011, 60.

[5] Karl Jaspers: La culpabilité allemande, Paris 1990, 47.

»Quand nous remontons à la source de notre propre culpabilité, nous finissons par nous trouver devant notre condition d'homme«.

Ainsi, affirme-t-il, que celui qui est resté passif sait qu'il s'est rendu coupable chaque fois qu'il a manqué à l'appel, faute d'avoir saisi toutes les occasions d'agir pour protéger ceux qui se trouvaient menacés, pour diminuer l'injustice, pour résister. C'est pourquoi, on se reconnaîtra, en tant qu'individu, moralement coupable d'avoir, par crainte, laissé échapper de telles chances d'agir. L'aveuglement devant le malheur des autres, cette absence d'imagination du cœur, et cette indifférence intérieure au malheur même qui frappe la vue, tout cela constitue une culpabilité morale.

Dans sa pensée sur la confession de la culpabilité, Jaspers distingue quatre sortes de culpabilité à savoir:

- La culpabilité criminelle: qui porte sur les crimes constitués par des actes objectivement établis qui contreviennent à des lois;
- la culpabilité politique: elle réside dans des actes des hommes d'état et dans le fait que, en tant que citoyen d'un état, je dois assumer les conséquences des actes accomplis par cet état à l'autorité duquel je suis subordonné et dont l'ordre me permet de vivre. Chaque individu porte une part de responsabilité dans la manière dont l'état est gouverné;
- la culpabilité morale: les actes que j'accomplis sont toujours en dernier ressort, individuels, et j'en suis moralement responsable;
- la culpabilité métaphysique: il existe entre les hommes, du fait qu'ils sont des hommes, une solidarité en vertu de laquelle chacun se trouve co-responsable de toute injustice et de tout mal commis dans le monde, et en particulier des crimes commis en sa présence, ou sans qu'il les ignore. Si je ne fais pas ce que je peux pour les empêcher, je suis complice. Si je n'ai pas risqué ma vie pour empêcher l'assassinat d'autres hommes, si je ne suis pas intervenu, je me sens coupable en un sens qui ne peut être compris de façon adéquate, ni juridiquement, ni politiquement, ni moralement. Que je puisse encore vivre, après que de telles choses se soient passées, pèse sur moi comme une culpabilité inexpiable.

Ainsi, les manquements moraux sont le terreau, dans lequel grandissent ensuite la culpabilité politique et le crime. D'innombrables petits actes comme la négligence, le conformisme facile, la justification à bon marché ou les encouragements imperceptibles de ce qui n'est pas juste, participation à l'établissement d'une atmosphère publique favorisant la confusion, l'injustice, la haine et créant par là même la possibilité du mal; tout cela a des conséquences qui contribuent à la culpabilité. On commet également une faute morale en refusant de voir clairement l'importance de la force, qui réside dans la vie en commun des êtres humains et toutes leurs relations. Telle est la culpabilité inévitable de tous, la culpabilité de la condition humaine. Ainsi l'atmosphère de soumission entraine-t-elle déjà une culpabilité collective.

Parlant d'une culpabilité collective, Karl Jaspers s'exprime en ces termes:

»Lorsque des membres de notre famille se rendent coupables par leur conduite, nous avons le sentiment de partager pour ainsi dire leur culpabilité. Cette culpabilité partagée ne se laisse pas objectiver. Nous rejetterions toute espèce de responsabilité tribale. Cependant nous avons tendance, étant du même sang, à nous sentir mis en cause quand un membre de notre famille commet une injustice. Et c'est pourquoi nous sommes enclins à réparer le dommage causé, compte tenu de la situation, de la nature de l'acte et de la qualité de ceux qui en ont souffert, même si nous ne sommes ni moralement ni juridiquement responsables«[6]

C'est pourquoi, comme l'auteur le dit aussi, tous, en tant que chrétiens, nous avons lieu de nous dire:

»Nous ne voulons pas si facilement nous sentir innocents, ni nous apitoyer sur nous-mêmes en nous disant victimes d'une fatalité, ni attendre des louanges pour notre souffrance; mais nous voulons nous interroger nous-mêmes, chercher impitoyablement à voir clair en nous: quand ai-je mal pensé, mal agi?«

Cet exercice introspectif permet d'aller plus loin dans la recherche de notre culpabilité et non dans celle des choses, ni celle des autres. Là on se tient devant Dieu comme individu et non comme réalité collective. La confession de culpabilité c'est une décision de conversion, de devenir meilleur chaque jour et de nous mettre en chemin vers la réconciliation. Le dialogue et le pardon découlent de cette confession qui conduit à la conversion et au renouveau.

Selon Dietrich Bonhoeffer, la vraie reconnaissance de la culpabilité ne résulte pas d'une expérience de la dissolution et de la déchéance; pour ceux qui l'ont rencontrée, elle ne peut provenir que de la personne du Christ même. Elle suppose que nous soyons dans une certaine mesure en communion avec lui. C'est pourquoi, l'auteur affirme que c'est un miracle même. Comment est-il possible que celui qui a renié le Christ soit en communion avec lui? Comment est-il possible que les ennemis d'hier peuvent être aujourd'hui des frères et sœurs, si ce n'est que par la grâce du Christ? Il s'agit ici de la grâce qui coûte que Dietrich Bonhoeffer distingue de la grâce à bon marché. En cela cette reconnaissance de culpabilité se distingue de toutes les autres, dont nous sommes les auteurs et qui demeurent stériles.

Tout ce que nous venons de dire nous révèle que la structure de l'action responsable comporte la disposition à assumer la faute et la liberté. Ainsi la confession de culpabilité ouvre les portes du dialogue, qui est l'un des éléments importants pour gérer et résoudre adéquatement les conflits. La confession de culpabilité permet de s'ouvrir, de se parler, de s'écouter et de décoder le langage d'autrui.

---

[6] Ibid., 88.

C'est dans la confession de notre culpabilité que peut sortir la disposition de l'autre pour le dialogue et la réconciliation, car la confession appelle et engage toutes les parties en conflit à une possibilité de communion et d'échange. Elle conduit ainsi à l'écoute, au dialogue, à l'entente et à la correction mutuelle. La confession de la culpabilité est ainsi une solution thérapeutique, une piste sûre et pratique pour que les groupes antagonistes puissent vivre ensemble. Par la confession de la culpabilité les personnes en conflit peuvent dans une liberté de parole retrouvée et partagée, dire tout ce qui leur tient à cœur. On acceptera que les frustrations, les revendications, les colères, les humiliations, les protestations et les cris longtemps cachés et étouffés fassent surface. La confession de culpabilité par sa qualité de libre expression est en même temps une occasion de guérison pour les personnes ou les parties en conflit. C'est une force qui libère et cette libération est nécessaire tant pour l'opprimé que pour l'oppresseur. Ainsi le cheminement vers la reconnaissance de la culpabilité et vers la repentance sous forme de dialogue est une thérapie pour les populations qui souffrent de divers maux liés aux différents conflits. Pour le cas du Rwanda l'esprit de la reconnaissance de la culpabilité doit être encouragé, car il est une véritable thérapie pour le peuple compte tenu du conflit qui a détruit la société et compte tenu des blessures non encore pansées après les événements tragiques du génocide commis contre les Tutsi en 1994. C'est ce cheminement seul qui permettra aux Hutus et aux Tutsis, groupes antagonistes depuis quelques années, à revoir leur histoire et à se dire la vérité face au drame qu'a connu le Rwanda. La confession de la culpabilité est ainsi pour les Rwandais une occasion de se frayer un chemin vers l'avenir à partir de la situation douloureuse qu'ils viennent de traverser. L'esprit de confession de la reconnaissance de la culpabilité est une invitation à une attitude d'ouverture, de dialogue et crée un chemin vers la réconciliation, car, en mettant en avant la reconnaissance de leur faute et en mettant en avant le respect de l'autre, il permet aux antagonistes de se parler, de s'écouter, de se voir et de s'accueillir mutuellement, ce qui devient pour eux une approche thérapeutique contre les angoisses traumatisantes du conflit. C'est ainsi qu'elle peut devenir le ferment de la redynamisation des relations humaines.

Pour Desmond Tutu l'objectif est la vraie réconciliation et il démontre qu'elle n'est pas facile, mais elle emmène la vraie guérison. Il dit:

»On ne peut pas feindre le pardon et la réconciliation. Ils ne représentent que ce qu'ils sont. On ne peut pas se donner des petites tapes dans le dos, se comporter sinon comme des aveugles. La vraie réconciliation dévoile la terreur, la maltraitance, la douleur, l'humiliation et la vérité. Parfois on aggrave même la situation. C'est un exercice risqué, mais à la fin il vaut la peine, car, quand on affronte la situation réelle, la guérison viendra. Une fausse réconciliation ne peut amener qu'une fausse guérison «[7]

[7] Cf. Desmond Tutu: No future without forgiveness, New York 1999, 86.

C'est pour quoi la vraie réconciliation repose sur une vrai confession de la culpabilité, comme l'a formulé Dietrich Bonhoeffer pour l'Eglise allemande pendant la guerre: Voici en effet, le texte de la Confession de la culpabilité de Dietrich Bonhoeffer, lui qui a vu en l'Eglise le lieu, où cette reconnaissance de culpabilité devient réelle. C'est au moment où l'Allemagne était confrontée à l'idéologie nazie et à la tragédie du génocide des juifs. Je cite textuellement:

- *L'Eglise confesse ne pas s'être acquittée avec suffisamment de clarté et de franchise de sa mission, consistant à annoncer le Dieu unique qui s'est révélé en Jésus-Christ pour tous les temps et qui ne tolère pas d'autres dieux à ses cotés. Elle confesse sa lâcheté, ses déviations et ses dangereux compromis. Elle a souvent renié sa mission, qui est de veiller et de consoler, et a fréquemment refusé ainsi la miséricorde qu'elle devait aux exilés et aux méprisés. Elle était muette alors qu'elle aurait dû élever la voix parce que le sang des innocents criait au ciel. Elle n'a pas trouvé la bonne parole, dite de la bonne manière et au bon moment. Elle n'a pas résisté jusqu'au sang au reniement de la foi; elle est responsable de l'impiété des masses.*
- *L'Eglise confesse avoir pris en vain le nom de Jésus-Christ pour avoir eu honte de lui devant le monde et pour n'avoir pas combattu avec assez de vigueur l'abus de ce nom à une fin injuste. Elle a toléré que violence et injustice fussent faites à l'ombre du Christ. Elle n'a pas protesté lorsqu'on insultait ouvertement le nom le plus sacré, et a ainsi favorisé le sacrilège. Elle reconnaît que Dieu ne laissera pas impuni celui qui, comme elle, a pris son nom en vain.*
- *L'Eglise se reconnaît coupable de la perte du jour du repos: désertion du culte et mépris du repos dominical. Parce que sa prédication du Christ était faible et son culte sans vigueur, elle est responsable de l'agitation et de l'inquiétude perpétuelles, comme de l'exploitation du travailleur au-delà des jours ouvrables.*
- *L'Eglise reconnaît avoir causé l'effondrement de l'autorité paternelle. Elle ne s'est pas opposée au mépris de la vieillesse et à l'adulation de la jeunesse, de crainte de perdre les jeunes et de compromettre ainsi l'avenir; comme si son avenir résidait dans la jeunesse! Elle n'a pas osé annoncer la dignité divine des parents face à une jeunesse rebelle et a essayé, d'une manière bien terrestre, »d'être jeune avec les jeunes«. Par là, elle est coupable de la dissolution d'innombrables foyers, de la trahison des pères par leurs enfants, de l'auto-idolâtrie de la jeunesse, qu'elle a ainsi laissé abandonner le Christ.*
- *L'Eglise confesse avoir vu l'usage arbitraire de la force brutale, la souffrance morale et physique d'innombrables innocents, l'oppression, la haine et le meurtre sans élever la voix, sans trouver moyen de se hâ-*

ter au secours des victimes. Elle s'est rendue coupable de la mort des frères les plus faibles et les plus désarmés du Christ.

- *L'Eglise confesse avoir manqué d'autorité au sujet de la dissolution de tout ordre concernant les rapports des sexes. Elle n'a pas su opposer une résistance ferme et valable au mépris de la chasteté et à la proclamation de la licence sexuelle. Elle n'a pas su dépasser le stade d'une indignation morale occasionnelle. Elle est ainsi coupable envers la pureté et la santé de la jeunesse. Elle n'a pas su annoncer avec suffisamment de poids la parenté de nos corps avec celui de Jésus-Christ.*
- *L'Eglise confesse avoir assisté en silence au dépouillement et à l'exploitation des pauvres, à l'enrichissement et à la corruption des forts.*
- *L'Eglise confesse être coupable envers d'innombrables hommes dont on a brisé la vie en les calomniant, en les dénonçant et en les privant de leur honneur! Elle n'a pas convaincu le calomniateur de son injustice, et a ainsi abandonné la victime à son sort.*
- *L'Eglise confesse avoir convoité la sécurité, la tranquillité, la paix, la possession et l'honneur auxquels elle n'avait pas droit, et avoir ainsi non pas freiné, mais favorisé la concupiscence des hommes.*
- *L'Eglise se déclare coupable envers les dix commandements, et confesse avoir ainsi renié le Christ. Elle n'a pas témoigné de la vérité de Dieu de telle manière que toute recherche de la vérité et toute science ne puissent reconnaître leur origine que dans cette vérité. Elle n'a pas annoncé la justice de Dieu de manière que toute vraie justice doive chercher en celle-ci sa source. Elle n'a pas su montrer la réalité de la sollicitude de Dieu de telle sorte que toute activité humaine voie en elle son origine.*
- *L'Eglise est coupable d'avoir fait disparaître, par son silence, toute action responsable, tout courage à faire face et toute disposition à souffrir pour ce qu'on a reconnu juste. Elle est coupable d'avoir laissé les autorités se détourner du Christ* [8]

Commentaires y relatif

Est-ce trop dire? Quelques justes se lèveraient-ils pour prouver que la faute n'incombe pas à l'Eglise, mais aux autres? Quelques hommes d'Eglise rejetteraient-ils ce que nous venons de déclarer comme une grossière insulte? Auraient-ils la prétention de se croire appelés à juger le monde et à peser la faute, l'attribuant à celui-ci ou à celle-là? L'Eglise n'était-elle pas entravée et liée de

---

[8] Bonhoeffer: Ethique, 87-89.

toute part? Tout le pouvoir temporel ne se lèverait-il pas contre elle? Pouvait-elle compromettre ses cultes et sa vie communautaire, ses derniers biens, en défiant les puissances anti-chrétiennes? Ainsi parle l'incrédulité, qui voit dans la confession des fautes non pas le retour à la figure de Jésus-Christ qui a porté le péché du monde, mais simplement une dangereuse dégradation morale. La libre confession des péchés n'est pas à bien plaire, mais elle marque l'irruption de la personne de Jésus-Christ dans l'Eglise, qui s'y soumet, faute de quoi elle cesse d'être Eglise. Qui étouffe ou altère la confession des péchés, se rend irrémédiablement coupable envers le Christ.

En confessant sa faute, l'Eglise ne dispense pas l'humanité de sa propre confession, mais l'engage à entrer dans la communauté de ceux qui confessent leurs péchés. L'humanité qui l'a trahi ne peut subsister devant le Christ qu'en étant jugée par lui. L'Eglise appelle à ce jugement tous ceux qu'elle atteint.

Nous apprenons de Dietrich Bonhoeffer que la vérité, qui inclut toujours la repentance, précède la réconciliation, non dans le sens moral, mais dans le sens logique. On ne peut pas grimper à la réconciliation par une échelle de moralité. La grâce à bon marché ne nous est pas permise. La réconciliation est inconditionnelle, mais appelle à la repentance . Dans ce sens c'est un important devoir des églises chrétiennes d'annoncer le message de l'Évangile de la vérité qui libère, de la justice pour tous, de l'amour du prochain, qui inclut l'ennemi, du respect absolu de l'homme, qui est créé à l'image de Dieu et qui est délivré par le sang de Jésus, et annoncer la bonne nouvelle du pardon, du dialogue et de la réconciliation. Cette constatation est particulièrement importante dans le contexte rwandais et a été adoptée par l'Eglise Presbytérienne au Rwanda dans sa Confession de la Culpabilité après le génocide.

Le texte de la confession de culpabilité du Synode Général de l'Eglise Presbytérienne au Rwanda (EPR) en 1996 après le génocide de 1994 contre les Tutsi (Texte traduit du Kinyarwanda en Français):

»Rwandaises, Rwandais et vous tous les croyants en Dieu, le moment vient pour nous évaluer parce que l'Eglise a une grande honte devant l'extermination de la race humaine qui est 'l'image de Dieu'; l'extermination qui a eu lieu dans notre pays et vis-à-vis de laquelle l'Eglise a affiché au grand jour ses faiblesses du fait qu'elle n'a pas pu empêcher ou stopper ces actes ignobles que ce soit au moment où ils se préparaient ou lors de leur mise en exécution. Comme le serviteur de Dieu, le prophète Néhémie l'a fait (Cfr Néh 1,5-11); au nom de tous les fidèles membres de l'Eglise Presbytérienne au Rwanda (EPR), le Synode Général demande pardon à Dieu et à tous les Rwandais. A cause de cette inexprimable faiblesse et du manque de bon témoignage au moment opportun, le Synode demande à tous les chrétiens du Rwanda et du monde entier de s'engager fermement dans la lutte contre tout ce qui est relatif au massacre et qui est contre la volonté de la Parole de Dieu. Le Synode appelle tous les chrétiens à lutter contre tous les crimes mettant en danger la vie des Rwandais dont: la ségrégation ethnique et régionale ainsi que les divisions relatives à la croyance,

étant donné qu'elles sont la source et la cause du malheur qui s'est abattu sur le peuple de Dieu, lui qui les a créés pour vivre en paix et en toute liberté. La Parole de Dieu nous rappelle qu'il n'y a ni Juif ni Grec, ni homme ni femme, ni Hutu ni Tutsi ou Twa mais que nous sommes tous un en Christ.«[9]

Resumée

On peut fonder une politique de la réconciliation de la société dans la réconciliation de Dieu avec les hommes. Etant donné que Dieu est l'initiateur de la réconciliation et de la paix, tous les chrétiens sont appelés dans son service de la réconciliation et de la paix (2 Corinthiens 5,11). Son objectif est de gagner des hommes pour ce message de Jésus Christ. La réconciliation entre les hommes se réfère à la paix et la réconciliation entre Dieu et sa Création et se concrétise dans la situation du moment.

Ce message biblique que Bonhoeffer a mis au centre de sa théologie et de son action peut être très significatif dans le contexte rwandais actuel. Les chrétiens sont appelés à suivre la pratique de la réconciliation de Jésus sur la terre, de façon à ce que la réconciliation devienne «un devoir de paix pour l'humanité». C'est ainsi que nous construisons des ponts entre les hommes et c'est ainsi que nous sommes solidaires avec ceux qui souffrent, c'est ainsi que nous sommes présents pour les autres, construisons la paix et la vie nouvelle et seront capables de nous sacrifier pour ce processus. Nous voyons par tout cela que la contribution de Bonhoeffer à la discussion sur la réconciliation à l'intérieur de l'Eglise et dans la société rwandaise sont fortement liées au Sermon de Jésus sur la Montagne (Mathieu 5-7)[10].

Ce processus de la réconciliation doit être porté par beaucoup de personnes et la majorité de la population doit être prête à le promouvoir.[11] Pour cela une vaste campagne politique et écclésiastique de formation et d'information sur les relations de la vie en société est d'une importance stratégique.[12]. Cela veut dire qu'on organise des actions de réconciliation à de nombreux endroits, pour ainsi promouvoir la cohabitation des différentes parties divisées de la population.

Les impulsions de l'éthique de la réconciliation de Bonhoeffer peuvent aider de trouver des solutions consensuelles pour une réconciliation, pour une gestion non-violentes de conflits et la création de relations équitables.[13]. La mise en pratique de ses convictions contribuent à démanteler la méfiance et la haine entre les rwandais et entre les hommes provenant de la guerre et du génocide et peu-

---

[9] Twubake No. 09, Kigali, 1997.
[10] Ibid., 107.
[11] Ibid., 136.
[12] Ibid.
[13] Ibid., 135, 136.

vent ainsi fonder les bases de la réconciliation et la paix.[14]

Dans ce cadre-ci, les églises du Rwanda, particulièrement l'EPR après la reconnaissance de la culpabilité en 1996 ont contribué,

- à rétablir la confiance entre les hommes
- à accompagner le bon déroulement des tribunaux traditionnels Gacaca, permettant ainsi de rétablir la co-existance entre les victimes et les auteurs du génocide et accompagner ces tribunaux dans la lumière de la parole biblique,
- à organiser les cultes annuels de mémoires,
- à organiser les commissions pour l'unité et de réconciliation au niveau national aussi dans les communauté locales,
- à construire des monuments en mémoire du génocide,
- à accompagner les auteurs du génocide et les rescapés sur le chemin de la réconciliation et à mener le dialogue entre eux parce que c'est la source de la guérison pour tous.

De plus les églises ont offert aux différentes parties des endroits sûrs et protégés pour une communication et interaction entre eux, en leur permettant de se rapprocher personnellement. Puisque la vraie réconciliation est basée sur le pardon, qui inévitablement va de pair avec la reconnaissance de la culpabilité et la repentance, comme cela était le cas, par exemple dans la paroisse presbytérienne de Remera-Rukoma.

Le processus de la réconciliation nécessite un long cheminement et sur ce chemin l'aide et l'accompagnement est indispensable. Le travail de l'église des vingt dernières années montre que la réconciliation entre des ennemis est possible. Cela signifie que le travail des églises pour la réconciliation et la paix est très important au Rwanda. Il est absolument nécessaire de continuer. Nous sommes sur la bonne voie dans l'esprit de l'éthique de réconciliation de Dietrich Bonhoeffer.

---

[14] Ibid., 137.

Culpability Confession as a Path to Reconciliation – It *can* start, but it can only *start* with Bonhoeffer...

Jannika Haupt

In the following, I will deal with the culpability confession of Dietrich Bonhoeffer and the culpability confessions that the German church formulated in the years directly after the end of the Second World War. First of all, it is important to emphasise that it took the institutional church forty years to begin dealing seriously with its immediate culpability for the genocide committed by the Germans against the Jews.[1] This is still – and it must remain – »work in progress«. Dietrich Bonhoeffer's culpability confession is a better starting point for this essay than any other theological documents whose origins lie in the so-called Third Reich (i.e. the National Socialist regime with Adolf Hitler, »The Fuehrer«, as its leader), but it is necessary to go beyond that too – this is what the title is trying to say. The aim of the following is to make this thought plausible.

The first section is a comparison of the confessional documents in the 30s and 40s with Bonhoeffer's culpability confession; the second is an introduction to the criticism of Bonhoeffer's writings as expressed from a Jewish perspective; and the conclusion will be an attempt to focus on the outcome of Bonhoeffer's thoughts. The pitfalls inherent in Bonhoeffer's claims of reconciliation, especially between Christianity and Judaism, must also be pointed out here. All of this should be understood as a catalyst for discussion.

1. Why Bonhoeffer is more valuable for finding a path to reconciliation than the other attempts of the church in the following decades

Stuttgart, Darmstadt, Barmen. Isn't it remarkable how all these documents dealing with culpability are named after the cities they were drafted in? Bonhoeffer is more concise and rigorous, not only in the content, but even in the title of his fragment. It is clearly and straightforwardly named »Culpability Confession«[2].

---

[1] That the roots for a German theology after the Shoa are to be found in Bonhoeffer is a late 20th century understanding. Cf. Asta von Oppen: Der unerhörte Schrei, Dietrich Boenhoeffer und die Judenfrage im Dritten Reich [Schalom-Bücher Vol. 5], Hannover 1996, 109.

[2] Bonhoeffer states that a veritable culpability confession can only be a confession of guilt *in extenso*. Cf. DBW 6, 136.

The heading means what it says. It transports a holistic demand without narrowing it down to a city's name. Why is it that the confessions which are mentioned above all have specific local names? Is there a first limitation in giving themselves specific names? Didn't the authors trust their claim to have formulated *the* valid Confession for the church? Maybe that wasn't even their aim. But what does a confession of guilt mean without the requirement of being entirely true and total?[3] Whether this specificity was intended or not, maybe there is a specific sense behind it, namely – not explicitly – that these are »not enough«. In the following, these confessional documents will be presented briefly and an attempt made to show why they all lag behind Bonhoeffer's Confession – in total or in some aspects. In contrast to Bonhoeffer's draft, they all had and/or have the status of official church documents to comment on the status of the church after the genocide in Germany.[4]

Before that, the situation of the Evangelical Church in the years of the so-called »Third Reich« in Germany will be briefly explained, to give an indication of the lines along which the church acted in the late 30s to the mid-40s and to give an idea of the reuniting problems it had to face after the end of Second World War.

During the rule of National Socialism in Germany, the church was split into two main parties – the »German Christians« and the »Confessional Church«. The German Christians were followers and supporters of the National Socialist ideology and politics. There were even moves to abolish the »Old Testament« and to de-Judaise Christianity.[5]

Although the Confessional Church was founded out of protest against the interference of National Socialism in the rights of the church, it was by no means the party of fierce opponents the German church would have needed in order to be a righteous church on account of its confession.

The Barmen Declaration[6]

The Barmen Declaration, written in May 1934 (one year after National Socialism legislated the Aryan clause / laws excluding Jews), is a very early confessional document. It is included here – even though it is not a culpability confession at all – because it was adopted by the German Evangelical Church after the

[3] Refering to Boenhoeffer – it means nothing at all. It would even be a poisoning of the community, cf. DBW 6, 136.

[4] »Barmen« and »Stuttgart« are to be found on the official homepage of the German Evangelical Church, listed as confessional documents: http://www.ekd.de/glauben/bekenntnisse/index.html (visited on 25th Novemeber 2014).

[5] Cf. Heiner Faulenbach: Art. Deutsche Christen. II. Ideologisch-theologische Grundansichten, in: RGG^4, 2008, 701.

[6] Translated text cited after: http://www.ekd.de/english/barmen_theological_declaration.html (visited on 25th November 2014).

end of the Second World War, without seeing the need for any changes or additions.[7] Bonhoeffer's culpability confession was yet to be written, but he had already made important remarks – problematic in themselves, because he argues with anti-Jewish traditions of the Christian church – on how the church should react to the Aryan clause, namely by distancing itself from the ideology that Jewishness is a question of race.[8]

The Barmen Declaration was formulated at a Synod of the Confessional Church, opposing the »German Christians«. It consists of a preamble, six theses and a short conclusion. It is printed on two sheets of paper. The theses all follow the same pattern. They start with a citation of the New Testament. Accordingly, they formulate an affirmative meaning for the church's historical situation. They conclude with a rejection.

Barmen deals with the following topics:

1) Jesus Christ as the Word of God, whom we have to obey exclusively

2) Jesus Christ as encouragement and demand, liberating us from the godless claims of this world

3) the church as institution with its own jurisdiction that must not be changed by worldly politics and ideologies

4) the offices of the church as functional positions for the community and not hierarchical leadership (which must not exist)

5) worldly politics are not the exclusive and total regime of human life, including church life

6) the word of God is in no other service than its own, it is free as it is given.

Not to be misunderstood – this was a great achievement. It was and is against political instumentalisation of church. And in this aspect it is a very important attempt to resist and deny the total leadership claim of Adolf Hitler in its time, and a reminder today to resist »being an ideological child of your time« and instead to reread and test contemporary trends and requests in the light of the message and requests of Christ himself.

---

[7] Even though (in the 1970s and 1980s – 30-40 years later!) there were German theologians who emphasised the shortcomings of Barmen; in this context prominently to be named Eberhard Bethge (e. g.: Eberhard Bethge: Christologisches Bekenntnis und Antijudaismus. Zum Defizit von Barmen I, in: Bethge: Bekennen und Widerstehen, München 1984, 113-140 and: Bethge: Barmen und die Juden – eine nicht geschriebene These?, in: Regina Claussen/Siegfried Schwarz (Ed.): Vom Widerstand lernen. Von der Bekennenden Kirche bis zum 20. Juli 1944, Bonn 1986, 147-166).

[8] Namely: Bonhoeffer's essay »The church and the Jewish Question« from April 1933, cf. Dietrich Bonhoeffer: The Church and the Jewish Question, in: Bonhoeffer: No Rusty Swords. Letters, Lectures and Notes 1928–1936, New York 1965.

But Barmen lacks any explicit confession of guilt. Of course, that is because it is not formulated and has no claims to be a culpability confession. But the church, which still uses this document as a confessional document today, is in need of that and should at least have made some additions in this direction. At the time the Barmen declaration was formulated, perhaps the »Jewish question« was not its top priority, and maybe it was impossible to see where the National Socialist regime would lead, but in the aftermath even one of its authors, Karl Barth, regretted that no word was found to refute the state's injustice against the Jews.[9]

Even in 1934, the church had already failed to protect its members who were baptised Jews. Not only did it not protect them, it even exposed them to exclusion from their chosen church and thereby denied their Christianity. Although this was one of the reasons the Confessional Church was founded, out of protest against the Aryan clause – particularly because of the state's demand to exclude pastors who had »Jewish blood« in their ancestry – there was no negotiation of the »Jewish question«. The Barmen Declaration mainly concentrates on emphasising that there is another authority for the church with a more legitimate claim than the »Fuehrer«, and on dissociation from the »party« of »German Christians«. It is a document in which the church reasserts its own rights, and as such it is insufficient for the German church – at latest after the end of Second World War.

Stuttgart Culpability Confession / Culpability Statement

To start with a short remark: There are two names for this document. It is known as the Stuttgart Culpability Confession and the Stuttgart Culpability Statement. On its website, the German Evangelical Church officially names it the Culpability Statement[10]. In the internal semantic of the church, however, the status of a »confession« is stronger than that of a (mere) »statement«.

The Stuttgart Culpability Confession was written in October 1945. The occasion was the visit of a member of the World Council of Churches. It was signed by the councillors of the German Evangelical Church who were already leading members of the Confessional Church during the »Third Reich«. The World Council of Churches expected[11] a full confession of guilt from the German Evangelical Church as a condition for reconciliation. This document was more a

---

[9] Cf. in a letter to Bethge May 22th 1967, published in: Karl Barth: Gesamtausgabe, Volume V: 1961-1968, 1975, 403. Problems expounded in Hermann Kalinna: War Karl Barth »politisch einzigartig wach«? Über Versagen politischer Urteilskraft, Berlin et. al. 2009, especially Chapter V.

[10] http://www.ekd.de/glauben/bekenntnisse/stuttgarter_schulderklaerung.html (visited on 25th November 2014).

[11] Cf. Gerhard Besier / Gerhard Sauter: Wie Christen ihre Schuld bekennen. Die Stuttgarter Erklärung 1945, Göttingen 1985, 17.

reaction than an act of free will and comprehension. It is a result of consultations between the German church and the WCC which started in 1942, and the main reason for writing this document down was to enable the German Church to confess a grave joint responsibility for the persecution of the Jews and the politics of National Socialism. This one sheet of paper consists of five clauses. The central statement is formulated:

»*We see ourselves with our people not only in a vast community of suffering but also in a solidarity of guilt. Through us, infinite wrong was brought over many peoples and countries. That which we often testified to in our communities, we express now in the name of the whole church: We did fight for long years in the name of Jesus Christ against the mentality that found its awful expression in the National Socialist regime of violence; but we accuse ourselves for not standing to our beliefs more courageously, for not praying more faithfully, for not believing more joyously, and for not loving more ardently.*«[12]

It is a »we« of church and people, formulated by the church making no noticeable difference between the responsibility of the church and that of the people in general. It even starts with »*we have fought long years against the spirit which expressed itself awfully in the National Socialist oppressive regime*«. This is not a confession of guilt but a self-recommendation.[13]

It does not confess a special responsibility, in which the church failed and for which it bears a specific guilt. It is not a radical questioning of the actions of the German church, it just states in comparatives that one could have believed *more* courageously, prayed *more* faithfully, believed *more* joyously and loved *more* ardently. This supports the mistaken image of a church in – at least mild – opposition during National Socialism. In the complementary close there is talk of a new beginning but there is no concrete formulation of *how* that should or could be done. No contents. And there is no confession of guilt concerning the genocide against the Jews. It says »through us infinite wrong was brought over many peoples and countries«, which surely includes Judaism, and the confession of »the infinite wrong« is to be valued, but it does not express a specific guilt for the industrialised genocide against the root of Christianity. It is to be kept in mind that Bonhoeffer already blamed himself and the church for letting »the weakest and most defenceless brothers and sisters of Jesus Christ«[14] down, words already written five years before. After the end of the war, German theology still dealt with Israel as a cursed people, punished by God because it doesn't believe in Jesus Christ as the Messiah and, even worse, crucified the Son

[12] My own translation.

[13] Cf. Dieter Schellong: Kirchliches Schuldbekenntnis. Gedanken Bonhoeffers und die Wirklichkeit des deutschen Nachkriegsprotestantismus, in: Ernst Feil (Ed.): Verspieltes Erbe? Dietrich Bonhoeffer und der deutsche Nachkriegsprotestantismus [Internationales Boenhoeffer Forum Vol. 2], München 1992, 28-57, 47.

[14] DBW 6, 139.

of God. The earliest formulation of a theology that states that the church has not replaced Israel as God's chosen people but joins the covenant with God is to be found in the 1950s. But from then it took about another 20 years, in a movement from the communities into the governing bodies of the protestant churches and universities in Germany as a theological requirement, and recognising the need to talk with Judaism and hear and learn about the Jewish roots and contents of belief in the New Testament. We are still in a learning process.

In its time, the WCC read this document as a »freeing word«, but its reception in the Evangelical Church of Germany was cautious.

German Theology started to write critically and reflected on this document in the 1980s.

Word of Darmstadt.

This has as its subheading »A Word of the 'Bruderrat' of the Evangelical Church in Germany on the political path of our people«. Unlike the Barmen Declaration and the Stuttgart Statement, the Word of Darmstadt shares the fate of Bonhoeffer's Confession: it is not regarded as »tradition« by the institutional Evangelical Church of Germany today. It was written in 1947 and immediately sparked off controversial discussions.

It consists of seven paragraphs, like the others filling one sheet of paper. Four of these seven paragraphs start with the phrase: »*We went astray, when we...*«[15], a phrase that assigns to it its confessional character. The first paragraph demands that we attend to the words of Jesus Christ and confesses that German politics and longings in the years of National Socialism (although unnamed) do not accord with the word of Jesus Christ. The second paragraph criticises the »dream« of a special German mission for the world which it had been attempted to realise by means of rigid political leadership and military missions both inside and outside Germany. The third paragraph confesses a betrayal of Christian freedom. The church was wrong in being a restorative force, resisting changes in forms of life where this was necessary to make »living together« possible. The fourth paragraph criticises too how the church politicised the free grace given by God. Political or social ideologies and convictions must not dictate to the offer of grace. The fifth paragraph states a failure of the church in dealing with economic problems. The church did not concentrate on the poor and disenfranchised. The sixth leads to a draft of what could be done to avoid going astray »*Turning back to God and turn to one's neighbour by the power of the death and resurrection of Jesus Christ*«. In the seventh and last paragraph, the authors put the emphasis on the freedom which lies within the Word of God against the demanding ties of the world. It states the responsibility of the individual »*to*

[15] This and the following citations are my own translations.

build a better German State which conduces to right, social welfare, inner peace and reconciliation«.

The Word of Darmstadt tried to name concrete guilt for the events during National Socialism that were supported by the church. It states the need for reconciliation with the nations of the world. It also shows *how* the church supported the structures for and the regime of National Socialism itself. It goes beyond the Stuttgart Culpability Statement[16] and was not accredited by the larger part of the church and theologians in its time. It later became an important document for the church of the German Democratic Republic.

It is a very specific document and it has a clear aim, to make Germany a better state. It is a politically sensitive document, but that is where its limitations lie, side by side with its progressiveness – it is a document of domestic policy.

In conclusion of this first part:

The German Evangelical Church was not willing to confess its joint responsibility for the genocide against the Jews without any cutbacks. It tried to distance itself from responsibility. It tried to qualify the guilt and blamed specific persons. But Bonhoeffer stated early after World War One »there is no guilt of single Germans and single Christians, there is just the one guilt of the Germans and the Church [...] not the individual needs to repent [...] but the church«[17]. In denying that, the German Church buried not only the need but also an opportunity for true beginnings of reconciliation. To quote Bertold Klappert: »A denial of joint responsibility and guilt for the Holocaust, no matter if it is intentional or unaware, shows that one still lives in the context of guilt and is part of all processes that lead to a new holocaust.«[18]

Bonhoeffer states similar theses in his culpability confession using different terms. He demands rigorous and concrete confession of guilt from the church. The foundation of his argumentation is the substitution of Jesus Christ. At least there are living problems within Jewish-Christian dialogue. This leads to my second part. As important as it is to acknowledge the contents of these familiar confessions, it is also important to observe what the church kept – and in my opinion still keeps – silent about too often.

---

[16] In fact it understands itself as an addition to the missing parts in the Stuttgart Statement. In this text too, no mentioning of the persecution and murder of the Jews of Europe is to be found.

[17] DBW 1, 75.

[18] Berthold Klappert: »Der Jude hält die Christusfrage offen«. Weg und Wende Dietrich Bonhoeffers in der Israelfrage, in: Klappert: Miterben der Verheißung. Beiträge zum jüdisch-christlichen Dialog [Neukirchener Beiträge zur Systematischen Theologie, Bd. 25], Neukirchen-Vluyn 2000, 58-104, 64.

2. Jewish voices on Bonhoeffer

When we seek reconciliation, the first thing to do is to listen to the group whom we wronged. This is not just a sign of respect, but a necessity in order to sharpen our sensibilities for true dialogue.

We are lucky if and that there *are* any voices to listen to. They open up the opportunity to lead a dialogue at all.

As a consequence, we have to listen to the critique the Jewish dialogue partners have formulated for finding a way to work with the opportunities Bonhoeffer offers. There are a few Jewish voices who comment on Bonhoeffer's theology. I will try to present their main arguments against and for a dialogue, based on Bonhoeffer's theology.

All of the critics put an emphasis on reading Bonhoeffer in his historical context, not in order to excuse his in parts anti-Jewish theology, but to understand him better within his theological tradition. But there is a strong willingness to reflect on his theology on »*the millennial Christian polemics against Jews*«. It is a question of seeing Bonhoeffer as a victim of his circumstances and of valuing his attempts to emancipate himself from them.[19] That leads to two different positions. The first one is to see Bonhoeffer »as the best of a bad lot« or as »a righteous Gentile« even though not acknowledged as one by Yad Vashem.

The position of »best of a bad lot«[20] is here represented by the arguments of Stanley Rosenbaum, professor for Jewish studies at Dickinson College in Pennsylvania. He argues against the theses that Bonhoeffer's attitude against Jews changed over the years from seeing Jews as being in need of mission to recognising Judaism »*as a legitimate bearer of God's continuing revelation*«[21]. His main observation is that Bonhoeffer does not deal with Judaism, but only with »the Jew« or Israel in a biblical sense[22]. Rosenbaum remarks that Bonhoeffer's mention of Jews in his Ethics – »*An expulsion of the Jews from the west must necessarily bring with it the expulsion of Christ. For Jesus was a Jew.*«[23] – does not go beyond Luther and therefore cannot be counted as an expression of a »man for all seasons«[24]. According to the readings of Rosenbaum, Bonhoeffer's main concern for Jews is in seeing them as a cursed people whose suffering can only come to an end by conversion.[25] He values Bonhoeffer's repudiation of the National Socialist oppression of Jews as a humanitarian act, but doubts that

---

[19] E. g. Pinchas E. Lapide: Boenhoeffer und das Judentum, in: Feil 1992, 116-130, 118f.

[20] Stanley M. Rosenbaum: Dietrich Bonhoeffer. A Jewish View, in: Journal of Ecumenical Studies 18 (1981), 301-307, 306.

[21] Ibid.

[22] Ibid.

[23] DBW 6, 89f.

[24] Rosenbaum: Dietrich Bonhoeffer. A Jewish View, 305.

[25] Cf. ibid., 302f.

Bonhoeffer, the theologian, sees much more in that than the concrete danger for baptised Jews.[26] He confirms the observations that Bonhoeffer becomes more related with the Old Testament and notes »tantalising signs of growth«[27] during Bonhoeffer's time after his arrest but states that »from the printed records we are constrained to glean our answers«[28] if there was a shift in Bonhoeffer's theology. So Rosenbaum resumes: »*His humility as well as his honesty are apparent in his writings as well in what is written about him. It is nonetheless sad to search his works, in vain, for references to Jews that are not ignorantly patronising or dogmatically conversionist*«[29]. It is very important to mention: Rosenbaum does not deny that there might have been a full acceptance of Judaism by Bonhoeffer after the Second World War, but he also refuses to find proof of that in the fragments of his works, and does not want to judge »out of silence«[30].

Richard Rubenstein, on the other hand, argues that it is precisely because Bonhoeffer sticks to his Lutheran teaching that he is able to say anything at all against the persecution of the Jews.[31] He says that, however great his anger and offense at reading passages such as, »*We should still show them the Christian doctrine and ask them to turn and accept the Lord whom by rights they should have honoured before we did [...] Where they repent, leave their usury, and accept Christ, we would gladly accept them as our brothers*«[32], he can think of no other possibility for Bonhoeffer to speak out for the Jews amongst his fellow pastors than with the authority of Luther. Rubenstein questions whether a political or humanitarian argument would have convinced colleagues within the church, but with the authority of Luther, »*well known for his antagonism to Jews*«, it was an attempt with some chances of success »*to argue that the Nazi attempt to exclude baptised Jews on racial grounds from Christian fellowship had no theological support*«. Rubenstein even strengthens the theological reasonability of Bonhoeffer's separation, though completely un-Jewish, of the two realms and emphasises, seeing it as the most striking remark, that Bonhoeffer formulates how, under distinct circumstances, the church can and has to legitimately criticise the state.[33] Only with the teaching of two realms can Bonhoeffer keep the church free from political influence and simultaneously be able to

[26] Ibid.
[27] Ibid., 306.
[28] Ibid.
[29] Ibid.
[30] Ibid.
[31] Cf. Richard L. Rubenstein: Was Dietrich Bonhoeffer a 'Righteous Gentile'?, in: International Journal on World Peace Vol. 17.2 (2000), 33-46, 36f.
[32] Ibid.
[33] Ibid., 37f.

criticise politics from the point of view of the church and aid »*the victims of any ordering of society, even if they do not belong to the Christian community.*«[34]

Rubenstein has read Rosenbaum and comprehends his arguments, but with his shifted focus he comes to another résumé. He follows Ruth Zerner in being of the opinion that, had Bonhoeffer survived, he »would have undertaken a radical rethinking of Christian thinking.« She judges that as being likely, because »Bonhoeffer's students and theological heirs in post-war Germany have taken the lead in the creative dismantling of the Christian legacy of anti-Judaism and its historical consequences«[35].

What can be learned for Christian theology now from these Jewish readings of Bonhoeffer? We have to listen. We have to listen to and learn from Rosenbaum's critique as to why Bonhoeffer is *not* »the saint« that some want to make him. We can learn from Rosenbaum where within Bonhoeffer's works the theological wrong for the Jewish-Christian dialogue lies. And avoid making these mistakes again.

We can listen to Rubenstein's relativisation of Bonhoeffer's anti-Judaism and be thankful for his willingness to read the best out of Bonhoeffer, but we must not adopt – or even worse, excuse – such anti-Judaism relying on the authority of Rubenstein. An heir of the victims is allowed to do that, we as the heirs of »*millennial Christian polemics against Jews*«[36] first have to emancipate our theologies from such attitudes.

3. The need to go beyond Bonhoeffer

For a start, we[37] have to watch our semantics. Thoughts are formed by language and I am convinced that no Jew – and quite rightly so – would accept such talk of him/her as a »weakest brother and sister of Christianity« as Bonhoeffer formulates. We have to pay due regard to the fact that there has been a vast improvement in Jewish-Christian dialogue and therefore in Christian theology – at least compared to Christian theology that was dominant in Bonhoeffer's times. Marking Judaism as a 'poor subject' is a first step towards stating a deficit. And stating deficits *for* others puts oneself in the status of having a deeper insight and therefore creating a gesture of supremacy. But the idea of supremacy leads to no dialogue and hinders partnership or learning.

One could argue that the German guilt against the Jews was just a contextual, historical one. But the pattern that Bonhoeffer describes and strengthens is that

[34] Ibid., 38.
[35] Ibid., 43.
[36] Rosenbaum: Was Dietrich Bonhoeffer a 'Righteous Gentile'?, 307.
[37] In this case especially contemporary »German Christians« (in the institutional church).

sinning against a fellow human being is sinning against Jesus Christ. In the act of not defending – or less active – protecting a victim, one abandons one's Christianity and, with it, one's humanity. Contextual wrongdoing is therefore a very direct problem of Christology.[38]

Bonhoeffer sees the scope of realising a space for reconciliation, as *the one and only* form of Christ's Substitution,[39] in the church. But in the years after the Second World War and of reform in the church, it was *not* the church which discovered the necessity to learn anew about its own belief content. It was a movement of individual theologians and members of the communities who founded Jewish-Christian dialogue circles, not the institutional church. Church can and must *only* offer[40] a space for reconciliation but it cannot demand this process in order to realise its own destiny and purpose[41].

We have to argue with Bonhoeffer against Bonhoeffer. In his culpability confession he says that a confession of guilt creates a space within which forgiveness becomes possible, but then goes on to state that there is a Christian imperative to forgive[42]. That brings along at least two problems. The first one is a specific one for my context: Christians were perpetrators, Jews were victims. We can't demand a forgiveness that 'naturally' follows if the confession of guilt is only entirely true by transferring a specific Christian imperative. We can emphasise this imperative for ourselves and we can – and maybe we must – emphasise this demand for forgiveness as realising the resemblance of Christ in the church. But this is something that we, as the heirs of the perpetrators, cannot demand from the religion we tried to annihilate. And a demand in this context would also be even the tiniest expectation of forgiveness as a »natural« process because of our willingness to confess our guilt. Bonhoeffer is too rigid in his certainty of the forgiveness that follows the confession of culpability.

And that leads to the second problem. It is not only in Jewish-Christian dialogue that there cannot be a demand for forgiveness. The same is also true in Christian-Christian dialogue after wrongdoing of the one against the other. There is

---

[38] Referring to Wolfgang Gerlach, it is argued for a very careful and sensitive dealing with the »Question of Christ« retracing and following Bonhoeffer's »The Jew keeps the question of Christ open«.

[39] Cf. DBW 6, 135.

[40] Or as Magdalene Frettlöh states, church has to/can act as an agent. Cf. Magdalene L. Frettlöh: Vergebung oder »Vernarbung der Schuld«? Theologische und philosophische Notizen zu einer frag-würdigen Alternative im gesellschaftlichen Umgang mit Schuld, in: EvTh 70.2 (2010), 116-129, 125. In her essay she picks up the picture of »cicatrisation of guilt« which is formulated by Bonhoeffer in his fragment »Guilt, Justification, Renewal«.

[41] Schellong reads Bonhoeffer the way that church only exists as a space of awareness of guilt, cf. Schellong: Kirchliches Schuldbekenntnis, 29.

[42] DBW 6, 142f.

already the trauma of being a victim, to which the church cannot add the trauma of being a bad Christian[43] because one is not able to forgive the perpetrator.

Confronted with the horror of the Nazi regime there were people who continued believing in God and people who stopped praying, who experienced the loss of God. Some said God/Jesus Christ was murdered in the crematories of the concentration camps. That we can go on to talk and think about God is justified because there was religious belief in the camps. But theology has also to deal with the religious silence. The imperative requirement is to incorporate both means of »coping«. We are allowed to hope, because there was hope, for the presence of God in the midst of history, but we must not be sure (anymore) because of the religious silence which also existed. All theology after the Holocaust has to focus on and do justice to both cases of religious expression – for falling religiously silent is also a religious expression.

There is no right to forgiveness. It only can be given and this giving cannot be a religious demand.

To emphasise Bonhoeffer again: a culpability confession creates the space for the *possibility* of forgiveness. It is also a very Jewish thought to first address the victim to ask for forgiveness before asking God. This is part of the liturgy of Yom Kippur, the day of reconciliation. Confessing one's guilt is the first step by the wrongdoer in the direction of the ones to whom he/she has be done wrong.

But an essential part of the reconciliation process must be an awareness of the real risk of not being accepted – and justifiably so – by the (former) victim. This also presents an opportunity for *not* perpetuating the roles of victim and perpetrator – whereas demanding by contrast, would set the trap of doing so. The only thing the confessor can do is to give time and ask again in full awareness of an open answer being possible.

[43] Or even being »a source of poison for the community«, DBW 6, 136.

Peace as a central task for Christians
Bringing about peace in the work of Dietrich Bonhoeffer and its importance for current ethics

Clemens Wustmans

Preliminary

This text deals with the topic »Peace as a central task of Christians. Bringing about peace in the work of Dietrich Bonhoeffer and its importance for current ethics«. It is divided in five parts and finishes looking ahead on current challenges speaking of peace in the German church.

In the beginning four parts do follow the biography of Dietrich Bonhoeffer from the mid of the 1920s to the 1930s and then to the passed-on fragments of his ethics,[1] written down at the arrest in the 1940s. It follows this chronological order as suggested by Reinhold Mokrosch et. al.[2] because there is a very strong link between Bonhoeffers biography and his theology. Nowadays it´s fascinating to see that the claim for ethics coping the precise situation is linked that immense way to the way his ethics developed during his life, a very special life and biography.

Picking up this impressive and inspiring close relation of opus and acting in life this text tries to explicate Bonhoeffers development in speaking of bringing about peace.

1. The (neo-) Lutheran tradition and its cultural imprint

In February 1929, the 23-years-old vicar Dietrich Bonhoeffer dealed in a lecture in front of his German Foreign parish with the question of whether in a Christian perspective a war is justified.

He brings forward the argument that we´re living in a dilemma. On the one hand side we´re told not to kill, we´re told to love even our enemies. On the other hand side it´s said you should live *more* than altruism, you shall *love* your next person. Following the young Bonhoeffer, *every* Christian finds himself between these two positions in case of war. Why that?

---

[1] Dietrich Bonhoeffer: Ethics. Translated from the German Edition, edited by Ilse Tödt, Heinz Eduard Tödt et. al., English Edition edited by Clifford J. Green, new English translation translated by Reinhard Krauss et. al., Minneapolis 2005.

[2] Reinhold Mokrosch / Friedrich Johannsen / Christian Gremmels: Dietrich Bonhoeffers Ethik. Ein Arbeitsbuch für Schule, Gemeinde und Studium, Gütersloh 2003.

If he loves his enemy and turns at him his other cheek, what about the love for his mother, his brother or neighbour? Isn´t he to blame for their suffer? Apparently Bonhoeffer argues that the command of love to your next person is a justification for a Christian to take part in the war.

He confesses as a person of his time: »The Lord had given me to my mother, to my nation; What I have, I owe to my nation; [...] this is divine order, because god created people and nations. [...] but the love to my nation will bless the murder, will bless the war [...] The Lord calls the people to fight and victory.«[3]

This justification of war shows us Bonhoeffer according to the lutheran or neo-lutheran ethics of order, according to their perspective on the authorities. For neo-lutheran theologians since the 19th century, so called orders (regimes) of creation were the foundation of their thinking about the world; God had created authority, nation, people, family, marriage, countrymen, soldiers, work, culture, etc. and ordered it from »top to bottom«: Authority superordinates the people, parents their children, the master his apprentice. A war just can be permitted, if the authority fights against the lower people; a war, started by the people against the authority – king or sovereign – is always a sin. But a war initiated by the authority can be necessary, e.g. if agitation or riots disturb the order.[4]

Reading the programmatic script oft Martin Luther, Ob Kriegsleut auch in seligem Stand sein können (1529), it becomes clear that the mandate of the soldiers during war is a sacred mandate. This means nothing less but the sacral justification of war itself and of course of the soldier. The task for the individual person is to behave righteous within this mandate constituted by god. The institution of war, according to Luther, can just be evil and wrong, if the acting person becomes acting and wrong. This typically differentiation between person and mandate is claimed for soldiers as well as for all other situations people can be put in by the Lord.[5]

The young Bonhoeffer picks up this theology, which causes a positive valuation of war. Another aspect that leads him to that position is his negative anthropology. He is convinced that mankind is ruled by the sin in such a way that even if a man tries to create peace, this could lead to the sin of the overestimation of one´s own capabilities. Even in 1932, as a lecturer in Berlin Bonhoeffer confesses: »There is no chance for mankind to build or organize peace; [...] There is no assured peace. A Christian can just dare peace because of his faith.«[6]

---

[3] Dietrich Bonhoeffer: Barcelona, Berlin, Amerika 1928-1931, ed. by Reinhard Staats und Hans Christoph von Hase (DBW 10), München 1991, 337-339.

[4] Mokrosch: Dietrich Bonhoeffers Ethik, 112.

[5] Volker Stümke: Das Friedensverständnis Martin Luthers. Grundlagen und Anwendungsbereiche seiner politischen Ethik, Stuttgart 2007.

[6] Dietrich Bonhoeffer: Berlin 1933 (DBW 12), ed. by Carsten Nikolaisen et. al., Gütersloh 1997, 233.

Although Bonhoeffer picks the speech of peace out as a central theme in different lectures and sermons, he strictly separates the kingdom of god from the kingdom of the world, he even separates the Christian faith and the human ethics.[7]

2. Protestation against the tradition: Bonhoeffer condemns war

During his studies at the Union Theological Seminary New York in 1930/31 there are principles laid for a change in Bonhoeffers position. Here he met Reinhold Niebuhr and the French Christian pacifist Jean Lasserre. From then on Bonhoeffer advocated uncompromisingly an ecumenical initiative of all churches for peace. Here, at this ecumenical context, it is where his ethics of peace begins. Quotes are totally different to what we heard before:

»But don´t you have to destroy life at war? Just because of that church doesn´t know anything about holiness of war. It´s a struggle for being – with dehumanized instruments. Church, praying to the Lord, is addressing God just for peace. [...] How shall a Christian act politically? [...] In every decision he experiences the inexpiably antagonism of the peace of Jesus Christ and the hate of the world.«

Now for Bonhoeffer universal peace is the precise order of God. Without any exception he claims in 1932: »The order of international peace today is The Lord´s order to us. In that way a precise awareness of the Lord´s will is declared for our time.«[8]

At the same time he denies any apology or justification of war through the churches. For Bonhoeffer now war is sin; a Christian participating at the war has to act so in awareness of bearing responsibility towards god´s order of peace.[9]

3. Bonhoeffer becomes a pacifist

An important step for Bonhoeffer turning to a pacifist was a re-lecture, a new way of reading the bible. He learned to hear in the bible the Lord´s categorical, unconditional demand and was convinced people have to show their obedience. Bonhoeffer emphasized that a man could only be justified and a conciliator if he stops trying to assert his own justice and his own ability for peace but asserting the justice and peace of God.

---

[7] Mokrosch: Dietrich Bonhoeffers Ethik, 113.

[8] Dietrich Bonhoeffer: Ökumene, Universität, Pfarramt 1931-1932 (DBW 11), ed. by Christoph Strohm et. al., Gütersloh 1994.

[9] Mokrosch: Dietrich Bonhoeffers Ethik, 116.

In 1932 Bonhoeffer became speaker of the Junior Secretaries of the World Alliance for the work on friendship in the Churches. In that position he got the task of preparation and leading through the Fanoe Conference of this World Alliance in August 1934. He worked on this task in London, where he had taken office as a pastor in October 1933. A major reason for him going to London was his immense disappointment about the deficient opposition of his church against Adolf Hitler and his »conquest« of the German protestant church through by establishing the so called »Reichsbischof« Ludwig Müller.[10]

Working in London, Bonhoeffer caught up information about the situation in Germany almost daily; this situation in 1934 had changed in favour of Hitler. Amongst others Hitler became »Führer« of Germany with apparently absolute power after the death of the president Hindenburg. Bonhoeffer felt himself confirmed in his opinion, Hitler was meaning war.[11]

Facing the drawing menace of war, Bonhoeffer had taken an uncompromising position against war. He focused the topic of the Fanoe conference – »church and world« – to the topic »war and peace« – which by the way provoked the clear protest of the conference leaders.[12]

Yet in his abstract for the conference Bonhoeffer had clarified the church´s position against the demands of the state: »Against the objection: War is creating peace. The answer of the church is: That´s not true, war creates bane and loss.«[13]

And in his speech at the conference on August 28th, 1934, he expressed absolutely that every justification of war has to be denied, even related to defensive wars. He called at the convention, »Peace shall be, because Jesus Christ is in the world, which means peace shall be, because there is a church of Jesus Christ, for their sake the world still exists. And this church of Jesus Christ is still living in all people and in addition beyond all borders of national, political, social or racial way. Christians cannot focus their weapons against each other, because they know they focus their weapons against Jesus Christ himself.«[14]

After that he started to attack politics and economy, in a way that had lead to an arrest at that time if it would have been expressed at German territory. But it´s still up to date: »How comes peace into being? Based on a system of political contracts? Based on international capital investments at the different countries? Based on major banks, based on money? Based on peacefully building-up of arms for the purpose of the protection of peace? No, based on all that not – be-

---

[10] Ibid., 117.

[11] Eberhard Bethge: Dietrich Bonhoeffer. Theologe – Christ – Zeitgenosse. Eine Biographie, Gütersloh [7]2001, 446.

[12] Mokrosch: Dietrich Bonhoeffers Ethik, 118.

[13] Dietrich Bonhoeffer: London 1993-1935 (DBW 13), ed. by Hans Goedeking et. al., Gütersloh 1994, 296.

[14] DBW 13, 299-301.

cause for one reason, because in every case peace is mixed with safety. There is no path to peace through the way of safety. Peace has to be dared. Fights are not won supported by weapons, but supported by God.«[15]

That´s why Bonhoeffer appealed for an ecumenical synod of peace.

It´s interesting to see – five years before the beginning of World War two he anticipated the war. At all these who hesitated protestations on the background of the gospel he called: »Should the Lord have told us to work for peace, but also to provide tanks and lethal gas for protection? No, the Lord did not say that, but he said, there shall be peace among all.«[16]

Bonhoeffer was supported by his friend, the French pastor Jean Lasserre, who took sides with him on Farnoe. Bonhoeffer had already got known Lasserre in 1930 in New York as an extreme advocacy of the Sermon on the Mount. Bonhoeffer was very impressed by Lasserres way of life, spending his life together with poor industrial workers in France as his way of succession of Jesus Christ. Lasserre can be seen as push and »kick-off« for Bonhoeffers change to pacifism and his readiness for *living* according to the Sermon on the Mount.[17]

In a second statement abstract for the Farnoe conference Bonhoeffer expressed a common pacifistic position beyond Christian pacifism. »The enemy of working on peace is war. War has to be understood a) as an aware act of human will, which is completely responsible for it, b) as the work of demonical powers in this world, such as disease disasters etc., c) as the exposure of a world addicted to war. [...] Secular pacifism answers: a) Peaceful welfare will not be created by the instrument of war. This is the reason why war is morally not to justify. b) A rational organisation has to be built which curtails the forces that are leading to war. c) War has to be eliminated, to uncover the world as a good world.«[18]

In opposite to his statements in 1928/29 now there is no longer a gap between the peace of God and the human peace in the world. It´s the symbol of a one-way street instead, understood as the empowerment to act for peace.

The christian pacifism, that was not shared by many others, had awaked an aspiration, which was appreciated by even less people: He wanted to travel to the Ashram of Mahatma Ghandi, getting to know his pacifistic way of resistance up close. – Bonhoeffers plans were called insane in Berlin. Instead he got the appointed position as the leader of the preachers seminary in Finkenwalde, Germany. And Bonhoeffer decided to stay in Germany, where he was convinced about the importance of taking part in the opposition.[19]

---

[15] Ibid.
[16] Ibid.
[17] Mokrosch: Dietrich Bonhoeffers Ethik, 122.
[18] DBW 13, 295-296.
[19] Mokrosch: Dietrich Bonhoeffers Ethik, 123.

In the German protestant church Bonhoeffer was struggling for peace more or less alone. The majority of protestants in Germany were attached to Hitler, the Nazi party and the forcible-coordination of the society (including the church). His protestation against the pogroms against Jewish people died away. His Betheler confession (July 1933), warning against anti-jewish attitudes in Germany, was ex post defused by the church leaders.[20]

At that time, during his stay in London and coming back to Germany, quitting his plans for India, he got more and more convinced by the principle of succeeding the Sermon on the Mount. Two beatitudes are fundamental for him: The nonviolent shall be blessed. The conciliators shall be blessed.

Bonhoeffer argues against any weakening of the Sermon on the Mount resolutely. He refuses any postulation, it´s demands could only count in private spheres, but not in public. Similarly he refuses the opinion, just inner ethos could be touched, without practical action. It´s interesting to see that in his lectures for the future vicars in Finkenwalde Bonhoeffer appears as a true Christian pacifist; his later inclusion in violent resistance seems unthinkable at that time. He still hopes the Lords justice and peace will take victory.[21]

4. Peace as topic in Bonhoeffers fragments of ethics

Bonhoeffer has written the fragments of his ethics during World War II – at a time of hate, murder, humiliation, indignity, repression and brutality. Topics as conciliation, understanding, dialogue or peace were not part of the agenda of Europe´s reality. It was even a time when the use of the term »peace« could have led to accusation because of treason or working against the armed forces. Pacifists who refused military service where executed. All that implied for Bonhoeffer: In contrast to his scriptures ten years ago he was not able to use the term »peace« in his ethics. He had to use synonyms. Doubting in public about the reasonable meanings of war could have been dangerous for his life.[22]

Bonhoeffer had received a ban of public speaking in 1940, he was no longer allowed to teach. He was observed by the »Gestapo«, the Nazi intelligence service. Altogether it was like a ban from his profession. For Bonhoeffer in 1940 it was clear to see that he could publish his ethics as recently as there should be a time after Hitler and the war.

In addition it was a common sense in Germany at this early time of war that the quickly achieved victories would strengthen peace. It was no real awareness for speaking of peace in Germany at that time. That was the time, Bonhoeffer worked on his ethics, alone and against the spirit of his time. And it explains,

---

[20] Ibid., 124.
[21] Ibid., 128.
[22] Ibid., 133-134.

why there is just a hidden ethic of peace in the passed down fragments of Bonhoeffers ethics.[23]

A major point in the ethics of Bonhoeffer is the task to act accordant to reality, accordant to truth and appropriate. This is framed by conditions. A man has not to act according to abstract, conceptional principles of moral, but according to the real situation he is confronted with. At this real situation there is not given any clearly good and bad. He has to approve, *but* to disagree a situation. On the other hand side every man has to accept the world as judged *and* affirmed by God. This includes opposition against a neo-lutheran concept of two divided orders of God and the world and also against any idealized dreaming of implementing the kingdom of God at this world.

This leads Bonhoeffer to a third condition: Responsibility has to be understood as restricted. As we heard before, there is no orientation at an abstract ethos, but at conciliation with the reality in Christ.[24]

This concept includes speaking of the responsibility for peace as task for the liberated conscience. This leads beyond the belief of Martin Luther, every man should be responsible for peace according to his very own profession. In contrast Bonhoeffer demands moral courage. Bonhoeffers speech of peace is linked closely to his demand of help for the repressed. The important – and according to Bonhoeffer the only – empowerment for this demand is God´s own order, as he declares for ethics at all.

5. Looking ahead: Current speaking of bringing about peace at the German church

Speaking of peace is a current topic for the church, especially in Germany. This year will be a special year of commemoration: In July it will 100 years ago that the first World War began, in September we remember the beginning of World War two 75 years ago. At present German soldiers are serving in Afghanistan. This very mission was motive for the Protestant church in Germany to publish a script discussing current challenges at struggling for peace.

The paper questions categorically that the path of military violence could lead to peace. Although there have been intense and commendable efforts today it is still not managed to guarantee safety, development and real constitutional legacy in Afghanistan. The military operation, started in 2001, apparently failed at developing »exit strategies«. In general struggling for peace *must* focus harder on the acceptance of cultural diversity, on protection, encouraging freedom and reduction of misery.

[23] Ibid., 135.

[24] Ibid., 165-177.

In January 2014 the German President Joachim Gauck opened the Munich Security Conference with a speech titled »Deutschlands Rolle in der Welt: Anmerkungen zu Verantwortung, Normen und Bündnissen« (translated vaguely »The German role in the world: Comments on responsibility, norms and alliances«). The speech caused a mixed echo because of its demand, Germany should take more responsibility in the world, if necessary with a higher military commitment. Indeed it is a dilemma, knowing about horror and killing which sometimes just can be stopped by military interventions. But justifying wars in that context seems cynical. This dilemma also leads into a discussion of fundamental attitudes about ethics: While the tradition of deontological approaches offers clear answers for a strict pacifism without looking closely on the consequences of acting or non-acting, are other positions even focused on these consequences. Rationally focusing on values almost every instrument can possibly be used for the recreation of human rights. A position highlighting the consequences within the overall situation can accept a double effect and legitimate negative side effects, which would not be tolerated as the main aim of action.

Martin Honecker shows another important point of view when he describes that »traditional« known wars more and more are replaced by »low intense conflicts«, a terminology marked by the US military. Especially the clear differentiation between combatants and non-combatants is often not longer given.[25]

Honecker highlights how in such conflicts the questions about personal identity and affiliation are set up.[26] Main characteristic of such »new« wars is their denationalisation by replacing government players by other organisations or even »private« persons who face more disadvantages in renouncing violence. Also the more and more asymmetric warfare according to a more asymmetric world order and the higher autonomization of wars and conflicts are important to be seen, when regular armies often lost control about the wars.

Traditional ways of fighting wars are not enabled to end such conflicts. They are addressing states and don´t work in above shown »low intense conflicts«, even if their intensity in reality isn´t low at all. Participants don´t even have to reach certain military victories to keep up high the level of danger and threat. New wars are characterized by a dislocation of forces in time and space.

Also in the way of their formal ending current wars differ from traditional known. Long processes of reaching peace are necessarily, during the danger of violence flaring up again has to be minimized. There have to be developed ethically responsible ways of facing these new kinds of war.

---

[25] Martin Honecker: Gerechter Krieg und/oder gerechter Friede, in: Peter Dabrock et. al.: Kriterien der Gerechtigkeit. Begründungen – Anwendungen – Vermittlungen. Festschrift für Christofer Frey zum 65. Geburtstag, Gütersloh 2003, 251-268, 258.

[26] Ibid., 260.

In a 2007 published memorandum by the German protestant church, EKD, a concept of »justified peace« is opposed to the traditional wording of »justified war«, but not in the way of a radical Christian pacifism.[27]

Instead it´s a thought out theory subordinating military tools under the civil primate. According to the memorandum just strongest severe acts of injustice can legitimize military interventions.[28] First it´s a task for the members of a community their self to provide their politically freedom.[29] Any emergency aid is subject to important criteria who let one think of the ones for a justified war – a reason, authorization, right intentions, the question of the last resort and the proportionality of the consequences.[30]

For the EKD legitimacy is given when the aim of an operation is to take tasks as the police or to enclose the heaviest violent conflicts within a society, the guarantee of a before negotiated armistice, the protection of a peace agreement, the demobilization of armed forces or to build a secure environment for a self-supporting political, economic and cultural reconstruction.[31]

All these aspects can according to the memorandum just be fulfilled by taking care of the codetermination of the parties involved.

There is still a sceptical view on the chance to create peace by military resources, which leads the EKD to emphasize that parallel to the creation of a secure environment a real recreation has to be started.[32] For a long time in history a more strictly successive approach of safety and recreation was usual.

The contribution to prevent violent conflicts have to focus on the treatment of the causes of violence. Four keywords are given in this context: peacekeeping, peace-making, peace-enforcement and peace-building.[33]

According to the memorandum the only authority which is entitled to approve interventions is the United Nations Security Council, according to the UN Charta.[34] As the UN has no armed forces on their own it is necessary to fall back on the support of its member states or organizations as NATO.[35] The memorandum allows and even emphasizes that the European Union and Germany have to join responsibility to participate in such interventions.[36]

---

[27] Aus Gottes Frieden leben – für gerechten Frieden sorgen. Eine Denkschrift des Rates des Evangelischen Kirche in Deutschland, Gütersloh 2007, 78.
[28] Ibid., 75.
[29] Ibid.
[30] Ibid., 68-69.
[31] Ibid., 78.
[32] Ibid., 90.
[33] Ibid., 113.
[34] Ibid., 84.
[35] Ibid., 90.
[36] Ibid., 95.

Evaluating the operation in Afghanistan up to now in the statement »Selig sind die Friedfertigen« (Blessed are the peacemakers), published by the EKD in December 2013, some aspects of the memorandum are pointed out which were failed.[37]

Nor have the local participants adequate been involved in the decision-making processes[38] neither can the operation be called as focusing on an civil primate and being part of a concept of peace-making and improving security at the time before 2010.[39] Furthermore there has not set enough energy on constructing state control, public authorities and constitutional institutions.[40]

Also it had to be more on mind to work on development projects in a way to compensate given social differences between regions and ethnic groups instead of increasing them. For the EKD this is the only way to support peaceful coexistence.[41]

The statement emphasizes how hard it is for the local people to differentiate between the United States »mission of self-defence« and the mission of stabilisation by the ISAF, which has negative influences on the acceptance by the local public.[42]

Accepting the standard that enforcing values has to step back for the protection of men and that we have to accept diversity in culture and different ways of social life,[43] the concept given by the EKD seems to be a reasonable ethically guideline.

It values the essential question of the sovereignty of states and cultural diversity by emphasising the United Nations Security Council and the international law as only source of legitimation. By focusing on development a path is shown to fight the causes of »new« kinds of wars.

Be orientated towards this guidelines one has to admit that there are situations which require military intervention. Although this seems incompatible to Christian pacifism at first glance, also according to Bonhoeffer, who represented this pacifism in his later writings, responsibility can´t be put aside in »pious escapism«. Not becoming guilty seems no option in facing realities in the world.

Speaking with Bonhoeffer and the current scripts of the EKD, the protestant church in Germany, there has to be a close relation between peace and justice.

---

[37] »Selig sind die Friedfertigen«, Der Einsatz in Afghanistan: Aufgaben evangelischer Friedensethik. Eine Stellungnahme der Kammer für öffentliche Verantwortung der EKD (EKD Texte 116), Hannover 2013, 16.

[38] Ibid., 18.-19.

[39] Ibid., 19.

[40] Ibid., 32.

[41] Ibid., 35.

[42] Ibid., 17.

[43] Honecker: Gerechter Friede, 263-264.

Military violence must be enhanced by strict legal norms and the regulations of the international law. Asymmetrical use of force can lead to an escalation of violence which hardly could be transformed into a legal normed life. The passed down theory of a justified war anyway has to be subordinated a concept of justified peace. The »ius ad bellum« should be replaced by speaking of the »ius contra bellum«. A future task is to develop a responsible completion of military operations. This includes a focus on the »ius in bello« as it is unavoidable, related closely to the international law.

Peace as a central task for Christians in the light of Dietrich Bonhoeffer
Bonhoeffer's Peace Ethics with a special focus on Churches and Peacemaking in Tanzania

Abednego Keshomshahara

1. Introduction

We are living in the world whose inhabitants cry for peace almost every day. Through media we learn that people have no peace due to religious conflicts although the central message of all religions is peace among the people. Through media one observes that peace has been scarce due to tribal and ethnic conflicts which lead to wars and disharmony. In other places there is lack of peace mainly due to socio-economic and political inequalities that lead to oppression, exploitation, drug abuse, discontentment and wars. Gabor Steingart in his book »Weltkrieg um Wohlstand« observes that we are living in the world where failure to share resources leads to sharing spears and bombs[1]. In other contexts, peace is disrupted by climatic changes which cause drought, floods, and winds of destruction, hunger and fear[2]. It is in this context that peace becomes one of the goods which are very scarce in the world. Due to scarcity of peace, Christians have been and still are challenged to view peace as their central task.

There are Christians who have set an example of how Christians should be engaged in peace issues in the light of the bible and Christian faith. One of those Christians and theologians is Dietrich Bonhoeffer who dedicated himself for peace theology during the 2nd World War in Germany when he struggled to defend the Jews against Adolf Hitler's regime which did not only burn shops and temples of the Jews but also tortured and killed them on the basis of racism, religion and cultural differences[3]. Bonhoeffer becomes important in the discus-

---

[1] Gabor Steingart: Weltkrieg um Wohlstand: Wie Macht und Reichturm neu verteilt werden, München 2006, 1-13

[2] Wilson Niwagila: Our Struggle for Justice, Peace and Integrity of Creation. A Quest for Theology of Reconstruction in Africa, in Jesse Mugambi (Ed.): The Church and Reconstruction of Africa: Theological Considerations, Nairobi 1997, 173; Elisabeth Gerle: In Search of a Global Ethics. Theological, Political, and Feminist Perspectives based on a Critical Analysis of JPIC and WOMP, Lund 1995, 11ff; cf. Abednego Keshomshahara: A Theology of Poverty Reduction in Tanzania. A Quest for Christian Socio-Economic and Political Vision in Tanzania, Dodoma 2008, 67-68, 190-191.

[3] Cf. Pascal Bataringaya: Versöhnung nach dem Genozid. Impulse der Friedensethik

sion about peace due to his ethics of actions that fills in the gap of abstract, dogmatic and theoretical ethics which does not confront concrete situations[4]. Bonhoeffer's shift from passive resistance and defenselessness to active resistance of being ready to kill the killers for the sake of the voiceless is a clear indication of his concrete, pragmatic and situational ethics[5]. He was even ready to be jailed, tortured and to die for the sake of peace just like Jesus Christ's readiness to die on the cross for salvation of humans.

In his work about Peace Ethics in view of Dietrich Bonhoefer, Paschal Bataringaya maintains that the Gospel is peace and Christ himself is peace. Hence, Christians are called to create and maintain peace in the world[6]. Christians follow Jesus Christ whose central task was and still is to bring peace to humanity and nature in general. Jesus came to bring about peace between humans and God. This kind of peace extends to peace among humans and between humans and nature, the surrounding environment and the whole creation[7]. St. Paul puts it very clearly that through Christians' salvation even nature will be liberated. This alerts people from the beginning to take care of creation which also takes care of humans in a number of ways. If nature is not taken care of, peace cannot be guaranteed as the ecological systems are part and parcel of human life, hence source of human peace as far as provision of human basic needs are concerned. The task of the Christians as far as peace is concerned is therefore of vertical and horizontal dimensions. The vertical dimensions of humans relationship to God determines and affects the horizontal dimensions of believers' relationship to their fellow humans and nature at large.

In this presentation we shall survey peace in biblical and theological perspectives. We shall be able to discuss peace in the light of the Sermon on the Mount where Christian pacifism is encouraged for the sake of peace as Christ's revolution that revolutionizes the world. For Bonhoeffer, the Sermon on the Mount is not a Utopia; rather it is realistic, concrete and practical in human lives for pursuit of peace[8]. Moreover, we shall be able to see the other side of theological interpretations in which active resistance against oppression is highly supported and recommended. Such different ethical and theological stances pose ethical and moral challenges to believers who ought to make difficult decisions for difficult situations as determined by Christianized free conscience that is responsible to God and neighbours[9]. A survey on peace in the context of the challenges

---

Dietrich Bonhoefers für Kirche und Gesellschaft in Ruanda, Kamen 2012, 130-136, 142ff.

[4] Ibid., 128-132.

[5] Ibid., 141-145.

[6] Ibid., 19.

[7] Ibid., 130.

[8] Ibid., 135-136.

[9] Ibid., 152-162.

experienced in Tanzania where the author of this article comes from; will be made to see how the Christians in Tanzania take peace seriously as their central task. Finally, some recommendations and conclusions will be made with regard to peace and the way forward.

2. Peace in theological and Biblical Perspective

2.1. Passive Resistance as a Way of maintaining Peace in the Light of the Sermon on the Mountain

Pacifism and Peacemaking

Dr. Mark P. Roberts in his book entitled *»Seeking the Peace of Christ: Christianity and Peacemaking«* argues that one of the problems that hinder Christians from pursuit of peace include pacifism or pacifistic anti-military stance[10]. This stance is taken from the Sermon on the Mount. In this sermon, Jesus Christ does not encourage the use of force or retaliation when one is offended. He does not even allow self-defense. For Jesus, loving the neighbor implies also loving the enemy with hope that love will change and lead enemies towards peace. This stance of pacifism is radically against use of violence or militarization. For Jesus love of neighbor without retaliation or self-defense becomes one of the fundamental ways to overcome violence and conflicts in society. Jesus Christ himself did not use force against his enemies. He wants his followers to follow the Sermon on the Mount as a way of maintaining peace in society. As Paschal Bataringaya observes, pacifism in the light of the Sermon on the Mount implies total dependence on God who is source of peace; it implies that God should do everything on behalf of the victims[11].

Dietrich Bonhoeffer applied this stance during World War II when Adolf Hittler had caused atrocities to the Jews on the basis of racism and religion. Although he did not advocate for the use of force or retaliation against Hitler's regime at the beginning, he at least challenged the church to speak against the evils of Hitler's regime[12]. Bonhoeffer was of the opinion that men and women in the church should be engaged in peace and justice against injustices, oppression and wars. He adds that Christians should stand against everything that destroys life in church and state systems besides taking care of the victims of oppression regardless of their religious differences[13]. Bonhoeffer's views on ethics of action show that the church of his time was pacifistic in terms of being quiet about the

---

[10] Mark D. Robert: Seeking the Peace of Christ: Christianity and Peacemaking, 2010 from http://www.patheos.com/blogs/markdroberts/ (visited on 1st December 2014).

[11] Bataringaya: Versöhnung nach dem Genozid, 14-20.

[12] Ibid., 16-20.

[13] Ibid., 19-20.

evils that were done by Hitler's regime. But Bonhoeffer's pacifism encourages prophetic voice against evils in society. He therefore encourages active non-violence as opposed to total passivity that allows oppression to prevail[14]. For him love of enemy does not imply love of enmity since love of enmity can harm the one who loves the enemy. Love of enemy should go hand in hand with hating and condemning enmity so that enmity may not prevail and cause more harm. Jesus himself was not quiet when he found that the temple of God was being misused for business purposes; he chased business people in the temple and he taught them to use the temple for prayers not for economic enterprises (Mathew 21:12-13).

Problems of Christian Pacifism

There are problems which are associated with Christian pacifism that is derived from the Sermon on the Mount. In their discussions about the Sermon on the Mount, St. Augustine of Hippo views this Sermon as a Christian way of life that aims at guaranteeing peace in society. For him, the Sermon on the Mount is a yardstick of Christian discipleship and realization of God's kingdom on earth. In his view, it is the »highest standard of morality and as a perfect measurement of the Christian Life«[15] The problem arises when not all the Christians can abide with the Sermon on the Mount due to its impracticability in daily lives. Some theologians think that the Sermon on the Mount is a Christian ideal which cannot be realized until the eschatological era has emerged. Another problem is when Christians are a minority while the majority is non-Christians who follow natural right systems.

Thomas Aquinas was of the opinion that the Sermon on the Mount is meant for few perfect Christians different from many ordinary or normal Christians. For him, ordinary Christians should follow natural laws based on Ten Commandments which give room for punishment of evil. During the medieval period it was held that the Sermon on the Mount was meant for clergy, especially those in monastic orders and not the laity. It was during reformation in the 16th century when stages of ethics for clergy and for laity were abandoned on the basis of priesthood of all believers. During reformation, ethics were meant for all Christians without differentiations[16].

Martin Luther argued that a Christian is both private and public. Hence, when he is in private life issues he/she should be guided by the Sermon on the Mount focusing on loving the enemy without making revenge or defending him/herself (Mt.5). But when one is in public life he/she should respect and support the

[14] Ibid., 104-106.

[15] Emmanuel Oyedomi: An Understanding of the Sermon on the Mount from African Ecclesiology, in www.biblicaltheology.com (visited on 1st December 2014).

[16] Referring to personal seminar notes about »Friedensethik« (Peace Ethics) held during Summer Semester 2007 at Bielefeld University by Prof. Dr. Dr. Heinrich Schaefer.

state laws (Rom.13) which punish the wrong doers for national interests[17]. Luther says that war against the oppressor or invader is less evil compared to long term evils of oppression. He discourages offensive or aggressive wars and accepts war for defending the national interests against invaders[18]. He discourages war based on arrogance and religious basis. The problem with this stance is to divide a person into two sections as if a person in personal business is an angel and in public issues is a worldly person; hence causing dilemma to the Christians as far as decision making is concerned.

On the weaknesses of Luther's position, Klaus Nuernberger says that Luther's emphasis on enduring evil done to the individual believer and doing good including resistance to evils done to others is not characteristic of biblical morality since the bible teaches people to love God and their neighbor as they love themselves. Hence, personal interests should be defended just like how social interests ought to be defended. He adds that Paul himself could not tolerate attacks on his authority and integrity. Nuernberger contends that the biblical teachings encouraging self-denial and those against self-assertion are not only directed to an individual, but also to the state or collective entity[19].

2.3 Christian Active Resistance for peace in the light of Bonhoeffer' ethics programme

Dietrich Bohoeffer was engaged in active resistance against Hitler's regime after his arrival in Germany from USA in 1938. During this time there were systematic killing of the Jews and other prisoners from the East. He decided to conspire against Hitler by planning to kill Hitler as a way of ending war that had led to many deaths of Jews. This was a radical decision which was contrary to the Lutheran tradition that discouraged resistance and killing from below upwards; instead the Lutheran tradition allowed violence and killing from above downwards, accepting the state's use of violence to its citizens when they violate the law[20]. Bonhoeffer was ready to be guilt of killing for the sake of freedom and peace of those who were being oppressed and discriminated. He saw himself like Jesus who became guilty for salvation of humans[21].

Bonhoeffer decided to break the law that forbids killing for the sake of peace and victims; he knew that the plan to kill Hitler was not justifiable. However, his conscience was not accusing him though that could not make him righteous;

[17] Klaus Nürnberger: Martin Luther's Message for us today: A perspective from the South, Pietermaritzburg 2005, 253-270. Later on, Martin Luther realized the necessity for individuals to defend themselves but not for selfish reasons, the same applies for individuals to protect victims and combat the evil if the government officials are not around who could do that job. Ibid., 255.

[18] Ibid., 252ff.

[19] Ibid., 269-270.

[20] Bataringaya: Versöhnung nach dem Genozid, 142.

[21] Ibid., 142-143, 157.

he only expected God's grace for the sin of planning to resist and kill the dictator[22]. Bonhoeffer decides to break the law in order to make the law meaningful just like how Jesus broke the Sabbath law by healing sick people on Sabbath so as to give law new interpretation in support of human life. In this case, Bonhoeffer rejects to run away from responsibility; he decides to take responsibility before God for the people and before people for God. The decision to take responsibility with risk of failing was concretized in his readiness to be guilt for the course of fighting the evil[23]. In this case Christians can be compelled to break the law in extreme or extra-ordinary situations[24]. For Bonhoeffer, Christian disciples who continue to suffer and become guilt due to other people's sins are a clear indication that Jesus Christ still lives in the world while experiencing what happened on the cross[25]. This goes hand in hand with self-dedication or self- sacrificing for others.

Peter Szentpetery finds out that the cost of discipleship in the light of Ditrich Bonhoeffer is somehow a radical critic of his contemporary Lutherans who emphasized cheap grace rather than expensive grace that made Jesus die on the Cross. He observes that Bonhoeffer wants not only justification of sin but also justification of sinner who ought to relate well with God and his/her neighbour. For Bonhoeffer, forgiveness of sin should not be offered without repentance of sin. In this case sin must be mentioned, punished and judged if at all justice and peace should prevail. In the views of Szentpetery, Bonheffer is against legalism but maintains that Lutheranism should not disregard good works since they have their place that focus on visible pain according to Mathew 5 and invisible righteousness such as hidden prayers and thanksgiving according to Mathew 6[26].

Christiane Tietz uncovers that for Bonhoeffer, justification by faith does not lead to ethical silence or quietism. For Bonhoeffer, she adds, faith without work is nothing (Jacob 2:19). She observes further Bonhoeffer's emphasis on good works on which the final judgment will be based as signs of faith that saves[27]. Bonheffer challenges the protestant ethics that has ignored the relevance and place of good works, hence leading to love of fatherland instead of loving Christ and the neighbor[28]. As such, failure to love Christ and neighbor leads to racism,

---

22 Ibid., 144-146.

23 Ibid., 144-146.

24 Ibid., 153ff.

25 Ibid., 142-145.

26 Peter Szentpetery: Ist die »Nachfolge« eine radikale Kritik des Luthertums?, in: Bonhoeffer und Luther. Zentrale Themen ihrer Theologie, ed. by Klaus Gründwaldt / Christiane Tietz / Udo Hahn (Amt der VELKD), Hannover 2007, 158ff.

27 Christiane Tietz: Rechtfertigung und Heiligung, in: Bonhoeffer und Luther 2007, 99ff.

28 Szentpetery: Ist die »Nachfolge« eine radikale Kritik des Luthertums?, 159.

discrimination and oppression based on religious differences and hatred. It is in this context of need of emphasizing faith and actions that Bonhoeffer and his fellow opponents of Hitler planned to take serious actions against Hitler and his regime.

On 20th July, 1944 the Christian resistance movement supporters planned to kill Hitler. As Christians, they trembled because it was murder. They went on with their plans to kill him physically. On 20th July, 1944 the Christian resistors tried to kill Hitler but in vain as Hitler only got small injuries at his headquarters. Hitler's state tortured the Christian resistors and gave them capital punishment[29].

3. Christians' task of maintaining peace in Tanzania

3.1 Harmonious Life among Tanzanians of different religions and ethnic groups

Tanzania has been a country of peace for many years despite the presence of more than 120 ethnic groups and different religious groups. Tanzania has been hosting refugees from Rwanda, Burundi, Democratic Republic of Congo and freedom fighters of South Africa during the times of apartheid. It has been involved in the movement of fighting for freedom of some African countries against colonialism bearing in mind that Tanzania would not be free if its neighbors were not free. People of different faiths such as Muslims and Christians have been living together and supporting each other during times of sorrows and joys. They stay together in families; they go to the same schools, markets, health centers, etc. The contribution of Christians in terms of dialogues, common projects like planning to teach religious education in schools and offering social services to all Tanzanians regardless of religious affiliations has been of cardinal importance in maintenance of peace in the country. Since justice is needed to guarantee peace, the Church in Tanzania has been prophetic by condemning corruption, drug abuse, grabbing of people's land, tax evasion and abuse of free market economy (e.g. importation of expired goods) as depicted in the Bagamoyo statement of 1994[30]. The contribution of churches worldwide to debt cancellation so as to release the poor from the burden of paying back the loan that had led to expensive social services in 2000 was remarkable.

All these efforts were made by churches to make sure that peace is maintained in the country in terms of people's access to basic needs and social services.

---

[29] Frederique Dantonel: Das Widerstandsrecht, in: Bonhoeffer und Luther 2007, 167-202.

[30] Godson S. Maanga (Ed.): Injili Kamili: Historia ya Kanisa la Kiinjili la Kilutheri Tanzania: 1963-2013, Moshi 2013, 569-578.

3.2. Conflicts between Muslims and Christians in Tanzania

Despite peaceful life that has been experienced in Tanzania, there have been underground conflicts between Muslims and Christians especially when there are intermarriages between Muslims and Christians. Conflicts arise when the motive for such marriages is conversion of a spouse and children. Other conflicts are based on the fact that Christians in Tanzania were able to access education in the missionary schools while Muslims missionaries established only madras for religious instructions without focus on secular education. Only a few Muslims were able to acquire secular education in missionary/church schools. This made the first President of Tanzania, Mwalimu Julius Kambarage Nyerere to nationalize mission schools to allow all Tanzanians access education equally irrespective of their religious backgrounds. As time went on, many Muslims also accessed secular education, hence giving them opportunities to hold positions in politics and government in the same way as Christians.

Of recent, things have changed when some radical Muslims started to preach in mosques that Tanzania is ruled by Christian dominated systems (*Mfumo Kristo*) on the basis of what was declared by sheikhs from all over Tanzania at Diamond Jubilee hall on 15th of January, 2011.[31]. Radical Muslims go on saying that from the time of colonialism the Christians got chances of education and positions of leadership in the country, the situation that they claim it discriminates the Muslims to date. Muslims go on to demand that they should be allowed to exercise their religious law systems as total expression of their freedom of faith and worship. The radical Muslims do not like the government to support church institutions of social services while those institutions serve all Tanzanians as per memorandum of 1992. The messages of hatred were being spread in the country through CDs, DVD, fliers and religious meetings[32].

The Sheikhs who spread messages of hatred instructed Muslims to kill religious leaders who seemed to hinder their demands but also to kill Christian leaders as a way to frustrate Christians in the country. On Christmas of 2012, Father Ambrose Mkenda of the Roman Catholic Church in Zanzibar was injured by an unknown person who shot him but failed to kill him[33]. In February 2013 there was conflict between Muslims and Christians at Buseresere, Geita, over the question about who should slaughter animals for human use. The conflict over slaughtering animals ended up with slaughtering the Pentecostal Pastor Rev. Mathayo Machila, leader of Christians who decided to slaughter animals without letting the Sheikhs to do that job. This incident led to serious

---

[31] »Jukwaa la Wakristo Tanzania (TCF)«, in: Kiongozi (news paper), March 22-28, 2013, 4; also: »Maaskofu sasa wacharuka«, in: Habari, Toleo Na. 275, December 26-January 1, 2013.

[32] Joseph Sabinus: Maaskofu walilia Amani, in: Kiongozi, Toleo Na. 13, March 29-April 04, 2013; also »Maaskofu sasa wacharuka« 2013.

[33] Ibid.

fighting between Muslims and Christians in Buseresere until when the police forces curbed the situation. Few weeks later, a Roman Catholic Priest in Zanzibar, Father Everist Mushi was shot and died few hours before the Sunday services were to begin[34]. As some Sheiks preached hatred against Christians, some church buildings were being burnt while threats to kill more pastors, priests and bishops were going on[35].

3.3 Christians' initiatives to restore peace and harmony between Muslims and Christians in Tanzania

Speaking out against evils made against Christians in Tanzania

Due to the aforementioned problems which took place between 2011 and 2013, Christians were of the opinion that the government of Tanzania was doing nothing to end religious conflicts in the country. The Roman Catholics, Protestants and Pentecostal churches formed a forum (Tanzania Christians Forum-TCF) to address those problems. This forum made statements which blamed the government of Tanzania for keeping quiet when radical Muslims preached hatred and made claims which were not true about the nation and Christians. Worse enough the Muslims' CDs and that proclaimed animosity between Muslims and Christians were being sold in markets without government intervention. This made the Christians blame the Government for failure to stop suppression of Christians by Muslims[36]. One hundred and seventeen Bishops (117) from Tanzania Episcopal Council (TEC), Christian Council of Tanzania (CCT), and Pentecostal Churches in Tanzania (PCT) in their declaration, wanted the government of Tanzania to protect Christians and their properties against the radical Muslims. In addition to that, the church leaders urged the government to make it clear as per national constitution that slaughtering of animals for butchery is not meant for Muslims, otherwise the silence of the government on such matters would imply that the Muslims' claims were true[37]. Church leaders disagreed with Muslims claim that the government was ruled by Christian systems. They said that was not true since 90% of top government leaders were Muslims while on Zanzibar Island 100% of leaders were Muslims as if Christians in Zanzibar had no qualifications to lead others[38]. If top leaders were Muslims, how could

---

[34] Rose Athumani: JK warns against incitement, Daily News, Tuesday, April, 2, 2013; »Jukwaa la Wakristo Tanzania (TCF)« 2013, 4.

[35] »Jukwaa la Wakristo Tanzania (TCF)« 2013, 4.

[36] Ibid.

[37] Ibid.

[38] It is estimated that Christians in Tanzania are 40% of the population while Muslims are also 40%. Other religions form 20% of the population. Cf. Keshomshahara 2008, 18. In Zanzibar, Muslims are over 90%. Note that in the census the question about religion is not asked to avoid religious fundamentalism based on number of adherents.

Muslims claim that the country was led by Christians' systems?, the Tanzania Christians Forum questioned. Bishops finished their response by saying that the government of Tanzania is principally ruled by democratic principles[39].

The church leaders went on saying that if the government of Tanzania fails to stop those who instigate religious hatred in the country and fail to search and catch those who cause atrocities of deaths of religious leaders and burning of church buildings, Christians would be told that the government of Tanzania favours Moslems, hence, compelling the church to rethink again its relationship with the government. Moreover, if nothing is done by the government, the churches would inform the international community that Tanzania was violating the basic fundamental human rights in terms of inactive response to systematic assassination of Christian religious leaders[40]. Bishops were aware that not all Muslims were against the Christians[41]. This is proved by the head of the Muslims Council in Tanzania (Abbreviated as BAKWATA in Kiswahili) who said that the government had not taken serious measures against the terrorists who distort peace in the country[42].

The President of Tanzania, His Excellence Dr. Jakaya Mrisho Kikwete who is a Muslim, addressed the nation and said that both Muslims and Christians were blaming him whereby Christians were saying that the President sides with the Muslims while Muslims said that the President was favoring Christians. He said that some Muslims in Dar es Salaam were praying for him to die[43]. With regard to religious conflicts he said that »the government was not interested in seeing anyone mocking faiths of others«. The President ordered the security officials in the whole country to take serious measures against those who make provocative statements against other religions[44]. The government pursued Muslim and Christian leaders who were making provocative statements to adherents of different religions. The Muslim and Christian media that broadcasted information of hatred or instigation of conflicts were closed[45]. After the government intervention the situation at least became calm. Hence, the role of churches in Tanzania for peace restoration cannot be underestimated. The churches' approach to speak out against evils without keeping quiet and also avoiding revenge against Muslims fits Bonhoeffer's programme of peace ethics.

---

[39] Also »Maaskofu sasa wacharuka« 2013.

[40] »Jukwaa la Wakristo Tanzania (TCF)« 2013, 4.

[41] Ibid.

[42] »Ugaidi wafichua udhaifu wa dola in Raia Mwema«, in: Alhamisi, May 15-21, 2013.

[43] »Kikwete: Misikiti mitatu imenisomea itikafu nife«, in: Nipashe, Jumanne, April 2, 2013.

[44] Rose Athumani: JK warns against incitement.

[45] »Redio za Waislamu, Wakristo zafungwa«, in: Habari, February 27- March 5, 2013.

Interfaith Dialogue for peaceful life between Muslims and Christians in Tanzania

Interfaith dialogues have been held in different parts of the country to help Muslims and Christians know each other and be able to tolerate each other as they address common challenges for development. On 26th of December, 2013, there was an interfaith symposium in Bukoba whereby the Deputy Minister for Communication, Science and Technology, Mr. January Makamba, a Muslim, was invited as guest of honour. In this symposium there were Muslims and Christians, sheikhs, pastors, priests, Muslim and Christian choirs. This symposium was initiated by the Roman Catholics who said that Tanzania was experiencing several problems which threatened peace. In that symposium it was noted that peace in Tanzania was distorted by factors such as drug abuse, robbery, HIV/AIDS, corruption and religious conflicts. Such problems, it was added, ought to be addressed by all Tanzanians of different religions cooperatively bearing in mind that if peace is endangered, all Tanzanians will be affected negatively. The guest of honor, Mr. January Makamba urged Tanzanians to live together in peace without discriminating each other; he cited an example from his own family whereby his father is a Muslim, his mother a Roman Catholic and his wife a Lutheran. He said differences of religions have never divided their family; instead they have been respecting and tolerating each other. It is only through dialogue that peace among Christians and Muslims can be maintained. This is what was also emphasized by President Jakaya Mrisho Kikwete when he was addressing the religious tensions between Muslims and Christians in Tanzania[46].

4. Conclusion and Recommendations

This paper has shown that peace is a central task of Christians. Christians like Dietrich Bonhoeffer did set a good example of how Christians should be engaged in peace making on the biblical and theological basis. His emphasis on Christian pacifism as a way of creating peace on the basis of the Sermon on the Mount in addition to speaking against evils was a revolutionary contribution and challenge against churches which keep quiet when evils were done. Bonhoeffer's radical and drastic change from pacifism to active resistance of even planning to kill the killer was a clear indication of his concept of pragmatic, concrete and situational ethics that was not bound to dogmatics and Lutheran traditions of leaving such punitive actions to the state only. The paper has shown how Christians and churches in Tanzania dedicate themselves to the tasks of peace in terms of living with tolerance among people of different religions, especially the Muslims, for the sake of peace. In addition to that, church-

[46] »JK aagiza Viongozi wa Dini wakutane«, in: Habari leo, Toleo Na. 02209, Jumatatu, January 7, 2013.

es play the prophetic role of speaking against evils while avoiding revenge. The fruits of the churches' prophetic voice are many among which are debt cancellations to relieve the poor and the government's intervention to stop instigation of religious conflicts among Muslims and Christians. The endeavours to make dialogue with Muslims indicate the churches' readiness to work for peace in the country. This task of making sure that peace prevails should be initiated and experienced at individual, family, community, church, mosques, national and international levels whereby churches and other religions should play their role as agents of peace in the world rather than escalators of conflicts, wars and disharmony in their respective areas of jurisdiction.

Responsabilité et Courage civique - Fondamentaux de l'éthique de Dietrich Bonhoeffer

Traugott Jähnichen

1. Introduction

Pendant les vacances de Noël 1942 - après une dizaine d'années de dictature inhumaine des Nazis en Allemagne, après trois années de guerre d'extermination en Europe, et environ trois mois avant son arrestation en tant que membre de la résistance - Dietrich Bonhoeffer écrit un essai méditatif d´abord adressé à lui-même et à ses amis. Bonhoeffer identifie le nazisme comme »la grande mascarade du mal« (DBW 8, 20 [RS, 26])1, parce que le National Socialisme a toujours présenté des visages trompeurs et a été ainsi en mesure de tromper beaucoup de gens sur ses véritables intentions. Au regard de cette expérience malheureuse, Bonhoeffer se demande: »Qui tient bon?« Sa préoccupation était, au regard de ces expériences avec »l'ordre du mal« (DBW 12, 166), incarnée par Adolf Hitler, de pouvoir clarifier les concepts éthiques d'une manière nouvelle.

Au terme de la dictature nazie Bonhoeffer a reconnu que ceux qui s´évertuent à soigner leur image ne peuvent pas résister au National Socialisme. Face à cette situation, Bonhoeffer conclue qu'enfin de compte ni la raison, ni son principe, ni sa conscience, ni sa liberté, ni même sa vertu personnelle ne peuvent apporter de réponse à la situation sociale actuelle, mais par contre »qui est prêt à sacrifier tout cela, dans la foi, lorsque, attaché à Dieu seul, il est appelé par la foi à une action obéissante et responsable; celui dont la vie ne veut être rien d'autre chose qu'une réponse à la question et à l'appel de Dieu« (DBW 8, 23 [RS, 28]) serait à même de résister.

Bonhoeffer approfondit cette pensée lorsqu´il définit le courage civil comme une libre responsabilité, qui finalement repose dans la foi en Dieu. »Celui qui exige le libre risque de la foi dans une action responsable et qui accorde pardon et consolation à celui qui, de ce fait, devient pécheur.« (DBW 8, 24 [RS, 29]) Ces considérations, Bonhoeffer les a d´abord introduites en détail dans les différentes sections de son »éthique«, mais avant tout, il les a rendues vraies dans sa propre vie. Dans ce qui va suivre, l´arrière fond biographique de ce chemine-

---

[1] Note préliminaire: Les citations en allemand sont de »DBW« »Dietrich Bonhoeffer Werke« en 17 tômes édition Christian Kaiser Munich. Il existe une traduction francaise basée sur DBW 6 »Ethique« édition Labor et Fides Génève 1965 et une traduction de la nouvelle édition de »Résistance et soumission – lettres et notes de captivité« basée sur DBW 8 (RS) édition Labor et Fides Génève 2006.

ment sera d´abord identifié, de quoi découlera une présentation de la logique de l'éthique de la responsabilité de Bonhoeffer.

2. Les prises de position de Dietrich Bonhoeffer vers la résistance politique de l´année décisive 1939

Grâce aux informations de son beau-frère Hans von Dohnanyi, Bonhoeffer est mis au courant, au moins à partir de 1938, que des hauts cadres militaires allemands planifient de renverser Adolf Hitler. Mais pendant ce temps, il sait que l'Allemagne nazie, indépendamment de l'accord de Munich de 1938 avec les démocraties occidentales, a aussi intensifié les préparatifs de la guerre. Hitler planifie une guerre d'agression en rompant le droit international avec l'objectif de soumettre toute l'Europe sous son pouvoir et de commettre des génocides contre les juifs et d'autres minorités, tout cela pour mettre en pratique l'idéologie raciste du National-Socialisme. Face à l´ampleur de cette escalade, Bonhoeffer, qui sympathise beaucoup avec des idées pacifistes et l'option pour la non-violence, est constamment préoccupé par la question de savoir s'il ne doit pas participer activement à la planification du coup d'Etat contre la dictature de Hitler. Dans le contexte de cette situation difficile, Dietrich Bonhoeffer pense à séjourner temporairement à l'étranger en vue d´activer ses contacts en Angleterre et aux États-Unis. Enfin, après une courte visite chez sa sœur et son beau-frère émigré juif, Gerhard Leibholz en Mars 1939 en Angleterre, il reçoit une invitation pour les États-Unis pour une rencontre le 12 Juin 1939 à New York. Beaucoup de gens en Europe auraient été heureux, vu la menace croissante de la guerre, de saisir l'occasion d'émigrer aux Etats-Unis. Mais Bonhoeffer est pris de profonds doutes intérieurs. Ses hôtes aux Etats-Unis pensent que Bonhoeffer souhaiterait émigrer et lui offrent une paroisse d'émigrés allemands aux Etats-Unis, ce qui aurait empêché ce dernier de retourner en Allemagne. Bonhoeffer essaie d´expliquer à ses partenaires qu'il ne pourrait rester à New York pas plus d'un an, voire même moins. Ainsi commence pour lui à New York un intense débat interne sur un possible retour rapide en Allemagne. Le 7 Juillet 1939 il s'embarque avec son frère Karl-Friedrich sur l'un des derniers navires avant le début de la guerre. Cette décision de retourner en Allemagne est pour lui comme une libération qu'il ne regrettera jamais, même lorsqu´il sera en prison2. Eberhard Bethge considère les quatre semaines à New York comme »la plus grave décision que Bonhoeffer ait dû prendre dans sa vie«3 parce que son

[2] Voir la lettre à Eberhard Bethge du 22/12/1943: »Tu dois savoir que je n´ai jamais regretté un seul instant mon retour en 1939, ou quoi que ce soit de tout ce qui est arrivé ensuite. C'est arrivé en toute clarté et avec meilleure conscience«. (DBW 8, 253 RS p.211).

[3] Dietrich Bonhoeffer avec témoignages personnels et documentations en image, présentés par E. Bethge, Reinbek 1976, 73 (en allemand).

retour en Allemagne marquait le tournant décisif pour son futur parcours dans la résistance active.

3. Les raisons qui ont amené Dietrich Bonhoeffer à retourner à l'Allemagne

Dans une lettre du 22 décembre 1943 écrite depuis sa prison à Eberhard Bethge, Bonhoeffer considère sa situation particulière en prison comme une »participation au destin de l'Allemagne« (DBW 8, 253 [RS, 211]) pour laquelle il a pris la décision de son retour de New York. Christoph Strohm a interprété ce motif comme une expression du patriotisme de Bonhoeffer4. Strohm entend le patriotisme comme une perception inextricablement liée à son propre peuple et pays. L'idée de vivre cette situation politique catastrophique en Europe depuis la sécurité de New York est pour Bonhoeffer presque comme un cauchemar : il se sent »déchiré« (DBW 15, 230) et découvre en lui des sentiments de nostalgie qu´il n´avait pas connus depuis sa jeunesse, même ayant souvent passé de longues périodes à l'étranger. En outre, il parle dans son journal qu´il écrit au cours de Juin 1939 à New York d´un sentiment massif d'expériences étrangères aux États-Unis. Bien qu'il souligne l´idée d´une civilisation universelle et fait constamment référence à la una sancta, le rassemblement de tous les chrétiens dans l´Église invisible, il se sent tout de même culturellement, politiquement et surtout ecclésiastiquement étranger. Pendant son séjour de 1939, Bonhoeffer demeure entièrement dans une perspective critique d'un observateur, c'est à dire compréhensif et amical envers les églises et chrétiens des Etats-Unis, mais lointain de leurs cœurs. En outre, il est par ailleurs rongé par l'incertitude quant à l'avancement des promotions de Vicariat qu´il dirigeait et sur le développement de l'Église en général en Allemagne. Il se demande constamment si on n'avait pas plus besoin de lui et de son travail de façon urgente en Allemagne. Dans cette situation, il reconnaît depuis New York le véritable lieu de travail qui lui est assigné par Dieu et il ne cesse d´évoquer son désir de retourner travailler en Allemagne, il utilise l´expression »travail à la maison« (DBW 15, 222). Intensément abattu par cette situation, c´est dans la lecture quotidienne de la Bible qu´il recherche des solutions à son incertitude et à son besoin d´orientation.

Les paroles bibliques vont rapprocher Bonhoeffer à ses propres questions intérieures, et vont l´aider à réfléchir sur ses ultimes décisions, tout cela à la lumière de la Bible. En fin de compte, il gagne beaucoup dans cette lecture de la Bible et rassemble des forces intérieures qui vont soutenir sa profonde conviction de se remettre en chemin pour retourner en Allemagne, retour pour lequel il a tant lutté intérieurement. Le 24 Juin, il reçoit confirmation de sa décision de revenir ra-

[4] Voir Christoph Strohm, »Participation au sort de l'Allemagne«, dans: Heuristique du monde de la foi, éd. par Karl Homann et Ilona Riedel-Spangenberg, Gütersloh 1997, 161-177 (en allemand).

pidement en Allemagne: De façon laconique, il fait la remarque suivante: »Les nouvelles de ce jour sont encore plus horribles. Solution: ‘celui qui croit ne s´enfuit pas’ (Esaïe 28, 16). Je pense au travail qui m´attend à la maison« (DBW 15, 233)

On peut voir dans ces phrases courtes comment sa situation se clarifie de façon substantielle : Compte tenu de la menace de plus en plus précise de la guerre, Bonhoeffer voit qu´un séjour supplémentaire aux États-Unis n'est plus possible, séjour qu'il interprète maintenant, avec l’aide de la lecture quotidienne des »Paroles et textes« de la Communauté morave comme une »fuite«.

A côté de ces considérations très personnelles, Bonhoeffer se donne à lui-même et surtout à ses hôtes américains une éthique sociale fondée de façon responsable sur sa décision propre. Dans une lettre à la fin de Juin 1939 à Reinhold Niebuhr, Bonhoeffer mentionne que sa décision de retourner est guidée par la pensée de »partager les épreuves de son propre peuple«. Il se voit en tant que chrétien en Allemagne face à une décision extrême: soit c´est la défaite de l'Allemagne, qui conduirait à la préservation de la civilisation chrétienne, soit c´est une victoire pour l'Allemagne, qui impliquerait la destruction de »notre civilisation« (DBW 15, 210).

Comme chrétien, il ne peut que souhaiter la défaite de l'Allemagne et il veut vivre cette expérience de la défaite en Allemagne même, afin de garder sa crédibilité envers ses compatriotes.

Avec la décision de quitter l´Amérique, Bonhoeffer fait un pas décisif, en partant de »l´étape du simple informé (qu´il était) au complice actif (qu´il deviendra)«5. Précisément parce que les conséquences d'un retour, c´est-à-dire la décision d'être complice actif avec un risque élevé d'échec, et avec lesquelles il avait tant lutté intérieurement, se précisaient de plus en plus. D'autre part, il était très sûr de lui, après que la décision fut prise, notamment aussi bien sur le chemin qui l’attendait que sur son engagement dans le complot d'assassiner Hitler, voie qu´il suivra en toute conscience.

4. Réflexion théologique sur le »lieu de la responsabilité«

A travers le contact avec son beau-frère Hans von Dohnanyi, Bonhoeffer avait pu être associé au bureau du renseignement militaire à Munich dès Octobre 1940, un département de contre-espionnage de l’armée allemande où beaucoup d’adversaires du régime s’étaient abrités. Presque en même temps, il commence à travailler sur »l´Ethique«. De ce fait, il lui a été possible, d'une manière unique dans ce genre de textes théologiques, de reconstruire la relation entre biographie et réflexion théologique-éthique. Bonhoeffer est actif dans la résistance contre

---

[5] Dietrich Bonhoeffer avec témoignages personnels et documentations en images présentées par E. Bethge, cité précédemment, 76.

le National-Socialisme, en travaillant officiellement comme agent du militaire allemand, mais en réalité faisant partie dans la conspiration contre le régime. En même temps il écrit une »Éthique«, dans laquelle il essaie de se rendre compte des motifs de ses actions. C'est ainsi qu'on comprend mieux comment dans son livre il détermine le »lieu de la responsabilité«, parce que .il comprend ses actions comme la prise de responsabilité face au »Mal absolu« du régime nazi.

Traditionnellement, ce problème, qui doit assumer quelle tâche, est discuté dans l'éthique protestante uniquement dans le cadre de la doctrine de la »profession«. La »profession« au sens théologique du terme détermine depuis Martin Luther le lieu où la personne est saisie par la grâce divine, en même temps qu´elle est rendue responsable par Dieu. Beaucoup de chrétiens pendant le temps des nazis ont refusé la résistance, avec l'argument que ce n'était pas leur »profession«, c.à d. leur tâche de combattre le régime. Ils se sentaient seulement obligés d'être »corrects« dans leur domaine de vie et de travail. Leur interprétation de la »profession« était une excuse pour ne pas joindre la résistance contre le National-Socialisme

L'interprétation de Luther par Bonhoeffer n'est ni une simple confirmation des obligations terrestres, ni le refus de celles-ci, comme le monachisme a pu le pratiquer en son temps. Le chrétien doit plutôt agir dans le monde et doit toujours se concentrer sur l'appel du Christ. Cet appel, dans chaque secteur de l'obligation professionnelle individuelle, est un appel limité, mais il reste »lié au Christ ... libéré de tout isolement« (DBW 6, 293 [Ethique, 211]). Cela signifie que le chrétien à travers l'appel du Christ sera d'abord obligé à l'action dans son propre milieu, là où il se trouve, mais qu'il sera en permanence confronté à de nouveaux défis au-delà des son milieu, et au besoin, être prêt à repousser les limites de son propre champ d'action. Bonhoeffer illustre cela par l'exemple d'un médecin qui non seulement est responsable face à ses patients à leur lit de malade, mais aussi, est tenu par la science médicale, dans ce sens où il doit être prêt à prendre publiquement position contre toute science médicale qui menacerait l'homme. Par conséquent, le milieu de la »profession« comme »lieu de la responsabilité« signifie le lieu d´une rupture potentielle de la responsabilité limitée, d´autant qu´il s'agit d'une responsabilité essentiellement libre :

»Qui dit vocation dit responsabilité, et puisque la responsabilité est une réponse entière de l'homme entier à la réalité entière, on ne saurait s'en tenir à son devoir professionnel au sens restrictif; une restriction pareille serait de l'irresponsabilité. La nature même de la libre responsabilité nous interdit de définir quand et dans quelle mesure un tel élargissement du 'champ d'action limité' est partie intégrante de la vocation et de la responsabilité envers le prochain.« (DBW 6,294 [Ethique, 211])

Bonhoeffer critique une réflexion éthique qui veut se restreindre seulement à un domaine étroit de responsabilité et qui n'est pas prête à regarder au-delà de son entourage. Cette réflexion s´illustre dans la situation même de Bonhoeffer. Tout d'abord, la »profession« veut dire: exercer ses fonctions là où on est engagé.

Ainsi, Bonhoeffer se comprend lui-même avant tout comme un théologien engagé dans sa responsabilité d'enseignant au service des jeunes pasteurs en formation de l'Église Confessante. Toutefois, la libre responsabilité doit s'occuper aussi des autres prochains, aussi des lointains, avec la conséquence que la libre responsabilité se trouve constamment devant le défi d'aller au-delà de la simple satisfaction du devoir à l'endroit où la profession est exercée. La responsabilité motivée par l´amour du prochain peut voir à travers d´autres fenêtres lorsqu´elle se rend compte d´une flagrante injustice en d'autres parties du monde et rend au moins possible un avis de contestation. Si en se référant aux »positions luthériennes sur la profession«[6] un tel engagement est rejeté, Bonhoeffer voit là un problème par rapport à l'intention originelle du terme profession. La responsabilité chrétienne libre doit être prête à s´ouvrir à d´autres possibilités de responsabilités même en dehors du lieu immédiat de l´exercice de la profession. Ces considérations peuvent aussi être interprétées comme un commentaire indirect sur son propre engagement dans la résistance. Bonhoeffer est conscient que son engagement dans ces actions transgresse la frontière de sa propre fonction professionnelle immédiate, mais il voit dans cet engagement de rejoindre la résistance une réponse à l'appel du Christ dans le cadre de l´acte libre de la responsabilité.

5. La compréhension bonhoefferienne de la responsabilité

En arrière fond de cette considération, se trouve développé dans »l'Ethique« un concept de la responsabilité dont l'obligation et la liberté sont les deux éléments constituants. La responsabilité, pour Bonhoeffer, est toujours à prendre dans une double orientation: premièrement dans la liaison de sa vie à Dieu et à celle des autres, qui comprend l'idée de l'action pour et au profit des prochains, adaptée à la réalité et orientée à la situation concrète et deuxièmement dans la liberté de sa propre vie, qui se traduit aussi dans la libre décision du risque qui inclut le risque d'échec et la volonté d´acceptation de la faute (Voir DBW 6, 256-276 [Ethique, 182-196]). En raison de cette tension entre l´obligation et la liberté, l'acte de la libre responsabilité repose sur le risque d'une décision individuelle, car sans un dispositif de sécurité de la part d'autres personnes ou une garantie par des principes et normes de base, chacun en soi individuellement, doit concrétiser l´acte d´»observer, juger, évaluer, décider et agir« (DBW 6, 284 [Ethique, 203]). Les difficultés de cette libre action et de chaque risque que comporte la décision, peuvent être supportées et trouvent ainsi leur point d´appui et leur orientation dans le regard de Jésus-Christ, dans lequel la réalité

[6] Bonhoeffer rappelle le cas d'une fausse justice à motivation raciale rendue aux États-Unis en 1931, lorsqu´il a voulu lui-même motiver l'un des principaux représentant de l'Eglise luthérienne à prendre part à une manifestation, qui s´en est refusé en se référant aux »dispositions luthériennes sur la fonction«. Voir DBW 6, 296 [Ethique, 213].

du monde est fondée:

»L'action du responsable s'accomplit dans l'engagement, qui seul le libère totalement, vis-à-vis de Dieu et du prochain tels qu'il les rencontre en Jésus-Christ; elle se déroule entièrement dans la sphère de la relativité, dans le demi-jour dont la situation historique entoure le bien et le mal, au milieu des aspects innombrables dont se revêt chaque donnée. Elle n'aura pas à se décider simplement pour le droit contre l'injustice, pour le bien contre le mal, mais elle tranchera entre le droit et le droit, entre l'injustice et l'injustice.« (DBW 6, 284 [Ethique, 203])

Une action responsable peut se dispenser de toute forme d'autojustification, puisqu´elle est entièrement orientée vers le Christ. Cela entraine toujours des situations de décision très difficile, dans lesquelles on ne peut pas distinguer entre le »bon« et le »mauvais«, bien plus souvent entre le juste et le juste, ou plus dramatiquement encore, entre l´injuste et l´injuste, c.a d. entre deux possibilités, où il faut choisir le moindre mal. Cette action responsable ne se passe souvent qu´au crépuscule, tardivement, comme Bonhoeffer a pu en prendre conscience dans son propre cheminement, puisque, en dernière analyse – au nom de l´appel de détresse de l'amour du prochain – on peut être prêt de prendre sur soi le rang du coupable.

Face à ce défi, Bonhoeffer se demande, si et dans quelle mesure il est nécessaire de respecter les limites de la responsabilité, d'une part du point de vue de l'acteur lui-même, et d'autre part, aux vus des normes fondamentales, telles que exprimées par exemple par la loi de Dieu dans les Dix Commandements. Le risque de responsabilité libre ne doit jamais conduire à la »destruction et anéantissement« de son acteur (DBW 6, 282 [Ethique, 201]): »la mesure de la capacité de l´homme en association avec l´action responsable et la prise sur soi de la culpabilité, a sa limite respective dans l'unité de l'homme avec lui-même. Il y a des responsabilités que je ne peux pas porter sans de ce fait en être brisé...« (DBW 6, 282 [Ethique, 201]). Pour le dire de façon positive, on peut seulement accepter de porter une telle responsabilité, et pouvoir la réaliser, si la personne qui la porte ne s´en trouve pas surchargée, c. à d. si la responsabilité n'est pas en contradiction fondamentale avec l'identité de la personne concernée.

L'autre limite de la responsabilité est donnée selon Bonhoeffer, lorsque que l'action responsable est face à la »Loi«, c'est-à-dire portée par »la loi de Dieu et l'amour du prochain, telle qu´elle se trouve clairement exprimée et interprétée dans le Décalogue, le Sermon sur la Montagne et dans l'exhortation (la parénèse) apostolique« (DBW 6, 282 [Ethique, 202]). En général, l´action de la libre responsabilité a lieu conformément au texte explicite de la loi. Parce qu´alors ce »n´est pas la loi mais bien Jésus Christ qui est la réalité dernière« (DBW 6, 283 [Ethique, 202]). La responsabilité concrète peut, dans certains cas, »enfreindre la loi« (DBW 6, 298 [Ethique, 214]). Une telle effraction de la loi ne doit pas nécessairement être considérée comme un outrage à la volonté divine, tel que Bonhoeffer essaye de préciser dans ses réflexions sur la difficile relation entre loi et liberté: vu que la loi ne peut pas être séparée de son auteur, Jésus-Christ en étant lui-même »l´ultime référence« (DBW 6, 298 [Ethique, 214]) à laquelle recourir, ce qui peut dans certaines situations, signifier respecter la loi dans sa substance, pour en venir jusqu'à être libéré »de la loi au profit d´une action responsable« (DBW 6, 298 [Ethique, 214]):

»Pour Dieu et pour l'amour du prochain, c´est-à-dire pour l'amour de Christ, il existe une liberté quand il s´agit du respect du sabbat, de l´honneur aux parents, bref de toute la loi divine, une liberté qui casse la loi, mais seulement dans la mesure où elle la rend plus forte, plus vigoureuse encore« (DBW 6, 298 [Ethique, 214]).

Bonhoeffer souligne à plusieurs reprises, et avec insistance, qu'une telle suspension temporaire »de la loi ... sert à son véritable accomplissement« (DBW 6, 298 [Ethique, 214]) et que une »effraction de la loi ...doit être reconnue dans toute sa rigueur« (DBW 6, 298 [Ethique, 214]). Contre tout cynisme d´infraction et surtout contre toute tentative de détourner la loi dans son principe, en particulier le Décalogue, comme le National-Socialisme (Nazisme) a tenté de le faire contre le commandement »Tu ne commettras pas de meurtre«, Bonhoeffer souligne le caractère ponctuel, l´inévitable obligation de la culpabilité et la gravité de la transgression:

»Mais il y a une différence décisive selon laquelle l'on considère une telle transgression de la limite posée comme sa suppression et qu'elle est ainsi abandonnée comme droit de nature particulière ou selon qu'on est conscient, lors de cette transgression, de commettre une faute, peut-être inévitable, qui ne sera justifiée que dans le rétablissement et le respect de la loi et de la limite«. (DBW 8, 30 [RS, 33])

Cela signifiait concrètement qu'il fallait farouchement combattre la politique nazie, qui refusait le droit de vie à certains groupes de personnes, comme des handicapés ou des Juifs, parce que cette politique était une suspension par principe de la Loi Divine. Par contre pour Bonhoeffer il était permis, par exception, de suspendre le commandement »Tu ne commettras pas de meurtre« ponctuellement, par exemple dans une guerre justifiable de défense ou dans la résistance contre une dictature sinistre comme le régime nazi, avec le but de mettre les commandements en vigueur par après, si vite possible. Bonhoeffer restait toujours convaincu de la primauté de la non-violence. Pourtant il se voyait forcé d'abandonner l'option pour la non-violence et de rejoindre la conspiration contre Adolf Hitler face à la guerre d'aggression déclenchée par le dictateur et face au génocide que le régime nazi commettait.

Chaque infraction de la loi est ainsi vue, en raison d´une ou des »situation(s) particulière(s)« comme une »ultima ratio«[7], un dernier recours dans lequel on

---

[7] DBW 6, 273 [Ethique, 194]. Ces considérations conduisent au thème de la reprise de la culpabilité voir DBW 6, 272-275 [Ethique, 195-196].

peut reconnaître la faute due au non respect de la loi. C´est uniquement en cela que, selon Bonhoeffer, est inscrit dans le sens profond du terme ladite »innocence d'une conscience liée au seul Christ« (DBW 6, 281 [Ethique, 200]) parce que »seule la conscience affranchie de la loi ne craindra pas de participer à la faute d'autrui« (DBW 6, 279 [Ethique, 199]), à cause de l'amour des prochains, pour pouvoir en faire preuve de sa pureté. De cette façon, la »volonté de Dieu dans l'acte issue de la liberté est ainsi sanctifié«, bien qu´il paraît assez souvent »insolite« (scandaleux), que l'homme libéré garde »l'unité avec lui-même et la certitude de sanctifier authentiquement la loi tout en la violant« (DBW 6, 299 [Ethique, 214]). Le fait de toujours vouloir préciser la formulation de ce concept théologique de la responsabilité, face à la tentative d´enfreinte à la loi8, illustre bien comment Bonhoeffer a lutté pour clarifier son propre chemin vers le complot, mais aussi et comment il s´est engagé de manière responsable sur ce chemin, dans l'espoir d´en être pardonné. Et non seulement cela, il a pu conseiller sur le plan éthique les autres conjurés dans la résistance contre Hitler à s´engager dans cette même voie et est devenu pendant les préparatifs du complot contre Hitler l´aumônier de ceux qui y avaient pris part.

Les réflexions de Bonhoeffer d'une éthique de la libre responsabilité et du courage civique sont difficiles et non sans problématique parce que dans des situations extrêmes elles se mettent au dessus des commandements bibliques, même si l'intention reste claire de remettre en vigueur les commandements bibliques. Pourtant, le risque est grand de tomber dans le piège d'un certain décisionisme, c.à d. de la décision arbitraire d'un individu ou de plusieurs individus, qui sont en danger de se tromper. Bonhoeffer a vu ce danger et a souligné le risque d'un échec et exprimé d'être prêt à assumer la faute et la culpabilité. Peut-être qu'on devrait réfléchir, que des décisions portant si loin devraient être prises non par des individus isolés, mais par des groupes de chrétiens, conseillés spirituellement par des pasteurs pour ainsi minimiser le danger d'une décision arbitraire et erronée. Pourtant, le risque de l'érreur subsiste, car il s'agit d'une décision libre et enfin personnelle.

Postface

Après l'échec de la tentative d'assassinat de Hitler du 20 Juillet 1944, qui impliquait ainsi le dernier espoir de la réussite de la résistance, Bonhoeffer écrit une lettre très personnelle le 21 Juillet à Eberhard Bethge, comme résumé de l'expérience de la vie dans le complot et en prison: »J'ai appris á connaître et à comprendre de plus en plus la profondeur de l'horizon terrestre (en allemand: die tiefe Diesseitigkeit) du christianisme« (DBW 8, 541 [RS, 437]). Cet engagement »avec l'horizon terrestre« signifie une vie qui ne vise pas sa propre sainteté à soi. »Vivre avec l'horizon terrestre« pour Bonhoeffer veut dire la prise en

[8] Bonhoeffer a discuté de ces questions, en particulier dans «l´Ethique» (DBW 6, 272ff. et 297ff. [Ethique, 191-215]) et dans l'essai »Après dix ans« (DBW 8, 22f, 29f [RS, 25-40]).

main de la responsabilité, se positionner au monde dans la perspective de la »multitude des tâches, des questions, des succès et des échecs, des expériences et des perplexités« (DBW 8, 542 [RS, 438]) dans l'horizon de la souffrance de Dieu et être à même de veiller »avec le Christ à Gethsémané« (DBW 8, 542 [RS, 438]).

Bonhoeffer identifie cette attitude avec la »foi«. De cette manière, on prend part à la souffrance de Dieu, dans laquelle »se trouve toujours présente la reconnaissance de la mort et de la résurrection« (DBW 8, 541 [RS, 437]), Bonhoeffer a appris de nouveau à croire, et d'une manière nouvelle, à devenir chrétien. Ce nouveau parcours et ces expériences, lui sont devenus infiniment précieux, surtout dans la situation d'échec: »C'est pourquoi je pense, écrit-il, au passé et au présent dans la reconnaissance et la paix.« (DBW 8, 542 [RS, 438])

Bonhoeffer est lui-même persuadé – étant en prison après l'échec de la dernière tentative d'un attentat contre Hitler – que la décision de retourner en Allemagne et à participer à la résistance avait été la bonne. Il espère à un salut, mais surtout il attend la direction de Dieu pour sa vie : »Que Dieu nous conduise avec bienveillance à travers notre époque; mais surtout qu´il nous a conduise à lui-même« (DBW 8, 543 [RS, 438]). C´est dans ce sens qu´il pouvait finalement mourir en paix avec son Dieu.

Church as »Church for Others«? Reflections on the Role of Church in Society and the Relevance of Society for the Shape of Church

Kai Horstmann

1. Introduction

With his life testimony, Dietrich Bonhoeffer became a guiding figure of German Protestantism in the post-war years. With his unselfish determination to action, his attitude in prison and his reflected piety he still impresses people today.[1] Since 1998 a statue of Dietrich Bonhoeffer amongst other ecumenical martyrs or even saints[2] from the recent past has been presented to us as a model of true Christianity on Westminster Cathedral's west front in London.

Personally, I found it difficult to find a way into Bonhoeffer's theology. Theology and biography interwoven in the character of Bonhoeffer seemed all too singular to me. And certainly it is not all too simple to get a hold on Bonhoeffer's thinking. It surely is right that Bonhoeffer's work is characterised by an inner unity.[3] But its coherence is not just the result of a ripening process.[4] The inner unity of his theology is some *lively* closeness of fragments.[5] The development of Bonhoeffer's thinking in his academic research, church and political

---

[1] Many churches, parish halls, schools and hospitals have been named after him in Germany. In the assortment of German bookstores you currently can find about a dozen biographies on Dietrich Bonhoeffer, including two graphic novels plus Eric Till's movie on Bonhoeffer (Agent of Grace, 1999/2000). Furthermore there are numerous books available trying to facilitate Bonhoeffer's thinking in layman's terms in the present, apart from a variety of editions of poems, biblical reflections, prayers, etc. written by Bonhoeffer.

[2] Cf. Stephen R. Haynes: The Bonhoeffer Phenomenon. Portraits of a Protestant Saint, Minneapolis 2004 and Wolfgang Huber: Dietrich Bonhoeffer – ein evangelischer Heiliger. Vortrag zur Eröffnung des Internationalen Bonhoeffer-Kongresses am 3. Februar 2006 in Breslau, in: Kirchenamt der EKD (Ed.): Dietrich Bonhoeffer. Vorbild im Glauben, Texte und Predigten anlässlich des 100. Geburtstages von Dietrich Bonhoeffer, Hannover 2006 (EKD-Texte 83), 6-12.

[3] Cf. Heinrich Ott: Dietrich Bonhoeffer, in: Martin Greschat (Ed.): Gestalten der Kirchengeschichte. Vol. IV: Die neueste Zeit, Stuttgart/Berlin/Köln/Mainz 1986, 270-289, 271.

[4] In this respect vs. Eilert Herms: »Kirche für andere«. Zur Kritik und Fortschreibung eines epochemachenden ekklesiologischen Programms, in: Herms: Kirche für die Welt. Lage und Aufgabe der evangelischen Kirchen im vereinigten Deutschland, Tübingen 1995, 19-77, 31.

[5] Cf. Rainer Mayer: Vollendung im Fragment, Gießen ^{2}2006.

activities from 1927, the year of his graduation, until 1945, the year when he was executed, was much too dynamic, to distil »Bonhoeffer«, to make simple abstracts of Bonhoeffer on this or that.

As a practical theologian, my academic studies on Bonhoeffer are embedded in the ongoing discussions in Germany about the reform of Church and the concept of pastoral identity and duties. This is correlated to my profession as a pastor of the Evangelical Church in the Rhineland and to being a member of my church's committee on social responsibility. In this context, I inquire into the meaning of the expression »church for others«.

The practical theologians Eberhard Hauschild in Bonn and Uta Pohl-Patalong in Kiel published a book on Church last year. They call attention to the fact that the concept »church for others« merged into the ecumenical process for justice, peace and integrity of creation.[6] In this movement, church tends to be understood as the avant-garde of society. The members of the in-group are those who have the right consciousness and habits, while the masses belonging to the establishment in church and society are and do wrong.[7]

I want to add a question mark to the phrase »Church for others« because it tends to break up the special social unity of the Church that was emphasised by the young Bonhoeffer. And I want to add a question mark to the phrase »church for others« because it puts the Church into contradiction with the world. With the reformation, Church and the worship of the common priesthood have always been located *in* the world. So why does Bonhoeffer make that confrontation?

2. »Church for Others«

The passage we read is part of the outline of a work, the concept of a small book Bonhoeffer intended to write after prison. It stems from a time when Bonhoeffer, as we know from letters he wrote in captivity, surprisingly did not miss the Sunday service and did not read in the Bible for weeks. In a way, Bonhoeffer is losing his religion. The existence that Christ has shared with humanity becomes more important to him, than »religion«. He becomes convinced that one becomes a Christian if one becomes human, just as God himself did in Christ.[8] What Bonhoeffer is maintaining in his Christian irreligion is a *christic* understanding of Church as a form of existence.

---

[6] With Bonhoeffer´s work as a youth secretary of the *World Alliance for Promoting International Friendship through the Churches* and his famous appeal for an ecumenical peace council in Fanö 1934 as the historical background.

[7] Cf. Eberhard Hauschildt / Uta Pohl-Patalong: Kirche, Gütersloh 2103, 136.

[8] Cf. the letter to Eberhard Bethge 21.7.1944 in: Christian Gremmels / Wolfgang Huber (Ed.): Dietrich Bonhoeffer Auswahl. Vol. 5, Briefe aus der Haft 1943-1945, Gütersloh 2006, 171-173, 171.

Christic is a term I have learned from Muriel Orevillo-Montenegro.[9] Labelling something as *Christian* marks the motivational background of something done or the cultural context of an artefact. However that's not the issue, particularly regarding Bonhoeffer. It would probably be more appropriate to speak of a Christological or *Christ-centred* conception of Church. However, this more common expression does not hit the nail on the head, because Church, according to Bonhoeffer, is a shape of the Word of God in itself. This is why I want to mark Bonhoeffer's ecclesiology as christic.

Peter Zimmerling, a practical theologian from Leipzig, has put the dogmatic point of our formula's background as follows: »If faith means participating in the being of Jesus and this making itself concrete in the habit of being-for-others ... it is a logical consequence that Church only can be Church being there for others.«[10] But it is not only a habit to be there for others. The Church simply cannot *be* anything else than for others *for the Church is Christ*. We can actually find this formulation of the essence of Church in Bonhoeffer's writing: The Church, he says, is the present Christ, Christ in existence as congregation.[11] Thus Church cannot be conceived of in any other way than for others, self-renunciated in its appearance, mere pro-existence of the *creatura verbi* that does not savour the Word of God even if Church derives all its being from it.

The young Bonhoeffer put his effort into the conceptualisation of a maximum of Church. With the concept of Church for others now – in terms of Ernst Lange[12] – a minimum of Church with a maximum of relevance is thought in a doubled demarcation from a liberal theology that sublates churchliness in morality or the state on the one hand. On the other hand it is demarked from a pietistic or revivalist piety that focuses on the personal relationship with God only. Church cannot be merged into something else or be privatised, because the Church is the indispensible premise or fundament of faith.[13] The consequence of this fact is that »Church is not a human community with Christ giving himself to it, or a fellowship of those seeking Christ or having found him singularly, but it is a confraternity created by Christ ....«[14]

---

[9] Cf. Muriel Orevillo-Montenegro: The Jesus of Asian Women, Maryknoll 2006.

[10] Cf. Peter Zimmerling: Bonhoeffer als Praktischer Theologe, Göttingen, 2006, 52.

[11] Cf. Dietrich Bonhoeffer: Sanctorum Communicatio, in: Christian Gremmels / Wolfgang Huber (Ed.): Dietrich Bonhoeffer Auswahl. Vol. 1. Universität, Pfarramt, Ökumene. 1927-1932, Gütersloh 2006, 32-55, 42.

[12] Cf. Ernst Lange: Kirche für andere. Dietrich Bonhoeffers Beitrag zur Frage einer verantwortbaren Gestalt der Kirche in der Gegenwart (1965), in: Lange: Kirche für die Welt. Aufsätze zur Theorie kirchlichen Handelns, ed. by Rüdiger Schloz, München / Gelnhausen 1981 (Edition Ernst Lange 2), 19-62.

[13] Cf. Dietrich Bonhoeffer: Akt und Sein, in: Gremmels / Huber (Ed.), Vol. 1, 2006, 59-92, 70.

[14] Cf. ibid., 65f.

3. »Church for the World«

Following its christic character, the Church has got a remarkable relationship – or should I say affair – with the world.

The first thing is that Church is taking the world seriously. Bonhoeffer disqualifies a fairly common attitude amongst Christians who are not able to stand the lowliness of the world. These Christians soar towards heaven, where all suffering is overcome; they flee from the seriousness of the world's realities because of weakness.[15] And Bonhoeffer disqualifies those that he calls the children of the world as well. Those that are addicted to a pious Christian secularism, following the device »We need to build a strong fortress where we can live with God in security. We build the kingdom!«[16] By way of contrast, he qualifies faith as an attitude aligned with the reign of God beyond all utopian dreams. »'Let thy kingdom come' is the prayer not of a single pious soul fleeing reality, and not the prayer of an enthusiast or do-gooder, it is the prayer of those that do not segregate themselves from the world, of those not having any better ideas to improve the world, but those enduring in the midst, in the deep, in the banality and in the state of being subjected.«[17]

Enduring is a passive attitude, is suffering, not action. But it is an »affirmation of the earth at the same time, is engagement in the world's order, communities, history.«[18] As Church. »The kingdom of God develops itself within the Church, as far as Church is giving witness of the wonders of God", that is the resurrection of Christ, i.e. the end of the rule of death. And at the same time this activity of enduring is not only Church but state »as far as the state accepts and keeps the order of upkeeping life.«[19] Thus it is clear, that any contribution of Church to political discussions must not have the form of taking sides. It is not the Church's task to take a stand.[20] This is the task of the individual or of humanitarian organisations.[21] The task of the Church is biblical propagation.

The mandate of the Church is to make the substantiality of Jesus Christ real in its preaching, its order and in Christian life. Ethically the obedience of faith in

---

[15] Cf. Dietrich Bonhoeffer: Dein Reich komme! Das Gebet der Gemeinde um Gottes Reich auf Erden, in: Christian Gremmels / Wolfgang Huber (Ed.): Dietrich Bonhoeffer Auswahl. Vol. 2. Gegenwart und Zukunft der Kirche. 1933-1935, Gütersloh 2006, 53-68, 54.

[16] Cf. ibid., 55.

[17] Cf. ibid., 59.

[18] Cf. ibid., 61.

[19] Cf. ibid., 62.

[20] Cf. in contrast Wolfgang Huber's popular Bonhoeffer interpretation. Cf. e.g. Wolfgang Huber: In der Verantwortung, in: Kirchenamt der Evangelischen Kirche in Deutschland (Ed.): Fürchtet Gott, ehrt den König. Das Magazin zum Themenjahr 2014. Reformation und Politik, Hannover 2013, 41-44.

[21] Cf. Dietrich Bonhoeffer: Die Kirche vor der Judenfrage, in: Gremmels / Huber (Ed.), Vol. 2, 2006, 69-79, 71.

the Christian life of the single believer is not observed in a special district but in marriage – the sphere of family and private life, work – the sphere of economy, and authority – the sphere of politics.[22] Likewise the Church must not realise its mandate by unworldly means. Bonhoeffer can call the Church into play as a critical corrective to the state. At all times the Church shall ask the state to adhere to the legitimacy of its actions. [23] And the Church must have the courage to state the concrete commandment not in absolute terms, but concretely, for today.[24]

An example is the concrete commandment to keep peace on earth[25] not because of good reasons but because of the Word of God. [26] And this »Word of God is the word of the congregation, it has existence in time and space. It is not weak and just human teaching, but the powerful word of the creator.«[27]

4. »Confessing«

I would like to interpret this courageously proclaimed word of full power in relation to what Bonhoeffer said about confession.

The concrete commandment is the venture of a confession of situation in fellowship.[28] A confession expresses a decision about a situation that in history can never be unmistakably clear. Saying the Word of God as commandment is therefore always a venture. The question is: »Can Church proclaim the commandment of God within the same certainty as it preaches the Gospel? Can Church proclaim with the same certainty: 'We need a socialist order of economics' or 'Do not go to war', as the Church can say 'Thy sins are forgiven?'« [29]

Actually, the characteristic of confession according to Bonhoeffer would be misunderstood if it would be taken as a solemn sum of theology in timeless righteousness. To Bonhoeffer this would only mean to theologise without any commitment.[30] Just like the venture of the concrete commandment, a confession is a request and invitation in a special situation. The confession is the statement

---

[22] Cf. Lange: Kirche für andere, 46.
[23] Cf. Bonhoeffer: Die Kirche vor der Judenfrage, 72.
[24] Vgl. Dietrich Bonhoeffer: Zur theologischen Begründung der Weltbundarbeit, in: Gremmels / Huber (Ed.), Vol. 1, 2006, 114-131, 119.
[25] Cf. Dietrich Bonhoeffer, Kirche und Völkerwelt, in: Gremmels / Huber (Ed.), Vol. 2, 2006, 89-93.
[26] Cf. Dietrich Bonhoeffer, Vorlesung »Christologie«. Nachschrift, in: Gremmels / Huber (Ed), Vol. 2, 2006, 139-170, 151.
[27] Cf. ibid., 157.
[28] Cf. Rainer Mayer quoted by Zimmerling: Bonhoeffer als Praktischer Theologe, 107.
[29] Cf. Bonhoeffer: Zur theologischen Begründung der Weltbundarbeit, 119.
[30] Cf. Dietrich Bonhoeffer: Die Bekennende Kirche und die Ökumene, in: Gremmels / Huber (Ed.), Vol. 2, 2006, 94-114, 102.

of the insight of being truly Church and from the perspective of this certainty with a view to invite others: »Come, here is the Church!«[31]

The manner in which the Church is proclaiming the concrete commandment and reflecting its restrictions in a confession giving orientation regarding the way of truth is far from pride or arrogance. Just the opposite is the case: The Church is expressing its restrictions. This is why the confessing Church is not confronting Churches of other confessions as an enemy, but is taking the blame for the brokenness of Christianity and accepts in all false theology its own guilt, its lacking of power of reconciliation.[32]

The confession states the restrictions of the Church in its credibility. And this restriction can also be discovered *within* the Church. Differences in teaching and denomination are marked by confessions.[33] However, these confessions do not necessarily need to split the unity of the Church. The unity given by Christ makes differences tolerable and negotiable. Even confessions are negotiable because essentially they are judgments on special factual issues because of theological decisions. In this constraint, that is distinguishing a confession from the summa theologiae, lies the claim for unity in confession with those dissenting, who are asked to return.[34]

In calling for repentance, the confession is quite similar to the concrete commandment.[35] The confession, too, is venturous, time-bound, is essentially kerygmatic. The confession Church is a call for repentance.

5. »Word of God«

Bonhoeffer is reflecting on the locus of confession, the restriction of Church, and he is reflecting on the reason for confession, the boundaries that Church experiences, he explicitly is not interested in reflecting the means. Bonhoeffer's homiletics and his liturgical teaching are marked by renunciation of any questions of presentation because stylisation could lead to a misunderstanding of the Word of God. Peter Zimmerling: »It has to be kept clear that it is not my but God's Word that I speak out as officiant in liturgy.«[36]

---

[31] Cf. Dietrich Bonhoeffer: Zur Frage nach der Kirchengemeinschaft, in: Christian Gremmels / Wolfgang Huber (Ed.): Dietrich Bonhoeffer Auswahl. Vol. 3. Entscheidungen. 1936-1939, Gütersloh 2006, 31-51, 33f.

[32] Cf. Bonhoeffer: Die Bekennende Kirche und die Ökumene, 108.

[33] Cf. ibid., 36.

[34] Cf. ibid., 39.

[35] Cf. ibid., 42.

[36] Cf. Zimmerling: Bonhoeffer als Praktischer Theologe, 119. Cf. Bonhoeffer in Akt und Sein, 76.

The background of this strict restraint is undoubtedly the abuse of rhetoric and dramaturgy by the National Socialist propaganda.[37] But if we take a look at his lectures in Christology we can also see that the reasons for Bonhoeffer's restraint lie deeper theologically. In these lectures there is rejection in principal of asking about the means of revelation. »Our asking about the ways of divine knowledge is nothing but an expression of us being bound to our own authority«, says Bonhoeffer, because it keeps us from asking *who* encounters us in Christ, revealing himself only in obedient faith as a question already answered.[38]

The restraint concerning techniques of practical theology corresponds to this Christological thinking about revelation. The Word of God shall be heard instantaneously. This is why Bonhoeffer takes confidence in the biblical texts as the best principle for their visualisation and realisation. Bonhoeffer argues: The biblical text is concrete because the most concrete is the Holy Spirit being present. And the realisation of the text depends merely on its credibility. A sermon is non-credible, when the preacher does not live up to his word. It is not the promise, but the credibility of a sermon, that one can experience: this is somebody existing in Christ.[39] Hence, the training of preachers has to concentrate on their personal credibility in the fellowship of Christ.

6. »Finkenwalde«

As an institution of the Confessional Church, the seminary at Finkenwalde was an act of confession in itself. The aim of the communitarian life of the ministerial candidates in Finkenwalde was to introduce them to an obedient life with the Bible. It is all about some kind of naïve obedience: »Follow the commandment that you know. Don't ask, just do it.«[40] It is all about credibility, not about the proof of truth. This is not dependent on the deeds of the preacher but on the Word of God alone. This is why Bonhoeffer, as I have already pointed out, exercises restraint concerning all techniques of practical theology. He relies on the self interpretation of the divine Word by Christ. But this divine Word demands

---

[37] Cf. Zimmerling: Bonhoeffer als Praktischer Theologe, 120.

[38] Cf. Bonhoeffer: Christologie, 142.

[39] Cf. Dietrich Bonhoeffer: Vorlesung über Homiletik, in: Gremmels / Huber (Ed.), Vol. 2, 2006, 171-189, 176. Also cf. Dietrich Bonhoeffer: Vergegenwärtigung neutestamentlicher Texte, in: ibid., 115-135, 135 »The existence of the preacher is the medium.« (Eberhard Bethge's note).

[40] Cf. Dietrich Bonhoeffer: Nachfolge, in: Gremmels / Huber (Ed.), Vol. 3, 2006, 109-172, 139.
Actually this prompt reminds one of the famous statement by the late Brother Roger of Taizé: »Live what you have understood of the gospel, even if it is very little.« Cf. Dieter Sagert: Protestantische Heilige? Gedanken zu Dietrich Bonhoeffer und Frère Roger, in: Forum Nr. 254, Luxembourg 2006, 31-32.

obedience and an unbelievable pastor becomes dysfunctional, as Sabine Bobert-Stützel puts it.[41]

The communitarian life in Finkenwalde is an exercise in the realisation of this obedience in the situation of illegality and therefore of existential threat. It is not a common congregation with its club life, but a community within the Confessional Church, a community of soon-to-be preachers of repentance. This community is interpreted by Bobert-Stützel as a centre of resistance. The entire pastoral theology of Bonhoeffer is convincingly interpreted by Bobert-Stützel in these terms. But this preparation for resistance is not to be taken as preparation of spies.[42] It is about the protest, the literally polemic witness opposite to the common Christianity and society. This aspect of monastic life was stressed in Finkenwalde.[43]

7. The sacramentality of the ministry and the loss of congregation

In Finkenwalde the constriction of ecclesiology developed, the concentration of what has to be said about the Word of God and of the christic existence of the Church on the ministry and the ministers. The ministry of the congregation for the congregation thus became a ministry opposite the congregation.

With this concept of a new work in which we find the prospect of a poor Church for others, Bonhoeffer wants to contribute to a new credible start after the war and the Nazi regime. The poverty of the pastors shall be poverty for Christ's sake, an expression of faith relying only on the Lord and thus being free for service.[44] Actually a faith literally relying on God *alone*.

In his lectures on homiletics, Bonhoeffer still incorporates the ministry into the congregation. According to Bonhoeffer, preachers have the right to know how their sermon was received.[45] All the more justified is the question of Eberhard Bethge who asked in their correspondence, where among all that, that is the radicalism of the concept, there is still room for the congregational Church. Does it not get lost?

---

[41] Cf. Sabine Bobert-Stützel: Dietrich Bonhoeffers Pastoraltheologie. Theologenausbildung im Widerstand zum »Dritten Reich«. Dargestellt anhand der Finkenwalder Vorlesungen 1935–1937, Gütersloh 1995, 96.

[42] Cf. accordingly Sabine Dramm: V-Mann Gottes und der Abwehr? Dietrich Bonhoeffer und der Widerstand, Gütersloh 2005.

[43] Cf. Bobert-Stützel: Dietrich Bonhoeffers Pastoraltheologie, 128f.

[44] Cf. Bonhoeffer: Nachfolge, 137f.

[45] Cf. Bonhoeffer: Vorlesung über Homiletik, 188.

In actuality the pastor in his ministry appears to be the single holder of the word of reconciliation and salvation for mankind and world that originally was given to the Church as a special social body in a sameness of the spirit.[46]

We have to state a sacramentality of the ministry that has developed from Bonhoeffer's dogmatic understanding of the sermon. The identification of the sermon as the christic venture of saying the Word of God leads to an almost priestly representation of Christ by the minister.[47] With this sacramentalisation of the ministry the unity of the congregation in the common priesthood is shattered. Instead, Word priests and those receiving the Word will be opponents.[48]

8. Church for others?

In support of the credibility of propagation, Bonhoeffer developed an understanding of ministry in opposition to the common churchliness of the congregation. The preacher is the official holder of the Word of God as a prophet, who tells the Word of God inviting others into discipleship. Bonhoeffer's practical ecclesiology intensifies in a minimum of Church within a maximum of its kenosis for others. So what is wrong about that?

It is correct that giving witness in everyday life is of highest importance if Church is not just any religious group but the Church of Jesus Christ. And it is also correct that this witness in the highly differentiated reality of the world has to be given by the life witness of the individual in the first place. But it can only be recognised as a Christian witness if there is a relation between the act of witnessing and the centre of the Christian community. This is stressed by Eilert Herms.[49]

Accordingly, he insists that – especially according to the reception of Bonhoeffer – a tendency can be identified to pit individual Christian doing against par-

[46] Cf. Dietrich Bonhoeffer: Gedanken zum Tauftag von Dietrich Wilhelm Rüdiger Bethge, in: Christian Gremmels / Wolfgang Huber (Ed.): Dietrich Bonhoeffer Auswahl. Vol. 6, Aufzeichnungen aus der Haft. 1943-1955, Gütersloh 2006, 153-161, 161.

[47] »The confessional documents talk about the ministry, about ordination as a sacrament. [...] One will be called into the ministry. This call is irrevocable. One cannot rid himself of God´s vocation. That is the right point of the catholic 'character indelibilis'.« Bonhoeffer, Vorlesung über Homiletik, 172.

[48] Cf., quite disconcerting, Dietrich Bonhoeffer: Ethik, in: Christian Gremmels / Wolfgang Huber (Ed.): Dietrich Bonhoeffer Auswahl. Vol. 4. Konspiration. 1939-1943, Gütersloh 2006, 67-182, 175: »The book of sermons and the book of prayer primarily are the books of the congregation, the Holy Scipture is the book of the preacher. This could be taken as an appropriate expression of the divine opposition of ministry and congregation.«

[49] Cf. Herms: »Kirche für andere«, 46.

ticipation in the common life of the community.[50] The task of the ministry is to present the Word of God to the congregation as its origin, fundament and guideline and to encourage and enable, i.e. to empower every single Church member to live his or her life under the Word.[51]

Is this what Bonhoeffer meant when he wrote that the Church has to tell every person in every profession that life with Christ means to be there for other?[52]

Bonhoeffer's concept for the reform of the Church aims at the »enthronement of the gospel« as Zimmerling puts it strikingly.[53] It is true that Bonhoeffer tried to maintain that the commandment of Jesus does not justify any reign of the Church over authority or of authority over family or whatever, because all the mandates are under the reign of Christ.[54] But this equalisation is subverted by the opinion that Church is a christic shape of the Word of God. This leads to the misunderstanding of a claim to superiority in an avant-garde understanding of Church.[55] This claim is not actually supported by Bonhoeffer. Nevertheless, a constructive criticism of Bonhoeffer's concept of mandate is necessary to prevent this attitude. Eilert Herms is doing so by presenting a concept in which all the mandates are consequently interactional related. Because we all take part in all mandates.[56] In allusion to Bonhoeffer, Herms writes: »Under the conditions of highly complex societies abandoning the cultivation of the Church experienceable, and the renunciation of its presence in the network of social powers, results in disobedience.«[57]

9. Church together and with others

The fortitude of Bonhoeffer's concept of pastoral theology lies in its contextuality. This is the conclusion of Sabine Bobert-Stützel in her doctoral thesis.[58] And I do agree. Trying to copy Bonhoeffer's spirituality of fellowship would mean to deny one's own context, she says sharply.[59] But this does not mean to lay him

[50] Cf. ibid., 52.
[51] Cf. ibid., 68.
[52] Cf. Dietrich Bonhoeffer: Entwurf einer Arbeit, in: Gremmels / Huber (Ed.), Vol. 6, 2006, 162-1966, 165.
[53] Cf. Zimmerling: Bonhoeffer als Praktischer Theologe, 68.
[54] Cf. Bonhoeffer: Ethik, 172.
[55] Cf. Christoph Bäumler: Kommunikative Gemeindepraxis. Eine Untersuchung ihrer Bedingungen und Möglichkeiten, München 1984, 40, 43.
[56] This is true for ministers as well. It would be wrong to allot a special position to them. Cf. Bäumler: Kommunikative Gemeindepraxis, 35, who likewise refers to the collective character of Church rejecting such a special position of ministers.
[57] Cf. Herms: »Kirche für Andere«, 55.
[58] Cf. Bobert-Stützel: Dietrich Bonhoeffers Pastoraltheologie, 354.
[59] Cf. ibid, 358.

aside. We are challenged to think about these problems continuously. Ernst Lange did so.

The historical background of Lange is the upheaval in German society after the restoration period in the fifties, early sixties. He criticises the concentration on the parochie for parochie did lose the connection to people's realm of experience and milieus. A theology emphasising the alienness, strangeness of the Church's existence in the world could not and cannot work against a further separation of Church and world. This is why Lange is arguing with Bonhoeffer against Bonhoeffer that the misery borne by Christ is the misery of the world to be overcome in order to prevent the world from perishing.[60] We must not construct Church and world in opposition to one another because this relation is defined by the Lord.[61] Thus the Church has to open itself as an organisation towards the world in devotion.

Opening the Church to the world means practically to take notice of the social reality in which the Church exists congregationally. But we have to keep in mind that the Church members do so in quite different ways. Lange goes along with Bonhoeffer when he states that the Church's participation in social, political, or economical questions is not an institutional task in the first place, but the task of every single member of the Church in the daily routines of society.[62] But Lange is far from sublating the Church into a minimum. He suggests the Church should be conceptualised as a room to exercise freedom.[63] He requests Church to be a congregation that prevents Christians to clear themselves from their earthbound existence, but rather instruct them to be earthbound.[64]

Ernst Lange gave an example with an experimental congregation meeting in a shop, a former bakery store, in Berlin; a congregation with a big window for everybody to look inside and – more important – out; a congregation meeting so to say in a setting of daily routines. The laypersons were not submitted under the minsters but were taken seriously as experts of diaspora, experts for the reality of the world. Their expertise was called upon in circles and group meetings and communicating their experience in the light of the biblical promises in order to find encouragement for the life beyond the inner life of Church, empowerment for a Christian life in work and consumption, family, leisure time and civil co-responsibility.[65]

The impulses Lange gave are still relevant for building and shaping Church in the social reality of Germany. Occasional services already lead the pastors over

[60] Cf. Lange: Kirche für andere, 39.
[61] Cf. ibid., 45.
[62] Cf. ibid., 56.
[63] Cf. ibid., 57f.
[64] Cf. ibid., 58.
[65] Cf. Ernst Lange: Aus der »Bilanz 65«, in: Lange: Kirche für die Welt. Aufsätze zur Theorie kirchlichen Handelns, München/Gelnhausen 1981, 63-161, 77.

the threshold of the congregation. These parochial services are way out of the life of the inner congregation. We do need much more than liturgical tuning to make our Sunday services more attractive. What we need is a more communicative practice in our parochies to make their congregational life open to others, to the experience they have, their everyday practice. We need to communicate the gospel within the world's reality. This is something completely different from clerical admonition as well as from unworldly glorification, praising the Lord detached from the world.

Under the Word we need world knowledge; it is constitutive for the concrete commandment. While we know that empirical knowledge is never unmistakably clear and that participation of Church members in social reality is multiform. A people's Church is not as homogenous as a brotherhood. It is to be taken seriously by the organisation of the Church that the Church members participate in the different areas of social activity, in the elements of the social system according to their personal mature responsibility.[66] All Church members are always part of the world they are sent in as Church. And this is why the dispute of the world is not carried out somewhere outside but *within* the Church and cannot be decided within the last but one reality we live in. Thus an avant-gardist understanding of Church has to be criticised. It does not observe the sameness of the spirit.

The intermediation of every Church member in the body of Christ actually enables the Church to overcome the mutual determination by enemy images.[67] It makes conflicts manageable. A waiver of consensus-building within the open parochie would result in an arbitrary particularism. Instead of a core of the parochie having the power to make ultimate decisions there would be various other groups claiming the truth. And these groups could assume the social functions of Church within the complex society just as little as a core congregation that is closed in itself.[68] It is inevitable to argue within Church about the steps necessary to be taken in public education and culture, economics and politics under the reign of Christ, even without any perspective of finding a full consent, an ultimate justification within the last but one reality we live in.

Special fellowships, communities, and actions of single Christians in their discipleship can be honoured within this understanding as a critical challenge for the people´s Church, a ferment for change.[69] But the standard of communication within these communities must not be paid dearly for with the disqualification

---

[66] Cf. Konrad Stock: Civilcourage. Gedanken zum ethisch-politischen Vermächtnis Dietrich Bonhoeffers, in: Stock: Die Gegenwart des Guten. Schriften zur Theologie, Marburg 2006 (Marburger Theologische Studien 96), 215-224.

[67] Cf. Bäumler: Kommunikative Gemeindepraxis, 37.

[68] Cf. ibid., 93.

[69] Cf. Bäumler: Kommunikative Gemeindepraxis, based on Moltmann, 23.

of other members of the one body of Christ.[70] Differences of ethical judgment need to be mutually tolerated. Still concrete commandments and confessions have to be clear, have to be precise. They have to be listened to within the one body of Christ as a call into sameness of spirit by seriously questioning my differing position.

Opening the Church, especially its parochial organisation, means embracing the world *we live in*. Thus Church not only for others, but *together*. And for the world as well, not by having a message but by proclaiming it in public, inviting into the Church. Thus Church not only for one another but *with others*.[71]

I already mentioned a still pioneering example of the experimental congregation of Ernst Lange out of my context, the late phase of the evangelical Church in Germany being a people's Church.[72] Being in Rwanda I would like to give another example for this communicative concept of Church within the world. On January 18th we had a meeting of those having personal or partnership relations with Rwanda within the German region of the United Evangelical Mission. The head of UEM's Africa Department, John Wesley Kabango spoke about neighbourhood groups within Rwandan congregations meeting for bible studies and prayer. And talking about the problems of everyday life together connected with this. We need such groups to discuss political questions in a broader sense, to face the reality even in its high complexity, as a way of the communication of the gospel. The engagement with our world and this is engagement in conflicts, is part of the communication of the gospel which surely is not to be avoided but full of promise.

---

[70] Cf. ibid.

[71] Following this we do not need an evangelistic church development only (cf. Michael Herbst: Kirche mit Mission. Beiträge zu Fragen des Gemeindeaufbaus, Neukirchen-Vluyn 2013; the missional conception of Herbst has a wide influence on German protestant Churches at present) but a more than diaconic but public, respectively conciliar church development no less.

[72] Cf. Christian Fechtner: Späte Zeit der Volkskirche. Praktisch-theologische Erkundungen, Stuttgart 2010.

Ecumenism and the Future of the Church

Ulrich Möller:

1. Ecumenism and the Future of the Church – where we come from

Dear sisters and brothers, for my contribution on the final day of this fascinating conference, I was asked to speak on »Ecumenism and the Future of the Church«. The history of the Evangelical Church of Westphalia (EKvW) – as well as the journey which brought our delegation to this conference itself – are both already expressions of this theme.

The profile of the Westphalian Church is ecumenical. One root of this is in the fact that, after 1945, we had to face up to the failure of the protestant church in its majority during the Nazi period. After World War II, caused by Germany, *vast* areas of Europe were devastated. Germany was responsible for the planned Holocaust, a genocide in which more than 6 million Jews were murdered. 80 million people were killed in World War II, especially among the peoples of Eastern Europe, which Germany under Hitler had attacked in order either to oppress or to extinguish its people. When Germany was finally defeated, our country was regarded as being an enemy of humanity. It was the Christian sisters and brothers of the ecumenical movement who offered a hand of reconciliation towards the German churches, ready to re-accept them as part of the international, ecumenical fellowship. This was due to the fact that the Confessing Church on the basis of its famous confession, the Barmen Theological Declaration of 1934 and some outstanding representatives of the Confessing Church, especially Dietrich Bonhoeffer who died as a martyr, had proved that not the entire Christian church in Germany had denied its witness to Jesus Christ.

However, and with good reasons, the ecumenical movement expected that the Protestant Church in Germany as a whole should show, in a public confession of guilt, that they were aware of how fundamentally they had failed to confess during the Nazi era, and that they were ready to learn out of this for the future. This led to the Stuttgart Confession of Guilt, as we heard yesterday evening, right before the founding of the World Council of Churches 1948 in Amsterdam. It was on this basis that thc protestant churches in Germany were accepted to become members of the WCC. For this we are grateful until today. And this has put a special responsibility on the German churches, not to forget the historical and theological lessons we had to learn, paid for with the sacrifice of the blood of so many victims. This is one reason why the Protestant Church in Germany in a special way feels close and committed to the World Council of Churches until today.

Soon after World War II, the former allies became enemies in the upcoming so called »cold war« between the western states under the leadership of the US and the eastern communist states under the dominance of the USSR. Once more on the brink of war, the Christian churches in East and West founded the Conference of European Churches (CEC) as a bridge of peace-building and ecumenical cooperation. The EKvW Church President was one of those church leaders who were very much engaged right from the founding of CEC. So in the following decades, this ecumenical dimension of being church became essential for my church's self-understanding – sometimes achieved by painful debates of our General Synod in order to achieve a joint witness, as during the era of Apartheid in South Africa. And this is also true for other EKD member churches. This is mirrored at the level of our church order as well as in the ecumenical commitment of our church in our region, working together with sister churches of other confessional tradition like the Roman Catholic Church, the Orthodox Churches, the Anglican Church and the many different protestant denominations, most of them members of the Communion of Protestant Churches in Europe (GEKE). Together we try to express this ecumenical dimension of our church life, not only in our relationships with our international partner churches in Europe, in South-America and the US, but also in a very special way in our relationship with our sister churches in the United Evangelical Mission (UEM), a communion of 35 Churches in Africa, Asia and Europe. Its origins go back the missionary work of the Rheinish Mission, the Bethel Mission and the Zaire Mission way back in the 19th century. In an intensive transformative process from the 1970 s to the 1990 s we have grown from a former cooperation of these churches on the basis of German Mission Societies into an international communion of churches of Lutheran, Reformed, United, Methodist, Baptist and Anglican tradition. In reconciled diversity of the different confessional traditions, this communion is united in a joint holistic understanding of mission, together taking part in God's mission – MISSIO DEI.

What does that mean? The UEM Constitution says:

»The United Evangelical Mission is founded on the Holy Scriptures of the Old and New Testament, and shall serve the purpose of joint action in mission.

The United Evangelical Mission operates within a network of churches in Africa, Asia and Europe and wherever it may be called upon to serve.

Together these churches shall proclaim Jesus Christ as the Lord and Saviour of all people and shall face the challenges of present-day mission.

In a world torn apart, they commit themselves to remain members of the one Body of Christ, and therefore to:

- *grow together into a worshipping, learning and serving community;*
- *share gifts, insights and responsibilities;*
- *call all people to repentance and new life;*

• *bear witness to the Kingdom of God in striving for justice, peace and the integrity of creation.«*

It is on this basis that we have joined this important theological conference as part of our visit to Rwanda and Eastern Congo: as members of the one Body of Christ, as a network of churches to grow together in worship and service, by sharing gifts and being accountable to one another, together giving witness in striving for justice, peace and the integrity of creation.

This is not something abstract. This is to be experienced in the life of our churches, when our sisters in Goma and Bukavu share their stories beyond imagination – stories about brutal gang raping by war parties destroying innocent people's bodies, traumatising their minds and souls.

This takes place, when we hear how a 14-year old boy from the Kivu was forced to watch how, in front of his very eyes, his father was tortured and murdered by soldiers at home. When he shares how this led him to join the militias full of hate to take revenge against the people he held responsible for killing his father. And confessing how out of this trauma then he himself as youth member of this militia terrorised people by raping women, torturing, slaughtering men, women, children… until the Baptist UEM church in Kivu opened up to him the path towards a new life. Now he is learning nursing and caring for people in need.

This takes place, when in the UEM together we support the Lutheran Church in Namibia in its fight for a basic income grant for the marginalised people as a start-up to get out of abject poverty and as the sign of hope for so many worldwide.

This takes place when together as churches we share our stories of hope that encourage us to give witness to Jesus Christ today; listening to the margins, from where the God of the poor and destitute calls us to follow him to transform the world: So that all may have life in fullness, caring for the precious gift of creation and striving for ecological justice.

2. Ecumenism and the Future of the Church – Bonhoeffer's vision and its relevance for today

Dear sisters and brothers, in the lectures and group sessions since Tuesday you have worked on the ecclesiology of Dietrich Bonhoeffer, which he developed as he faced the specific context and challenges of his times.

In his foundational lecture »*On the theological justification of the work of the World Alliance*« at the Youth Peace Conference in Cernohorske Kupele on 26 July 1932, Bonhoeffer said the following, which is still true today:

»The church us the one community of the Lord Jesus Christ, the Lord of the world, has the mission to tell out his Word to the whole world. The parish of the

one church of Christ is the whole world. Every single church has territorial borders to its proclamation, while the one church has no borders. And to express their claim to the whole world, or rather, this claim of their Lord to the whole world, the churches have joined in the world alliance. ... It is not one holy, sacred district that belongs to Christ, but the whole world.« (DBW 1, 140-158)

And 1934 in »Church and Nations« Bonhoeffer said in his famous Fanö speech:

»The church lives in all nations and yet beyond all national, political, social and racial borders, and – through the command of the one Lord Christ, which they hear – the brothers of this church are more inseparably linked than all bonds of history, of blood, of class and of language could bind people. All these internal worldly bonds are valid, not indifferent, but before Christ they are also not final bonds. Hence the members of the ecumenical movement, if they stay with Christ, find his Word and command of peace more holy, more durable than the most holy words and the words of the natural world could be. ...These brothers through Christ obey his word and ... keep his command of peace... they cannot aim weapons at each other because they know that they would thereby be aiming the weapons at Christ himself.« (DBW 13, 298-301)

Bonhoeffer formulated his Theological Vision in 1932 in the year before the National Socialists seized power in Germany and again in 1934, shortly after the first synod of the Confessing Church and the adoption of the Barmen Theological Declaration. Only a long time later – after the unimaginable mass murders of millions of Jews and others by Nazi Germany, after 80 million deaths during the Second World War started by Germany – only then was this ecumenical vision really taken seriously.

With the founding of the World Council of Churches in 1948, a pilgrimage of worldwide Christians began, on the basis of the insight: »War is contrary to the will of God!«

Bonhoeffer's vision has time and again inspired the ecumenical movement. It was the vision of an ecumenical community of churches that – worldwide and across the denominations – takes the Word of God, God's command of peace and justice, in a relevant and practical way to the churches and the world, up until today.

His call for an ecumenical worldwide peace council inspired the ecumenical movement in the 1970 s up till the 1980 s in the conciliar process for justice, peace and the integrity of creation.

»It is God's will that the whole of creation lives together in unity and peace, reconciled in the love of Christ through the transforming power of the Holy Spirit«(Ephesians 1)

From the 1990 s until now, step by step the threats and challenges of globalisation have become the framework in which the churches together have to give witness.

The churches of the Global South in this process insisted that the question of justice has to be the core question. In the context of human-induced climate change, this has led to the common challenge of *climate justice*. And with all the complexity of factors which deny fullness of life to all people now the ecumenical movement is aware of both: it is complex and needs answers which can cope with this complexity; and it is a spiritual and practical challenge where we as churches have to be clearly at the side of the victims.

It is time that the churches together testify to God's mercy and God's peace to the societies in Africa and Europe and worldwide. This ecumenical mission is rooted in the heart of the Gospel.

What is our ecumenical vision really like?

The ground of our ecumenical bonds becomes clear in Paul's Letter to the Ephesians, chapter 4, verses 4-6:

»There is one body and one Spirit, just as you were called to the one hope of your calling, one Lord, one faith, one baptism, one God and Father of all, who is above all and through all and in all.«

This biblical confession testifies to an ecumenical reality that we do not produce, but which is given by our faith itself. The question to us is then whether we match up to the reality given to us or whether we miss the mark. We are asked whether we express this foundation in the form of our church fellowship, whether we are recognisably guided by the Spirit of the one God, whether we are witnesses to the one hope in our time. The one Lord calls us to be one body, as well. The one faith commits us to be guided by one Spirit. The one baptism makes us witnesses to the one hope.

Yet just as baptism forms the starting point of the Christian life, just as faith is the basis of a Christian way of life, just as the Lord of the faithful always goes ahead – so it is too with the ecumenical community. It is not a matter of take-it or leave-it. The fact that Christians and the churches belong together is, rather, given with the foundation of their confession: one Lord, one Faith, one Baptism.

The hymn to unity in Ephesians 4 ends up in praise of the one God and Father, who fills the cosmos and »fills all in all«.

This passage starts with what we *are* ecumenically, before it expresses the challenge of what we are to *become* ecumenically. Through the memory of what has been entrusted to us together we clearly perceive the calling to be the body of Christ together.

Such unity does not mean uniformity. This is our daily experience in the UEM family of churches: as quite different churches in our joint mission we are guided by the same Spirit and testify to the same hope. This is an ecumenism from below – in the UEM, our churches are bound together by more than 100 partnership relations on a church district to church district level, between churches in Africa, Asia and Europe, filling with life what it means being in mission together. And this goes not as one way traffic but in reverse programmes. Presently, pastors from Congo, Ruanda, Namibia and Cameroon are working in our Westphalian Church.

This kind of ecumenism gives space to diversity but trusts in the power of unity. Grateful for the unity we experience as a gift given by the Holy Spirit by confessing Christ, we seek ways to bring together the different gifts for common witness of this unity.

On this basis we receive as a gift of God our ecumenical cooperation which is expressed in the sharing of our common mission. We therefore must particularly preserve our ecumenical togetherness when responding to the major crises of our age as challenges to confess Christ today. The irresponsible mistakes that led to the crisis on the financial markets in 2008, the still acute danger of a climate disaster and the continuing war in many parts of the world call for us to give common witness.

This is why it has to be our common concern to contribute to shaping a just society that recognises overcoming poverty as its central assignment, and the transitioning to a sustainable economy in response to the threats of climate change. Therein lays a joint ecumenical task that we have to focus on particularly in the years ahead.

The ecumenical communion we are engaged in to form is not a stiff template but a living process. It is a path on which we time and again come to crossings and forks on the way, where we need to get out our compass to get our bearings again.

What crossroad are we standing at today?

Like many churches worldwide, we as UEM churches are in the process of redefining our place in society. In view of the drastic social changes in the process of globalisation, we are redefining our responsibilities and priorities of ecumenical commitment. We have to find a new balance today between the common message that has been entrusted to us and the many ways of expressing it in the lives of our churches. As Christians we are convinced that our picture of humanity as made in the image of God, our trust in the power of forgiveness and reconciliation and our hope for a life in justice and peace can unfold great power for the future of living together in the One World. Yet to achieve that we must again link up the diversity of our traditions and what we hold in common in our faith.

This brings me to the Milestone set by the recent General Assembly of the World Council of Churches (WCC) 2013 in Busan, South Korea:

It is a sign of maturity and strength that the very hotly debated, controversial dialogue process on threats and challenges of globalisation since the late 1990 s has now reached a point of a new consensus, based firmly on a theological basis that integrates the question of church unity into the broader perspective.

Let me close by introducing to you the spirit of the WCC Busan decisions:

3. God's Gift and Call to Unity – and our Commitment

Dear sisters and brothers in Christ, the WCC assembly of Busan marks an important milestone on the ecumenical journey. If time would allow, it would be worthwhile to give a detailed interpretation of its outcomes. In a groundbreaking way, the statements on *unity*, *mission* and the *pilgrimage of justice and peace* together have an inner coherence strengthening each other in their holistic witness. One important dimension of it is that the unity statement is unfolded in the context of God's love and passion for His creation and His people throughout history, starting with creation, aiming at the eschatological coming again of Jesus Christ and the new heaven and earth. It is in this context that the question of church unity is being addressed and unfolded – not as an end in itself but under the perspective how the unity of the church can serve the Missio Dei.

Bishop Professor Heinrich Bedford-Strohm has been very instrumental in this important approach as the chairperson of the WCC-Assembly Committee which developed the Unity Statement »*God's Gift and Call to Unity – and our Commitment*«, adopted unanimously by the assembly (WCC 10th Assembly, 30 October to 8 November 2013, Busan, Republic of Korea, Document No PRC 01.1).

I close my presentation by quoting from this essential WCC Unity Statement, because it can give us direction as theological foundation when we ask, how to give witness together to Ecumenism and the Future of the Church:

»God's Gift and Call to Unity – and our Commitment

1. 'In the beginning God created the heavens and the earth' (Genesis 1:1) Creation is a gift from the living God. We celebrate creation's life in its diversity and give thanks for its goodness. It is the will of God that the whole creation, reconciled in the love of Christ through the transforming power of the Holy Spirit, should live together in unity and peace« (Eph. 1).

Our experience

»2. Today, the entire creation, the world and its people, live in the tension between the profoundest hope and the deepest despair. We give thanks for the diversity of human cultures, for the wonder of knowledge and learning, for the enthusiasm and vibrancy of many young people, for communities being rebuilt and enemies reconciled, for people being healed, and populations fed. We rejoice when people of different faiths work together for justice and peace. These

are signs of hope and new beginnings. But we grieve that there are also places where God's children cry out. Social and economic injustice, poverty and famine, greed and war ravage our world. There is violence and terrorism and the threat of war, particularly nuclear war. Many have to live with HIV and AIDS and suffer from other epidemics; peoples are displaced and their lands dispossessed. Many women and children are victims of violence, inequality and trafficking as are some men. There are those who are marginalized and excluded. We are all in danger of being alienated from our cultures and disconnected from earth. Creation has been misused and we face threats to the balance of life, a growing ecological crisis and the effects of climate change. These are signs of our disordered relations with God, with one another and with creation, and we confess that they dishonour God's gift of life.

3. Within churches we experience a similar tension between celebration and sorrow. There are signs of vibrant life and creative energy in the growth of Christian communities around the world with rich diversity. There is a deepening sense among some churches of needing one another and of being called by Christ to be in unity. In places where churches experience anguish and constant fear of persecution, solidarity between Christians from different traditions in the service of justice and peace is a sign of God's grace. The ecumenical movement has encouraged new friendships forming a seed bed in which unity can grow. There are places where Christians work and witness together in their local communities and new regional agreements of covenanting, closer fellowship and church unions. Increasingly, we recognize that we are called to share with, and learn from, those of other faiths, to work with them in common efforts for justice and peace and for the preservation of the integrity of God's beautiful but hurting creation. These deepening relationships bring new challenges and enlarge our understanding.

4. We grieve that there are also painful experiences of situations where diversity has turned into division and we do not always recognize the face of Christ in each other. We cannot all gather together around the Table in Eucharistic communion. Divisive issues remain. New issues bring sharp challenges which create new divisions within and between churches. These must be addressed in the fellowship of churches by the way of consensus discernment. ...

5. ... Whenever we abuse life through our practices of exclusion and marginalization, our refusal to pursue justice, our unwillingness to live in peace, our failure to seek unity, and our exploitation of creation, we reject the gifts God holds out to us. ...

Our shared scriptural vision

6. As we read the Scriptures together, under the guidance of the Spirit, our eyes are opened to the place of the community of God's people within creation. ...

God's call to unity today

9. On our ecumenical journey we have come to understand more about God's call to the Church to serve the unity of all creation. The vocation of the Church is to be: foretaste of new creation; prophetic sign to the whole world of the life God intends for all; and servant spreading the good news of God's Kingdom of justice, peace and love. ...

13. The unity of the Church, the unity of the human community and the unity of the whole creation are interconnected. Christ who makes us one calls us to live in justice and peace and impels us to work together for justice and peace in God's world. ...

Our commitment

14. ... We confess our failures to do justice, to work for peace, and to sustain creation. Despite our failings, God is faithful and forgiving and continues to call us to unity. Having faith in God's creating and re-creating power, we long for the Church to be foretaste, credible sign and effective servant of the new life that God is offering to the world. It is in God, who beckons us to life in all its fullness that joy, hope, and a passion for unity are renewed. Therefore, we urge one another to remain committed to the primary purpose of the fellowship of churches in the World Council of Churches:

to call one another to visible unity in one faith and in one Eucharistic fellowship, expressed in worship and common life in Christ, through witness and service to the world and to advance towards that unity in order that the world may believe.

We affirm the uniqueness of our fellowship and our conviction to pursue the visible unity of the Church together, thankful for our diversity and conscious of our need to grow in communion.

15. In faithfulness to this our common calling, we will seek together the full visible unity of the One, Holy, Catholic and Apostolic Church when we shall express our unity around the one Table of the Lord. In pursuing the unity of the Church we will open ourselves to receive the gifts of each other's traditions, and offer our gifts to one another. We will learn to commemorate together the martyrs who witnessed to our common faith. We will continue theological conversations, giving attention to new voices and different methods of approach. We will seek to live out the consequences of our theological agreements. We will intensify our work for justice, peace and the healing of creation, and address together the complex challenges of contemporary social, economic and moral issues. We will work for more just, participatory and inclusive ways of living together. We will make common cause for the well-being of humanity and creation with those of other faith communities. We will hold each other accountable for fulfilling these commitments. Above all, we will pray without ceasing for the unity for which Jesus prayed (John 17): a unity of faith, love and compassion that Jesus Christ brought through his ministry; a unity like the unity Christ shares with the Father; a unity enfolded in the communion of the life and love of the Triune God. Here, we receive the mandate for the Church's vocation for unity in mission and service.

16. We turn to God, the source of all life, and we pray:

O God of life, lead us to justice and peace, that suffering people may discover hope; the scarred world find healing; and divided churches become visibly one, through the one who prayed for us, and in whom we are one Body, your Son, Jesus Christ, who with you and the Holy Spirit, is worthy to be praised, one God, now and forever. Amen.«

Dear sisters and brothers in Christ,

It is with this spiritual power uniting us all that we are asked to commit ourselves as churches to go side by side in the pilgrimage of justice and peace.

May our churches within the UEM family and beyond experience the uniting power of God's spirit on this pilgrimage!

May our revisiting of Bonhoeffer's important contributions for such journey ahead strengthen our faithtogether to face the challenges on our common pilgrimage!

L’œcuménisme l’avenir de l’Eglise à la Lumière de Jean 17

Vincent Muderwa Barhatulirwa

1. Introduction

»Au commencement était l’unité«. C’est par cette affirmation on ne peut plus surprenante que je voudrais introduire mon exposé pour dire une chose que je juge importante dans le développement de ma réflexion. L’unité est une réalité qui nous a précédés parce qu’elle fonde son origine en Dieu. Il suffit de lire le récit de la création pour s’en convaincre et même se référer à l’histoire du salut à travers laquelle l’Église, vue comme un rassemblement d’hommes et de femmes de toutes races, de toutes nations, de toutes tribus, de toutes langues sont unis par la foi en Jésus-Christ. Or Jésus-Christ est considéré comme le centre de l’histoire divine du salut. Unis à Christ, celui par qui l’unité entre le Père et Fils fait irruption dans l’histoire, les croyants n’ont pas d’autre choix que de vivre et de travailler pour l’unité sans laquelle l’évangélisation du monde risque d’être un leurre.

Nous essayerons de montrer, à la lumière de Jean 17, que l’immanence réciproque entre le Père et le Fils conduit, dans l’histoire de la révélation de Dieu, à l’unité entre le Christ et les croyants. Cette unité détermine la réussite de l’évangélisation du monde dans la mesure où les hommes et les femmes de tous les temps, au vu de l’unité réellement vécue, peuvent reconnaître que Jésus est incontestablement l’envoyé de Dieu et faire, pour ainsi dire, l’expérience de l’amour de Dieu. Il y a donc un lien entre l’œcuménisme, la réussite de l’évangélisation et donc l’avenir de l’Église.

Cependant, avant d’y parvenir, nous commencerons par constater que l’histoire du mouvement œcuménique est au creuset de l’histoire de l’Église. En deuxième lieu, et principalement, nous concentrerons notre attention sur un passage biblique pour tenter de montrer que l’unité est une création de l’Esprit et un don de Dieu. Nous devrions nous saisir de ce don en tant qu’Église, dans le partage pour faire aboutir la mission de l’évangélisation. Nous terminerons par une brève conclusion.

2. L’histoire du mouvement œcuménique au creuset de l’histoire de l’Église

L’idée œcuménique est issu directement des diverses formes de réveil et de l’engagement subséquent de certaines églises occidentales dans l’entreprise missionnaire mondiale. Le premier exemple le plus frappant fut l’apparition du mouvement piétiste au début du 18ème siècle. Luthériens, réformés et anglicans, tant en Allemagne qu'en Scandinavie, Pays Bas et Grande-Bretagne, ont redécouvert que l'unité chrétienne transcende les différences de dénominations, et se sont sentis poussés à s'engager dans un mouvement missionnaire nouveau, transdénominationnel. L'esprit œcuménique se manifesta entre autres dans les sociétés bibliques et, à la fin du 19ème siècle, dans des mouvements de jeunesse tels que les Unions chrétiennes de jeunes gens (UCJG-YMCA) et de jeunes femmes (UCJF-YWCA), et la Fédération universelle des associations chrétiennes d'étudiants (FUACE-WSCF). Cette conviction se fonde sur la parole de Jésus en Jn 17,21 »que tous soient un comme toi, Père, tu es en moi et que je suis en toi, qu'ils soient en nous eux aussi afin que le monde croie que tu m'as envoyé«.

Le terme OIKOUMENE, qui originellement désignait »le monde habité«, plus précisément le monde de la culture grecque ou romaine, a pris le sens du mouvement vers l'unité chrétienne ou tout simplement et au sens large, tout effort de créer l'unité parmi les églises séparées (catholique-romaine et non-catholiques). Cette unité n'est pas une simplification abusive qui confond unité et uniformité; c'est-à-dire elle n'est pas un effort de nivellement, d'uniformisation complète de toutes les confessions chrétiennes, elle n'est non plus une manifestation d'indifférence ou mépris à l'égard des différentes doctrines religieuses[1]. C'est un effort de faire coexister pacifiquement les églises catholique-romaine et non-catholiques dans un élan de complémentarité réciproque des charismes, portant à l'esprit que l'Esprit agit dans l'une et l'autre. Au niveau le plus restreint, et dans le sens contemporain, il s'agit des efforts déployés pour rapprocher les églises chrétiennes séparées.

Vatican II, dans son décret sur l'œcuménisme, notamment Unitatis Redintegratio, a décrit le mouvement œcuménique de la manière suivante:

Très nombreux sont partout les hommes qui ont été touchés par cette grâce – c'est-à-dire le repentir de la division et le désir de l'union – et, sous l'action de l'Esprit Saint, est né un mouvement qui s'amplifie également de jour en jour chez nos frères séparés en vue de rétablir l'unité, qu'on appelle le mouvement œcuménique, auquel prennent part ceux qui invoquent le Dieu Trine et confessent Jésus comme Seigneur et Sauveur, non seulement pris un à un, mais aussi réunis en des communautés dans lesquelles ils ont entendu l'Evangile et qu'ils appellent leur église et l'Eglise de Dieu. Presque tous cependant, bien que de façon diverse, aspirent à une Eglise de Dieu, une et visible, vraiment universelle, envoyée au monde entier pour qu'ils se convertissent à l'Evangile et qu'ils soient ainsi sauvés pour la gloire de Dieu.

A la lumière de ce décret, on peut noter qu'un élan de repentance pour stigmatiser les divisions entre croyants et un élan de bâtir l'unité ne sont possibles que sous l'action de l'Esprit Saint. Le mouvement œcuménique est donc un élan de

[1] Cf. Oscar Cullmann: L'unité par la diversité, Paris, 1986, 15-16.

cœur vers le rétablissement de l'unité parmi tous ceux qui, en tous lieux, invoquent Dieu et confessent Jésus comme Seigneur et Sauveur. Cette unité est de haute portée dans la mesure où elle contribue au salut du monde.

Comme l'a si bien vu David J. Bosch, Vatican II fut presque miraculeux au regard d'un esprit nouveau qui se fit sentir dans presque toutes les délibérations et tous les documents du Concile[2]. L'on pourrait noter que le »rétablissement de l'unité entre chrétiens« constitua l'une des préoccupations principales du Concile lorsqu'il déclare que la division des chrétiens »contredit la volonté du Christ, scandalise le monde et compromet la cause des plus sacrées qu'est la prédication de l'Evangile à toute créature«[3]. En fait, le mouvement œcuménique est fondé sur le fait que tous les baptisés, conscients de rendre un témoignage unanime au Christ, leur Seigneur devant les nations, sont appelés à se considérer comme un peuple qui forme un seul troupeau dans le monde où ils sont appelés à transcender les divisions souvent construites sur des différences confessionnelles. Le Décret, prenant une orientation réaliste, déclare que »s'ils ne parviennent pourtant pas à rendre pleinement témoignage d'une foi commune, qu'ils soient au moins remplis d'un respect et d'un amour mutuel«.

C'est dans ce sens qu'il faut que chaque église prenne conscience de ses propres charismes, les affirme tout en gardant à l'esprit qu'il existe toujours un danger de déformation[4]. Ensuite chaque église doit s'engager à respecter les charismes de l'autre, y relever ce qui est positif, sans toujours chercher à critiquer mais au contraire en tirer un enseignement à valoriser. Les dons accordés par l'Esprit aux différentes églises ne doivent ni être abolis, ni amputés au nom d'une uniformité, ni imités mais ils doivent se compléter mutuellement. Les charismes typiques au protestantisme, c'est l'importance accordée à la Bible (sola scriptura) et la liberté chrétienne. La dégradation de ces charismes peut se manifester dans l'étroitesse d'esprit qui consiste à éliminer les éléments prétendus étrangers à la Bible alors qu'ils sont conformes à l'esprit biblique. L'absence de tout magistère chez les protestants conduit à une sorte d'éparpillement doctrinal et lorsque la liberté dégénère en anarchie ou permissivité, on agit sans frein. Quant à l'église catholique, il s'agit de l'universalisme dans le sens du rayonnement de l'Evangile sur le plan spatial et temporel. Le danger qui guette l'église catholique-romaine, c'est l'institutionnalisme et le totalitarisme de l'organisation qui risquent d'étouffer l'Esprit.

---

[2] David J. Bosch: Dynamique de la mission chrétienne: histoire et avenir des modèles missionnaires, Genève, 1995, 619.

[3] Ibid.

[4] Pour lire en détails, cf. Cullmann: L'unité par la diversité, 23-30.

3. Au-delà des efforts humains, l'unité des croyants: une œuvre de l'Esprit et un don divin

L'Eglise, dans la compréhension paulinienne, est un organisme analogue au corps humain où chaque membre, en vertu de sa structure particulière et de sa fonction propre, contribue à former une entité foncièrement une. En 2 Co 12,4-31, Paul montre clairement que *le Saint-Esprit crée l'unité non pas malgré mais par la diversité*[5]. La méconnaissance de l'action de l'Esprit qui crée l'unité a des conséquences néfastes pour la cause de l'unité, dont les deux principales sont: *l'œcuménisme anarchique* au nom duquel les illuminés ou les fanatiques croient tout se permettre au mépris de l'ordre établi mais aussi un *raidissement confessionnel* entretenu par un intégrisme religieux qu'on retrouve aussi bien dans l'église catholique que dans les églises protestantes. Il s'agit ici de ne voir l'action diversifiante du Saint-Esprit que dans sa propre église[6]. Trois positions sont souvent prises:

mon église est l'unique Église, les autres sont dans l'erreur (position apologétique où le dialogue cherche à faire admettre à l'autre son erreur);

mon église est vraiment l'Église du Christ, les autres églises sont également des églises chrétiennes (voie médiane: à partir d'une conviction ferme, il y a une place réelle donnée aus autres, sans qu'on cherche à les ramener à son propre point de vue) mais il y a le risque de prétendre que la mienne a mieux conservé la totalité de la foi chrétienne;

toutes les églises sont également valables, il n'y a pas de différence importante entre elles (cette position se situe au-delà de l'appartenance à une tradition religieuse donnée).

Les partenaires dans le dialogue doivent prendre au sérieux ces positions.

C'est dans cette logique que les intégristes catholiques exigent le »retour« des »autres« dits frères égarés dans le berçail tandis que les intégristes protestants entretiennent une idée que depuis le 16ème siècle le Saint-Esprit se serait retiré de l'église de Rome et que l'unité ne peut être restaurée que si les catholiques se convertissent au protestantisme.

Pourtant, catholiques et protestants lisent le même livre sacré qui indique la prière dite sacerdotale où Jésus prie pour l'unité des croyants dans Jn 17,20-23 en ces termes:

(20) Mais je ne prie pas pour ceux-ci seulement, mais aussi pour les croyants en moi par la parole d'eux, (21) *afin que tous soient un*, comme toi, Père, en moi et moi en toi, afin aussi eux soient en nous, afin que le monde croit que toi tu m'as envoyé. (22) Et moi j'ai donné à eux la gloire que tu as donnée à moi *afin qu'ils soient un comme nous sommes un*. (23) Et moi en eux et toi en moi, *afin qu'ils*

---

[5] Ibid., 20-21.

[6] Ibid., 22-23.

soient complètement un, afin que le monde connaisse que tu m'as envoyé et que tu les as aimés comme tu m'as aimé.

Le fait d'être un est fortement souligné dans ce passage comme un but à atteindre parce que l'avenir de l'évangélisation du monde, mission principale sinon essentielle de l'Eglise, dépend essentiellement et peut-être exclusivement de l'unité des croyants. Or cette dernière, selon la première affirmation de Jésus (v.21), ne peut se modeler que sur l'unité entre le Père et le Fils (toi Père en moi et moi en toi). Selon sa deuxième affirmation, ladite unité est l'œuvre du Fils qui a donné la gloire reçue du Père aux croyants (v.22). La troisième affirmation de Jésus, c'est que l'unité qui s'étend sur les croyants par le fait que le Christ est en eux et le Père dans le Fils (v.23), fera que le monde connaitra que le Père a envoyé le Fils et que par cet envoi est signifié l'amour du Père vis-à-vis des croyants.

Le v.20 montre à quel niveau Jésus, au-delà de ses compagnons historiques, porte à l'esprit tout disciple potentiel qui croirait en lui par la proclamation de la parole. De même que Jésus a été envoyé par le Père dans le monde, de même le Fils envoie les disciples dans le monde, selon le v.18. La notion importante transmise par le v.20, c'est que la parole de Dieu dont le Christ est l'annonciateur privilégié et mandaté par le Père (vv.6.8.14.17) se manifeste désormais à travers le témoignage des disciples. L'activité missionnaire amorcée par Jésus connaît une continuation à travers les disciples qui transmettent la parole de Dieu et qui provoque la foi en Jésus[7]. Chaque génération est tributaire d'un héritage de la foi. Elle a la responsabilité de la transmettre à son tour à d'autres pour que Dieu qui était en Christ, réconciliant le monde avec lui, comme l'a dit Paul en 2 Co 5,20-21, trouve des hommes et des femmes disposés à se tourner vers Dieu. Dans un élan de repentance et armés à travailler pour l'unité trouvée en Dieu trine, une réalité doit être vécue qui transcende les clivages et les différences qui ne sont plus un obstacle à la cohabitation mais une richesse.

Dans le v.21, par la prière de Jésus, on peut noter que l'avenir post-pascal de la communauté des disciples et donc de l'Eglise dépend du témoignage des disciples. Leur mission consiste à proclamer la parole dont l'aboutissement est l'unité des croyants qui, en fait, est au cœur de la vision de Jean pour les croyants (Jn 10,16; 11,52 ; 17,11.21-23)[8]. Et c'est sur cette unité que se construit l'avenir de l'Eglise. Or, la nature de cette unité est explicitée par la proposition comparative-causale qui introduit une pensée de poids non négligeable. Les disciples seront »un« comme le Père est dans le Fils et ce dernier dans le Père. Une manière de dire que *cette unité n'est pas de type institutionnel issue de négotiation ni d'une démarche pour atteindre un consensus*[9]. La vision de

---

[7] Jean Zumstein: L'évangile selon Saint Jean (13-21), Genève 2007, 183.
[8] Craig S. Keener: The Gospel of John Vol.II, Peabody2003
[9] Cf. Bultmann, 393 et Barrett, 512, cités par J. Zumstein: L'évangile selon Saint Jean.

Jésus de l'unité de la communauté transcende une simple unité institutionnelle dans la mesure où elle inclue autant les croyants présents que futurs[10]. A mon avis, l'unité dont il est question est le fait de l'immanence réciproque entre le Père et le Fils et celle entre les croyants et le Fils par le Père qui a envoyé le Fils. Elle est une démonstration de l'amour du Père vis-à-vis des croyants de tous les temps. La formule d'immanence réciproque, dit Zumstein, a comme signification profonde la relation achevée d'amour et d'action qui unit le Père et le Fils. Comme le Père est actif dans et à travers le Fils (Jn 10,38 ; 14,10-11.20), de même le Fils est actif dans et à travers les croyants (Jn 15,4 ; 1 Jn 1,3 ; 2,5-6). Le résultat de cette immanence réciproque, c'est que »le monde croie que tu l'as envoyé«.

Il convient de noter que l'exposé de cet authentique amour (entre le Père et le Fils, et le Fils et les disciples), l'exposé de leur authentique unité fournit un témoignage contraignant à la vérité de l'évangile[11]. L'unité qui s'affirme entre le Père et le Fils, et par conséquent entre Jésus et les disciples de tous les temps, a un but, c'est que le monde arrive à connaitre à travers cette vérité que la mission de Jésus s'accomplit dans le fait d'avoir été envoyé par Dieu[12]. La mission de Jésus qui consiste à la réconciliation du monde est en jeu à travers l'unité des croyants. La vérité de l'évangile est établie dans le tribunal cosmique en accord avec le témoignage que la vérité est exposée par l'unité des témoins. Ce n'est pas simplement, poursuit Lincoln, que l'unité des témoins n'est pas un simple miroir de l'union entre le Père et le Fils, mais leur unité participe actuellement dans l'unité qui définit la relation entre Jésus et Dieu[13].

Dans ce sens, *l'unité dont il est question, ne doit pas être comprise dans un sens substantialiste mais dans un sens relationnel*, car, comme le Père parle et agit à travers le Fils, ce dernier est en parfaite communion de pensée et d'action avec le Père[14]. L'unité des croyants est, en retour, enracinée dans la propre unité de Jésus avec le Père. Le vivre ensemble qui doit caractériser la vie des croyants avec amour, tolérance et respect, transparaît en Jn 13,34-35 ; 15,12-13 ; 17,26, comme une invitation à l'unité qui n'est pas purement une unité d'amour. Elle est fondée sur l'acceptation et la transmission de la révélation transmise ou communiquée aux disciples par le Père à travers le Fils (Jn 17,6.8.20)[15].

Dans cette perspective, *l'unité pour laquelle Jésus prie est un don de Dieu, et*

---

[10] Andreas J. Köstenberger: John, Grand-Rapid 2004 , 498. Carson d'ailleurs maintient qu'une telle unité est achevé non par le fait de trouver »le plus bas dénominateur théologique commun, mais par une adhésion commune à l'évangile apostolique, par l'amour qui est un sacrifice personnel offert dans la joie, par un imperturbable témoignage aux buts partagés de la mission«.

[11] Köstenberger: John,.498.

[12] Andrew T. Lincoln: The Gospel according to Saint John, New York 2005, 439.

[13] Ibid.

[14] Barrett, cité par Zumstein: L'évangile selon Saint Jean, 183.

[15] Köstenberger: John, 499.

non le résultat des efforts cumulés des hommes. Il ne s'agit pas ici de la déresponsabilisation de l'homme mais une manière d'affirmer que le modèle que Dieu offre, dans l'histoire de la révélation, est un modèle d'unité. L'Eglise, comme rassemblement des croyants, n'a à offrir que le modèle de l'unité pour réaliser sa mission de l'évangélisation du monde. Ce n'est donc pas pour rien que le Diable s'acharne sur l'église pour la diviser davantage, afin que son témoignage cesse d'être crédible et donc inefficace. Tous ceux qui entretiennent la division et l'exclusion, au nom des intérêts inavoués et des idéologies, ne peuvent prétendre travailler pour la promotion de l'évangile.

Parler de la promotion de l'évangile ou de l'évangélisation ne consiste pas à transférer les croyants au ciel alors qu'ils vivent sur la terre dans la pauvreté, dans un environnement ravagé par les conflits et les guerres. Travailler pour l'unité, c'est aussi rassembler les populations de différentes confessions et traditions religieuses pour discuter des questions de paix. Tous les croyants de diverses religions aspirent à la paix, et ils sont convaincus que la violence va à l'encontre de l'essence même de leur foi. Ils ont ainsi, dans la foi un terrain d'entente qui rend le dialogue fructueux. Ces rencontres sont aussi un moyen pour chercher à guérir les blessures du passé, relire l'histoire de façon sereine et transformer les conflits en opportunité pour le vivre et le travailler. En plus, il y a des questions d'intérêt commun, notamment la justice, le développement, les droits humains et le statut de la femme qui transcendent les divisions religieuses. Au fur et à mesure que les populations de différentes tendances religieuses et de cultures différentes se retrouvent pour discuter des questions d'intérêt commun, elles abandonneront les préjugés, les stéréotypes, la désinformation ou l'ignorance.

La prière sacerdotale de Jésus vaut son pesant d'or dans l'invitation de l'Eglise d'être à l'image du Père et du Fils »pour qu'ils soient un comme nous sommes un«. Cette unité tient à la vie de Dieu transmise et donnée en partage aux croyants[16]. Le rayonnement des croyants dans un monde émietté dépendra essentiellement de cette immanence réciproque (i) entre le Père et le Fils, (ii) entre Jésus et les croyants et (iii) enfin des croyants entre eux. Les disciples sont activement associés à l'amour achevé caractérisant la relation entre le Père et le Fils et leur agir commun à l'égard du monde[17] et donc au projet de la révélation du Père dans le Fils. Le projet salvifique de Dieu réalisé par le Christ se poursuit à travers le témoignage et le vécu des croyants.

L'appel à l'unité est d'autant plus important parce que les disciples vivent dans un monde divisé (cf. 7,43 ; 9,16 ; 10,19 ; 12,42-43) et donc ils n'ont pas d'autre choix, pour avoir un impact, que d'entretenir une certaine cohésion (13,34-35 ; 17,21-23). L'absence d'unité a, depuis la nuit des temps, caractérisé la culture

[16] Claude Tassin / Jacques Hervieux et al: Les Evangiles: textes et commentaires, Paris, 2001, 1050.
[17] Zumstein: L'évangile selon Saint Jean, 183.

au sens large. Les rivalités étaient communes à tous. Dans le monde greco-romain, un appel à l'unité était adressé à l'Etat (Dyonisus), aux familles (Valerius Maximus), aux armées (Babrius) et l'inimitié personnelle était un standard dans les politiques partisanes et cette inimitié était étendue sur les enseignants dont les disciples se disputaient (le conflit autour de Philon et Paul), dans la compétition littéraire (Plutarque).

Vv.22-23: l'idée telle qu'énoncée au v.21 est continuée au v.22, est d'une dimension théologique, parce que l'unité se cristallise d'une part dans l'immanence réciproque entre le Père et le Fils et est affirmée au v.22 comme un don. Le don de la gloire que le Père a fait au Fils n'est rien d'autre que l'être divin dans le Fils qui devient le récipient de la gloire de Dieu sur la terre. En Jésus, le révélateur de Dieu transcendant, se révèle la plénitude de la réalité divine[18]. La gloire dont Jésus avait été gratifiée, dans le but d'accomplir sa mission sur la terre (Jn 1,14 ; 2,11 ; 11,4.40) et même visible à la croix (13,31-32 ; 17,1.24), c'est cette gloire que les disciples doivent partager, dans l'annonce de la Bonne Nouvelle, en tous temps et en tous lieux, pour être un comme le Père et le Fils sont un. Si donc le Christ dans l'évangile de Jean est paradoxalement glorifié à la Croix, tout croyant digne de ce nom doit être prêt à souffrir pour une cause juste et rester soumis à Dieu, lorsque portant le témoignage du Christ, il lui arrive de passer par la souffrance. Il ne doit pas idéaliser la souffrance ni s'imposer une quelconque souffrance, mais la recevoir de la main de Dieu sans murmures ni lamentations mais avec dignité comme le Christ, qui a affronté la mort pour libérer l'homme du péché et de tout ce qui l'asservissait.

La gloire dont il est question, ne doit pas être comprise de façon abstraite. Cette gloire, au regard de Jn 17,1-5, c'est l'indicible communion que le Fils a avec le Père et qu'il partage avec les croyants. La gloire de Dieu est donc manifeste dans une communauté de foi lorsque l'unité s'opère concrètement par l'amour que les uns ont vis-à-vis des autres.

Le v.23 est le verset dans lequel il est clairement défini que l'avenir de l'évangélisation du monde dépend de l'immanence réciproque. Il existe un parallélisme entre le verset 22 et le verset 23. On constate cela par exemple à la fin du v.22c (»qu'ils soient un comme nous sommes un«) et au v.23b (»et qu'ainsi le monde puisse connaître que c'est toi qui m'as envoyé et que tu les as aimés comme tu m'as aimé«). Il y a lieu de comprendre que l'unité parfaite à laquelle parviennent les disciples est le résultat de l'œuvre de la révélation de Dieu dans le monde, œuvre à laquelle les croyants sont associés[19]. L'unité parfaite, à laquelle parviennent les croyants, se construit sur l'unité entre le Père et le Fils et a été révélée dans le ministère terrestre de Jésus. L'unité entre le Fils et les croyants en est la conséquence directe. Comme l'a si bien vu Köstenberger »à moins qu'ils soient unis, comment peuvent-ils attendre offrir un authentique et

[18] Ibid., 184.
[19] Ibid., 184.

crédible témoignage au Père, qui est uni avec le Fils et l'Esprit dans sa propre révélation et le salut en Christ«[20]. La désunion de la communauté chrétienne dénie par elle-même le message qu'il proclame. Pour que le monde découvre que Jésus est l'envoyé de Dieu et qu'il fasse l'expérience de l'amour de Dieu, comme il est révélé à travers Jésus et l'amour de Dieu vis-à-vis du monde, le monde a besoin de voir transparaître la gloire de Dieu telle qu'elle s'exprime dans l'unité des croyants.

Au regard de Jn 12,37-43, une opportunité est offerte au monde qui a refusé de croire en la révélation apportée par Jésus terrestre, qui passe par le témoignage de la communauté. C'est là qu'elle découvrira la réalité de l'amour de Dieu, par l'envoi du Christ et, de façon subséquente, la réalité de l'amour de Dieu pour les disciples[21]. Dans ce sens, poursuit Zumstein, l'amour inconditionnel dont Dieu a aimé le Christ n'est pas un privilège réservé à la communauté mais il s'étend tout aussi sur le monde.

4. Conclusion

Au regard de l'utilisation concentrée de l'expression »que tous soient un« (v.21a, 22b et 23b), en dépit du fait que l'unité des croyants n'est pas motivée par une crise réelle à laquelle la communauté serait en train de faire face, le thème de l'unité est d'une intensité unique dans le passage. La proclamation de la parole doit être orientée en termes d'identité – une identité qui rassemble, une identité qui structure et une identité qui unit.[22] L'identité des croyants dans le monde divisé se reconnait à travers une identité de l'unité. *Celle-ci, au lieu d'être pensée dans le cadre d'une négociation institutionnelle en termes de formulation d'un consensus de doctrine et de pratique*[23]*, elle doit plutôt être comprise comme un don manifesté à travers le Fils*. Ce don n'est pas à thésauriser mais à partager avec les autres pour que le monde soit conduit à la foi en Jésus, l'envoyé de Dieu mais aussi à faire l'expérience de l'amour de Dieu.

L'unité devient un appel à l'ouverture, au dialogue sincère et franc, au respect des valeurs de l'autre, au respect et à la valorisation de la différence qui est une chance unique à saisir pour un enrichissement mutuel, pour la promotion de la justice et des droits humains, pour l'équilibre du genre en vue d'unir les compétences des hommes et des femmes pour le développement. Là où les églises sont divisées par des divergences insurmontables, qu'il s'agisse des doctrines, des vérités chrétiennes ou de la place qu'elles occupent sur l'échelle des vérités généralement reconnues, qu'il s'agisse des déformations non encore éliminées, la règle d'or qu'énonce Paul, c'est la tolérance (cf. 1 Co 8,4ss ; 8,7ss ; 1 Co

---

[20] Köstenberger: John, 499.
[21] Zumstein: L'évangile selon Saint Jean, 185.
[22] Ibid.
[23] Ibid.

10,27ss ; Rm 14,1ss), pourvu que la vérité principale soit gardée intacte (Ga 1,9 ; 2,4). Toute tentative d'exclusion des »faibles dans la foi« est à bannir, autant que cela est possible, parce que c'est dans l'inclusion que l'Eglise doit remplir sa mission de l'évangélisation, mission à laquelle elle ne peut se dérober et prétendre survivre. L'Eglise reste et demeurera une institution, au sein de laquelle toutes les différences ne sont pas ignorées mais accueillies et valorisées pour porter haut l'étendard de l'unité entre le Père, le Fils et le Saint-Esprit, qui a agi dans l'événement de la création, dans l'histoire du salut et qui est à l'œuvre dans le mandat de réconcilier l'homme avec son Créateur, avec lui-même, avec le prochain et avec l'environnement. Dieu qui était en Christ réconciliant le monde avec lui est depuis Pâques dans l'Eglise pour continuer la mission de la réconciliation à travers son Eglise.

Bonhoeffer, comme figure œcuménique, reste pour nous aujourd'hui une icône de la résistance non-violente fondée sur les valeurs de l'évangile, au nom d'une juste compréhension des écritures et de la théologie, qui conduit à l'action dans un environnement d'oppression et de suppression de l'homme créé à l'image de Dieu. On se rappellera de lui, comme martyre de l'intolérance, mais il ne s'est pas laissé porter dans la passivité et la contemplation mais plutôt par l'action même tout en étant en prison.

Expériences de réconciliation et responsabilité pour la paix dans le contexte allemand

Albert Henz

Frères et sœurs en Christ,

Je voudrais vous saluer chaleureusement au nom de l'Église Evangélique de Westphalie, dont une délégation de dirigeants de l'église est venue dans le cadre de nos relations de jumelage. Au cours de ce voyage, je représente Madame Präses Kurschus qui n'a pas pu venir pour des raisons de santé. Que la communauté autour de cette table, à laquelle nous avons invité aujourd'hui, soit, comme dans les temps bibliques, l'expression de notre communion spirituelle dans le Corps du Christ.

Vous m'avez demandé d'apporter une contribution de fond à votre colloque. D'autres parleront de Bonhoeffer pendant ces jours. Moi ici, je veux donner une contribution aux deux sujets qui ont occasionné notre voyage à nos églises sœurs: la commémoration du génocide contre les Tutsi il ya vingt ans et la situation conflictuelle entre les deux pays, le Congo et le Rwanda en tenant compte des expériences que notre église a faites avec des problèmes semblables. Je veux raconter comment nous pensons et argumentons au sein de l' Eglise Protestante en Allemagne, en ce moment, en ce qui concerne notre responsabilité pour la paix. Alors prenez ceci comme un mot d'acceuil et un mot de circonstance un peu étendu.

Tout d'abord, quelques réflexions au sujet de *nos* expériences et *notre façon de traiter le thème du génocide que nous les Allemands ont commis contre les Juifs et le peuple des Sinti et Rom.*

Ici, je vais me limiter au génocide perpetré contre les concitoyens juifs pendant le temps nazi. Malheureusement jusqu'à aujourd'hui, le thème du génocide perpétré contre les Sinti et les Rom est encore très peu évoqué. Nous constatons cette lacune en observant la discussion publique comment réagir à l'immigration des citoyens Rom venant des pays de l'Europe Sud-Est.

Le génocide contre les Juifs a eu un prélude dans nombreux pays européens depuis le Moyen Age. Les églises chrétiennes y ont une grande responsabilité et ont malheureusement pris part d'une façon désastreuse par leur interprétation traditionnelle des textes bibliques. La lecture anti-judaiste était la source de diffamations, de persécutions et de pogromes tout au long de l'histoire européenne. En Allemagne, après la première guerre mondiale, les hostilités contre les citoyens juifs avaient fortement augmenté en même temps qu'une campagne anticommuniste.

Après la prise de pouvoir des nazis, pendant les années trente, la privation du droit de citoyenneté du Reich, l'idée d'une émigration à Madagascar, les expropriations et expulsions, et enfin le déclenchement de l'agressivité dans la soi-disant »Nuit de Cristal«, ont finalement conduit à la soi-disant »Solution Finale«. La destruction progressive et précisément planifiée de la population juive a eu lieu dans tous les terrains occupés par l'armée allemande. La déportation dans des camps d'extermination et finalement l'exécution d'au moins 6 millions de Juifs sont notre responsabilité terrible au sujet du génocide.

Après la fin de la guerre et du régime nazi, le 19 Octobre 1945 à Stuttgart les églises protestantes se sont exprimé au sujet de leur échec moral. Pour beaucoup de membres de l'Eglise Confessante allemande et du mouvement œcuménique une déclaration sur la complicité des églises protestantes dans la politique meurtrière des nazis était inévitable et nécessaire. On trouvait des mots très prudents, sans faire une référence spécifique au génocide. »Nous confessons que nous n'avons pas eu plus de courage, que nous n avons pas prié plus fidèlement, que nous n avons pas plus joyeusement fait témoignage de notre foi et que nous n'avons pas aimé avec plus de ferveuer« était le message clé. La déclaration plus critique et plus spécifique de Darmstadt en 1947 n'a pas été acceptée par le Conseil de l'Eglise Protestante en Allemagne (EKD). La déclaration de Stuttgart avec son aveu de culpabilité était accueillie d une façon hésitante dans les Eglises membres en Allemagne. Peut-être que c'est lié à l'expérience qui a été décrite par nombreux observateurs après guerre comme psychologiquement compréhensible, qu'une société ayant commis de telles atrocités, doit »oublier«, pour pouvoir retrouver son équilibre.

En Allemagne, le procès contre les criminels d'Auschwitz en 1963 a conduit à la discussion active sur l'histoire de la culpabilité dans la société allemande. Dans nos églises le dialogue judéo-chrétien avait commencé à grande échelle. Ce furent des grands moments théologiques! Ils ont, par exemple, conduit, dans notre église de la Westphalie, á la décision du synode de mentionner l'Alliance éternelle de Dieu avec le peuple d'Israël dans notre constitution. C'était une longue route avec de nombreux arrêts! Aujourd'hui, il existe une culture commémorative bien établie et acceptée dans notre société. Cependant, une journée de commémoration de l'Holocauste, le 27 Janvier de chaque année est encore récente. Notre histoire nous accable si bien que, lorsque nous percevons les conflits actuels dans et autour d'Israël, nous ne prenons pas position sans gêne

Une dernière remarque: Si vous voulez réussir un tel travail de réconciliation, ceci n'est pas seulement un acte intellectuel. En particulier en Afrique du Sud, Nelson Mandela a pratiqué le concept de Commission de Vérité dans l'Après-Apartheid. Il comprend, sur fond chrétien, en particulier la rencontre entre les auteurs et les victimes. Les victimes ont le priorité de raconter. Les auteurs parlent enfin et demandent pardon. Notez bien: Cela se fait individuellement! La promesse du pardon n'est bien sûr possible que par les mots des victimes ayant subi l'injustice.

Deuxièmement - la réconciliation après le conflit frontalier.

Le fait que je ne peux pas m'exprimer en français d'une manière fignolée, ceci est lié à mon origine d'une région frontalière franco-allemande. Mon grand-père et mon père ont vécu encore la guerre entre les deux pays ainsi que le pénible changement répété de nationalité de nos voisins Alsaciens. Il me semble que ce qui s'est passé et se passe encore entre le Rwanda et le Congo, ressemble par beaucoup d'aspects à l'histoire mouvementée entre la France et l'Allemagne.

J'ai eu l'occasion d'être le témoin de la phase dans laquelle les églises, mais aussi Adenauer et de Gaulle en tant que représentants des deux Etats ont cherché à surmonter la soi-disant hostilité séculaire franco-allemande, à travers des gestes publics visibles, tels qu'à Reims et Verdun, mais aussi dans le Traité de l'Elysée de 1963. J'ai participé à des programmes d'échanges. Je me souviens des visites de groupes de jeunes Français dans ma ville natale. Et en effet: Ces mesures de politiques scolaires ont conduit non seulement moi, mais aussi ma famille, nos voisins, le groupe de jeunes de notre paroisse, surtout nos écoles et nos enseignants dans une solidarité qui ; aujourd'hui; rend impensable une confrontation violente entre nos deux pays.

Nos deux pays ont été les forces motrices dans le développement de la Communauté Européenne. Espérons que la Communauté Européenne reste sur le chemin vers une union non seulement économique mais aussi politique pour assumer sa grande responsabilité sur le plan mondial

Dans les années soixante les églises protestantes allemandes ont assumé leur responsabilité en déclenchant un débat sur notre relation avec les peuples de l'Est de l'Europe par la »Ostdenkschrift«, un Mémorandum, qui était au début fortement controversé mais qui a aidé à préparer la politique d'ouverture vers l'Est des gouvernements allemands et enfin la chute du Mur de Berlin et la fin du »rideau de fer« en 1989.

De l'expérience de l'Allemagne nazie est né également, certainement vous en savez quelque chose, l'idée d'un concile œcuménique pour la paix, la justice et la sauvegarde de la création, qui a conduit au processus conciliaire et aux nombreux services pour la paix. et aux initiatives au delà de l Allemagne. Un processus dans lequel nous sommes loin d'atteindre la destination.

Je arrive, en troisième lieu, aux discussions éthiques actuelles pour la paix dans notre Eglise. Elles tournent autour du concept *de la paix juste.*

La promesse de paix que nous avons devant nos yeux spirituels comme vision que le prophète Isaïe a formulée dans le deuxième chapitre de son livre: *»Et les peuples, de leurs glaives ils forgeront des charrues et de leurs lances des serpes: Car aucun peuple ne soulèvera l'épée contre un autre, et on n'apprendra plus à aller à la guerre. Allons, maison de Jacob, marchons à la lumière du Seigneur* «. (Esaïe 2, 4.5)

Nous, aujourd'hui, voudrions peut-être ajouter: on n'apprendra plus la terreur, les attentats suicides, les prises d'otages. Et la guerre et les expulsions seront oubliés! Merveilleux....

Bouleversé par les conséquences dévastatrices de la Seconde Guerre Mondiale, le Conseil Œcuménique des Eglises à Amsterdam en 1948 a formulé : »La guerre n est pas la volonté de Dieu«. Cette déclaration demeure obligatoire pour l'éthique protestante pour la paix. Nous savons qu'il n'existe pas de guerre juste et surtout pas de guerre »sainte«. Cependant, la promesse et la vision d'Esaïe ne sont pas réalisées dans un monde non délivré. Je mentionne quelques-unes des menaces actuelles:

- Le terrorisme international
- La menace venant du cyber
- La menace des armes de destruction massive
- La pauvreté et l'injustice
- Le changement climatique, qui conduit aux mouvements migratoires accrus, mais aussi aux plus grands conflits sur les ressources rares telles que l'énergie et l'eau
- La faiblesse des Etats, qui ne remplissent pas leurs obligations de souveraineté vis-à-vis de leurs citoyens
- La guerre civile croissante en Syrie

Ces expériences sont sous-adjacents à d autres types de conflits qui sont différents de la »guerre totale«, qui a conduit le COE (Conseil Œcuménique des Eglises) à sa déclaration en 1948. Politiquement, nous sommes témoins à l'heure actuelle d’une ouverture aux discussions sur la façon dont une paix juste peut être conçue et quel rôle jouent les opérations militaires. L’objectif reste la création d'un ordre mondial global de paix qui crée la justice sociale, économique et environnementale dans le monde entier.

Le Mémorandum de la Paix de notre Eglise de la Westphalie identifie quatre facteurs qui peuvent promouvoir le processus de la paix:

1. Protection contre la violence
2. Promotion de la liberté
3. Réduction de la misère
4. Reconnaissance de la diversité culturelle

Pour cela, les devoirs suivants pour un ordre mondial de paix sont formulés:

- *un système fonctionnel de la sécurité collective*
- *la garantie des droits de l'homme universels et indivisibles*
- *les règles minimales de la justice transnationale*
- *la facilitation de la diversité culturelle*

Pour la vision éthique de paix juste, il faut que le droit règne pour sa réalisation. Elle doit être concrétisée dans les institutions, les règles et les procédures d'un statut juridique international, qui répond aux exigences éthiques de la paix. Cela inclut, si nécessaire, une force de préservation de la loi dans le sens d'une police internationale, bien sûr, comme un dernier recours lorsque tous les autres moyens ne seront pas efficaces.

Les exceptions à l'interdiction de la force sont alignées sur la Charte des Nations Unies:

- C'est le droit des États à la légitime défense
- C'est le pouvoir d'imposer des sanctions contre les Etats qui menacent la paix mondiale
- L'utilisation de la force comme la *responsabilité de protection* pour des raisons humanitaires

Cette responsabilité internationale de protection est tripartite: une responsabilité de prévenir, une pour la réaction et une pour la reconstruction. La décision incombe au Conseil de Sécurité des Nations Unies ou à l'Assemblée Générale. Pour l'approbation de la force militaire, il y a cinq critères de légitimité:

1. Gravité de la menace
2. Légitimité des motifs
3. Utilisation comme un dernier recours
4. Proportionnalité des moyens
5. Adéquation des conséquences

Selon le contenu, la souveraineté est liée ici à une obligation de protection des citoyens. Il engage la Communauté Internationale à intervenir, si nécessaire, dans la phase précédente et suivante. La responsabilité de reconstruction (désarmement, mise en place d'une administration civile et d'un système juridique) est une nouveauté dans le cadre juridique international.

Conclusion

la force militaire ne crée jamais une paix juste, mais accorde seulement le temps nécessaire pour permettre une paix juste par des moyens civils. Cela veut dire aussi, l'opération militaire doit être accompagnée par les services civils de paix. Que ce principe n'ait pas été mis en exécution pour l'instant, tout au moins en ce qui concerne les dépenses financières, cela a été clairement constaté. Mesdames et Messieurs, voilà mes remarques ce soir. Je souhaite à votre colloque un bon déroulement. Je souhaite à cette région une paix juste. Et je souhaite à nous en Europe et en Allemagne la forme appropriée, d y apporter notre contribution.

Merci!

Reflections on commemorative practices in Rwanda and Germany

Katharina Peetz

1. Introduction

On the eve of the 20th commemoration of the genocide in Rwanda in 1994, I had the opportunity to participate in a focus group on commemorative culture and practices in Rwanda and Germany. This focus group was part of the international conference on »Reconciliation and Sustainable Peace – Impulse of the theology of Dietrich Bonhoeffer for the European and African context« in Karongi (Bethany). Our discussion took place on February 27th 2014 and focused mainly on three topics:

- What practices of commemoration exist in Rwanda and Germany?
- What functions do these practices fulfil?
- What significance do these practices have inside the commemorative discourse?

As we tried to answer these questions, we mostly spoke about Rwandan commemorative practices and Rwanda's process of coming to terms with the past. Yet the Holocaust and the German process of coming to terms with the past (»Vergangenheitsbewältigung«) were our benchmark in debating the Rwandan experiences.

2. Practices of commemoration in Rwanda (and Germany)

For a start we discussed the churchly practices of commemoration. The Presbyterian Church of Rwanda (EPR) holds remembrance services twice a year at churches in Remera and Gitarama where massacres were perpetrated.[1] Elisee Musemakweli, President of the Presbyterian Church of Rwanda, illustrates that at first only the survivors attended the remembrance services. »But, then, little by little, we had others join us and stand beside those who had suffered and little by little more people took part.«[2] During these remembrance services the confession is read that the General Synode of the EPR in Kigali passed in

---

[1] Cf. Jessica Denson: Rwanda: 20 Years Later - An interview with Dr. Elisee Musemakweli, President of the Presbyterian Church of Rwanda, March 6th 2014. Available from http://www.pcusa.org/news/2014/3/6/rwanda-20-years-later/ (visited on September 25th 2014).

[2] Cf Denson: Interview.

1996.[3] This confession emphasises the failures and omissions of the church in preventing, opposing or condemning the planning and execution of the genocide. »... we, the Synod, in the name of the members of the Presbyterian Church of Rwanda, repent and ask forgiveness before God and the nation for our weakness and lack of courage when these were needed.«[4] Some participants pointed out that no such confession had yet been made by other churches but would be appreciated. The testimonies of genocide survivors are another important feature of the services. The group underlined the importance of gathering personal testimonies of the 1994 genocide to commemorate victims.[5]

The official national commemoration in Rwanda is held during the national mourning week (April 7 to 14).[6] Participants described the mourning week and especially the central genocide commemoration ceremony in the Amahoro Stadium in Kigali as important but also as challenging for survivors. »... memory can feel like an affliction, and the greater imperative has often been to learn how to forget enough for long enough to live in the present for the rest of the year.«[7] The public commemoration ceremonies are also criticised by some scholars as a politicisation of individual mourning. According to Susan Thomson, this mourning week is dedicated only to remembering and memorialising Tutsi lives lost.[8] »Lives lost – Hutu, Tutsi and Twa – in the violence before and after the genocide are not memorialised.«[9] It is therefore an important task for the churches to favour inclusive practices of commemorating and to grant free space for all victims and their testimonies. The recognition that there have been victims of all ethnic groups at different historical epochs facilitates the contextualisation of guilt. For though the distinction between perpetrators and victims can easily be made in the case of a concrete historical situation such as the genocide, this distinction becomes blurred if one takes into view the violence be-

---

[3] Cf. Tharcisse Gatwa: The Churches and Ethnic Ideology in the Rwandan Crises 1900-1994, Eugene 2005, 227. See also Gerard van't Spijker: The Churches and the Genocide in Rwanda, Exchange Vol 26:3 (1997), 233-255, 253-254.

[4] The Confession of the EPR quoted after Gatwa: The Churches and Ethnic Ideology, 227-228.

[5] The Kigali Genocide Memorial Center is a particularly impressive example of this. Victims are commemorated as real individuals through testimonies told by survivors from their families.

[6] Cf. Susan Thomson: Whispering Truth To Power: The Everyday Resistance of Rwandan Peasants To Post-Genocide Reconciliation, African Affairs Vol. 110:440 (2011), 439-456, 443.

[7] Philip Gourevitch: Remembering in Rwanda, The New Yorker April 21th 2014. Available from: http://www.newyorker.com/magazine/2014/04/21/remembering-in-rwanda (visited on September 20th 2014).

[8] Cf. Susan Thomson: Resisting Reconciliation: State Power and Everyday Life in Post-Genocide Rwanda, Scotia 2009, 172-73.

[9] Thomson: Resisting Reconciliation, 173.

fore and after the genocide.[10] In addition, some of the genocide victims were Hutu who were trying to save Tutsi.

As to Germany, we mentioned three days per year dedicated to the commemoration of the Holocaust: the official Memorial Day for the Victims of National Socialism on January 27th, the Memorial Day for the »Reichspogromnacht« on November 9th and the 10th Sunday after Trinity. We discussed that although related to the liberation of the largest National Socialist death camp Auschwitz-Birkenau there is little notice of this official Memorial Day among the German population. Indeed, one out of five young Germans under 30 do not know the meaning of the word Auschwitz.[11] Participants gave two reasons for the higher perception of the national mourning week in Rwanda: 1. Perpetrators and victims are forced to live in the same country. 2. Unlike the three German commemoration days, the national mourning week is a public holiday period and thereby an intermission of everyday life. In relation to the problem of public awareness, the necessity of making remembrance visible in the public square was stated. Authenticity of testimonials and visibility of memorials were seen as helpful to build a commemorative community with post-genocide and future generations. Participants also mentioned the »Stuttgarter Schulderklärung« of the Evangelical Church in Germany and the Dietrich Bonhoeffer's confession of 1940 as models for the EPR confession in 1996. And yet the »Stuttgarter Schulderklärung« was seen by scholars either as a clear confession of guilt and a breakthrough in Jewish-Christian dialogue[12], or as an evasive and general text without a clear confession of the church's guilt in relation to the Holocaust and Israel[13].

3. »In remembrance of the victims« and »Never again«

Participants described the function of the Rwandan and German commemorative practices in two ways. First, these practices were interpreted as an opportunity to both remember and re-humanise those victims who have suffered or died in dehumanising circumstances. The importance of these two features in commemorative ceremonies is shown by the analysis of the centrepiece of the

---

[10] Cf. Sebastian Friese: Politik der gesellschaftlichen Versöhnung. Eine theologisch-ethische Untersuchung am Beispiel der Gacaca-Gerichte in Ruanda, Stuttgart 2010, 170–171.

[11] Zeit-Online, Umfrage: Jeder Fünfte unter 30 kennt Auschwitz nicht. Available from: http://www.zeit.de/gesellschaft/2012-01/umfrage-auschwitz (visited on September 26th 2014).

[12] E. g. Gunnar Heinsohn: Post-Genocidal Reconciliation in Rwanda: Are there lessons from Germany? Bremen 1997, 23.

[13] E. g. Siegfried Hermle: Evangelische Kirche und Judentum. Stationen nach 1945, Göttingen 1990, 267-268.

latest genocide ceremony in Amahoro Stadium in Kigali. Six hundred and thirty persons performed a song-and-dance spectacle that focused on the history of the genocide. During the play, its narrator denoted the arrival of white colonisers as the starting point of dehumanisation, the genocide as a fundamental denying of human dignity. The audience had to endure representations of killing acts on stage but at the end of the spectacle, lifeless the bodies were brought back to life by the symbolic act of lifting them tenderly.[14] At the same moment the spectacle demonstrates that the act of commemoration is not easy but often painful, especially for survivors. Philip Gourevitch describes the reactions of observers to a survivor's testimonial: »The first voice was like a gull's, a series of wild, high keening cries; the next was lower and slower, strangled with ache, but growing steadily louder in a drawn-out crescendo ....«[15] And yet participants saw commemorative practices as a necessary way to avoid fast oblivion and transport the reality of genocide to those who had not been directly involved.

Secondly, participants saw commemorations practices as a tangible, visible and mental statement in favour of the »never again«. To adhere to this »never again« we argued for multiple forms of commemoration and confession such as remembrance services, national ceremonies and individual acts like the prostration of the German Chancellor Willy Brandt in front of the Memorial to the Heroes of the Warsaw Ghetto. Some participants also commented on forms of commemoration through art[16] and fiction[17]. The question of how to transmit the »never again« to the later-born led us to a discussion about the Rwandan and German process of coming to terms with the past. German participants reflected their parents' or grandparents' silence about the Holocaust. »I never talked with my grandfather about what he did during the period of war and National Socialism« an attendee remarked. Also, the victims often remained silent in the face of their unspeakable dehumanising experiences. It was not until the third generation that the German process of coming to terms with the past began. Our group saw the reason for this lag partly in the common repression of the Holocaust: While the genocide in Rwanda was committed in broad daylight on the streets, the National Socialist extermination camps with their industrial killing machinery were located outside of Germany. This facilitated suppression and the claim of ignorance, even though in reality lots of Germans knew about these extermination camps.

Rwandan participants pointed out that the process of coming to terms with the

---

[14] Cf. Gourevitch: Remembering in Rwanda.

[15] Ibid.

[16] Further information on commemoration through art see: Amanda Breed: Performing reconciliation in Rwanda, Peace Review: A Journal of Social Justice (2006), 18:507-513.

[17] Further information on commemoration through fiction see: Nicki Hichtcott: Memorial Stories: Commemorating the Rwanda Genocide through fiction, in: Nigel Eltringham / Pam Madean (Ed.), Remembering Genocide, New York 2014, 54-70.

past in Rwanda started sooner, because no one could ignore the dead bodies in the streets and in the churches. Nonetheless the challenges of the Rwandan coming to terms with the past resemble the German process: e.g. most perpetrators remain silent or ignore their guilt and the majority of the Rwandan population in 2014 was not born in 1994. Also, the number of witnesses will slowly decrease. Our group agreed that the testimonials and stories of contemporary witnesses were central in the transmission of the »never again« to the post-genocide and future generations. In addition, several participants shared their experiences with contemporary witnesses.

4. Commemorative practices and commemorative discourse

There are some further questions of our discussion that might be significant for the commemorative discourse. When we talked about the different commemorative practices this enfolded the question of adequacy. e.g., can practices of commemoration that do not include all victims be adequate? In addition, these practices point to the question of how societies as a whole remember human-made catastrophes.[18] They also allude to the role of individuals in the collective process of commemoration and the question of possible manipulation of commemorative practices. Julia Viebach interprets the Rwandan commemorative ceremonies as a battle over interpretative authority in regard to history.[19] In her view, the ceremonies create hierarchies of suffering and exclude Hutu.[20] In this context it might be interesting to analyse in depth the churchly remembrance services to see if and how they are more inclusive than the public ceremonies. Furthermore, the commemorative practices mentioned point to the ambiguous relation between remembering and forgetting. Gourevitch's description of the central genocide commemoration ceremony in the Amahoro Stadium illustrates the pain of remembering which often results in re-traumatisation. In this context, Björn Krondorfer argues in favour of »...deliberate performative practices of forgetting [that] might benefit communities affected by a genocidal past.«[21] Last but not least, there is the question of how the reconciliation process is affected by commemorative practices that perpetuate dichotomies between perpetrators and victims, and that construct hierarchies of suffering as well as a one-sided narrative of the genocide's history.[22]

---

[18] See Julia Viebach: Die Transformation des Bruchs. Grundlagen einer Raumsoziologie nach Massengewalt, Marburg 2013, 15.

[19] Cf. Viebach: Die Transformation des Bruchs, 184.

[20] Cf ibid., 193.

[21] Björn Krondorfer: Is Forgetting Reprehensible? Holocaust Remembrance and the Task of Oblivion, The Journal of Religious Ethics, Vol. 36:2 (2008), 233-267, 233.

[22] See Filip Reyntjens: Constructing the Truth, Dealing with Dissent, Domesticating the World: Governance in Post-Genocide Rwanda, African Affairs 110:438 (2010), 1-34, 28-29.

5. Final remark

As we discussed quite touchy topics, I would like to thank all those students, theologians and clergy from various African and European countries for the eager and open exchange of opinions and viewpoints.

The question of guilt and confession of the young generations after the genocides in Rwanda and Germany – An experience Report

Christine Jürgens & Maximilian Schell

1. Introduction

Within the scope of the conference »Reconciliation and sustainable Peace« in Karongi, Rwanda, a group of 15 students from the Ruhr-University Bochum, and 10 students from the University of Piass, Rwanda, came together in February 2014 to form a discussion forum. The main focus of this discussion was the »Detmold confession of guilt« of 1996, which was published almost immediately after the genocide in Rwanda.[1] This conference was the first opportunity for students of similar ages, with different stories and experiences from their respective home-nations to convene in order to exchange views. Considering that the events of World War II only date back three to four generations, and to which we therefore can only bear witness through the stories of our grandparents, the distance to the horrific events in Rwanda is significantly smaller for our African fellow students. Consequently the critical questions and impulses on the topic of »Confession« were to be very different, but would nevertheless, or perhaps even because of this, lead to an exciting and prolific discussion. Despite completely different temporal distances: Both groups shared, that they were both sensitized in regard to the question of guilt, as well as collective and personal responsibilities for the future.

The following serves to give an insight into the important impulses, suggestions, questions, and concurrences of our discussion. These rudimentary elements of the discussion were continued especially during personal communications in between the lectures and have, even up to this day, continued to contribute to a dialogue and subsequent sensitization and appreciation for the stories and opinions of others.

---

[1] Cf. the lecture of Pascal Bataryingaya in this volume.

2. The Confession – A Definition

For the purpose of establishing a fundamental definition of the terms »Confession/Confessing«[2] it is first required to differentiate between a confession of *guilt* and a confession of *faith* or the confession towards a certain perspective on the world. Both types of confessions deal with the disclosure of a specific and personal perspective on truth. The work at hand concentrates on the confession of *guilt*, yet also often based on a specific confession of faith or truth. A confession of guilt is in this sense a verbal event, which occurs between one giving and one receiving party, which must redefine their relationship after the clarification of their experienced history in order to allow a social coexistence.

The individual and the collective confession of guilt and their relationship to one another

A confession of guilt can either be proclaimed by a collective (usually consisting of a group of people that claim to be representative of those involved in the event in question), or it can be declared by an individual.[3] It is important to note that a confessed statement is inseparable from its originator. Therefore, the originator of a confession of guilt can also be held accountable for it.

A confession that is borne by a group can constitute an *opportunity* and a *risk* simultaneously: An opportunity, in the sense, that it prompts reconciliation and peace processes. For example, this may occur when a representative group of involved individuals proclaims the fault of a certain party/group/institution in a specific event, speaking out loud difficult facts in order to enable the first steps towards reconciliation.

On the other hand, it can be a risk, if a majority of persons cannot relate to what is revealed in the confession and if this opposition is not heard. One example of this is the discontent of a Rwandan student regarding the Detmold confession of guilt, since he considered this collective confession to be unsatisfactory in spe-

---

[2] For a description using the example of the »Stuttgarter Schuldbekenntnis« see Werner Krusche: Schuld und Vergebung – der Grund christlichen Friedenshandelns, in: Martin Greschat (Ed.): Im Zeichen der Schuld. 40 Jahre Stuttgarter Schuldbekenntnis. Eine Dokumentation, Neukirchen-Vluyn 1985, 87-114, 91ff.

[3] The individual can either confess their own guilt or experience, or do so for an entire group or institution. With regards to the latter, it is worth mentioning the confession of guilt of Dietrich Bonhoeffer, who addressed the question of guilt of the church in World War II. Despite having been only verbalized by a single person, this confession is of particular importance, especially considering the fact that it was written during a time in which the atrocities of World War II were still occurring. It details the active resistance against the National Socialist regime, during the time at which the events were occurring, and is not simply a product of retrospection (compare the paper of Jannika Haupt in this volume). This confession of guilt was also mentioned in the discussion, alongside the Detmold and the Stuttgart confessions.

cific points, and he did not feel adequately represented by it.

A confession of guilt in the form of a publically exclaimed acknowledgement can set in motion a process, in which the individual is led to clarify his own view regarding the situation, and to subsequently either affiliate themselves with this »collective confession« or to begin critically questioning it. Thereby, the process of confession constitutes a strong *intentional element*, which seeks to incite a change from the »status quo«.

A confession of guilt does not however spell the end of the issue by saying that »what is past is simply over and everything that could be said has now been said«. A confession should *not serve forgetting*, and additionally it should *not force forgiveness*. To regret and to forgive are two divine processes. The confession is thereby a first step on a long way to reconciliation, and its real power is manifested especially in a change of future conduct. Ideally it reveals the respective misconducts and failures and thus reminds of bygone misguidances and their consequences. It enables the search for other ways of communication and the formation of personal relationships.

The Detmold confession was immensely important, both as a signal and for the way in which it improved the political situation. The fact that it was produced shortly after the 1994 genocide event, as well as its precise and detailed description of the crimes, allowed a dissociation of public opinion and enabled an open discussion about the taking of responsibility and the perpetration. Nevertheless all those involved share the task of having to turn the formalities of such a document into a harmonic coexistence in everyday life. Should any contradictions to it occur, they must offer sufficient opportunity for *open discourse* to avoid excluding anyone from the communal conversation.

3. The question of guilt of the »uninvolved generation«

Before someone personally recognizes and subsequently speaks their confession of guilt, they will have asked themselves to what extent they are responsible and to what extent they are guilty. This question is slightly different for our generations that were not directly and actively involved. Should we feel guilty for the actions of our ancestors? Are we guilty because of our connection to the events based on the place in which we have grown up and the connection to our ancestors, who shaped the history of our country?

The German students among us noticed that because of the larger temporal distance to the event in question, we are only infrequently confronted with the question of guilt in our daily lives. The question of guilt of our ancestors is also often not easily clarified: either all contemporary witnesses have passed away, or an involved person finds it too difficult to talk about that which they experienced. Furthermore, in Germany we are not faced with the situation that perpetrators and victims live in the same region as one another. A large number of those that were persecuted emigrated during or after the events occurred. Therefore, we are not confronted on a daily basis with the perspective of the victims and their descendants.

In Rwanda, the situation is substantially different. The process of systematic discussion between perpetrators and victims has only just begun. For the African students, the clarification of their own accountability has a much larger topicality, because they invariably have persons in their circle of acquaintances or in their family that were directly involved. Perpetrators and victims share a common living environment and so, the question of guilt is more frequent than in Germany.

What the students from both countries have in common is their lack of understanding for the terrible actions of the genocide. A majority of students does not feel specific guilt (or accountability) for what has happened. The notion that the accountability for the specific actions are handed on to one's descendants and that we, the successive generations, should feel accountable for these actions, is one which we found unreasonable. Nevertheless, we feel a connection to the occurrences. It is not a *question of guilt*, but rather a *question of responsibility*[4] that must be considered in the process of collective reconciliation and regeneration of relationships. The past, and thereby the history of our relatives puts a special responsibility on us. It is the responsibility to critically evaluate and form an opinion on the occurrences, which should prompt each one of us to *voice their position* and to dedicate their energy to the process of reconciliation through the *establishment of a dialogue*. As a young generation, the way in which we *become guilty* of such events, is, if we allow the events to be *forgotten,* and consider the past to be irrelevant to the present. It is our responsibility for the present and the future, that such things won't ever happen again.

It is therefore our collective and special obligation to deal with the history of our ancestry in a sensible and responsible manner.

As students we are very grateful that the Bonhoeffer conference offered a forum, which allowed for this contemplation process to occur and in which we were able to collectively approach the issue of forgetting. The goal to actively help shape our future and to avoid letting past mistakes repeat themselves has allowed a conversation that was characterized by openness and reciprocal interest by all participants. For this, we would especially like to thank our fellow Rwandan students.

---

[4] Wolbring proposes »Stigma« as a value-free, but also less continuative term for German sense of being peculiar, cf. Barbara Wolbring: Nationales Stigma und persönliche Schuld. Die Debatte über Kollektivschuld in der Nachkriegszeit, in: HZHZ 43 (2009), 325-364.

Méditation

Samuel Mutabazi

Je voudrais commencer cette méditation matinale en rendant grâce à Dieu pour cette conférence internationale. Elle constitue une occasion d'échanges et de discussion pour nous, théologiens et théologiennes, hommes et femmes d'Eglise, sur les thèmes d'actualité »la Paix et la Réconciliation«. Les thèmes sur lesquels nous allons réfléchir tout au long de cette conférence en essayant de nous inspirer de la vie pratique, des principes éthiques et chrétiennes de cet éminent chrétien engagé, le théologien Dietrich Bonhoeffer, un pasteur qui a su mettre sa foi chrétienne en pratique dans les moments les plus difficiles de l'histoire en Allemagne.

Je voudrais partager avec vous la Parole de Dieu que nous lisons en Josué 1, 6-9.

Josué fut appelé par Dieu pour devenir successeur de Moise. Moise venait de mourir. Le peuple de Dieu était encore sur la route vers la terre promise. Il campait encore dans les vallées de Moab, tout près du fleuve Jourdain. Dieu appela Josué pour succéder à Moïse en ces termes: »Moïse, mon serviteur, est mort; maintenant donc, lève-toi, traverse le Jourdain que voici, toi et tout ce peuple, vers le pays que je leur donne – aux fils d'Israël«. (Dt. 1, 2)

Après avoir entendu cette Parole divine, Josué fut bouleversé et eut peur de succéder à Moise. Il discuta avec Dieu et trouva des prétextes: Comment puis-je remplacer Moise, un homme fort, qui parlait avec toi? Un homme qui a pu affronter Pharaon, le roi d'Egypte? Un homme talentueux qui a fait quitter les Hébreux de l'esclavagisme en Egypte? Un homme qui a défiée Pharaon par sa foi et sa confiance en Dieu? Un homme qui a pu conduire le peuple d'Israël de l'Egypte en traversant la mer rouge et en passant par le désert? Comment puis-je donc remplacer Moise? Comment puis-je conduire ce peuple si difficile et si désobéissant?

Josué voyait que la tâche n'était pas facile. Devant le peuple d'Israël, il y a encore le fleuve du Jourdain qu'il faut traverser, il y a les pays très forts comme Jéricho, le pays des Amorites, la Transjordanie, le Canaan… Tous ces pays possédaient une armée très forte avec des armes et des chars de combat…

Josué avait raison d'avoir peur. Cependant, il ignorait que son Dieu est plus fort que tout cela. Il avait oublié tout ce que Dieu avait fait pour le peuple d'Israël et dont lui-même était témoin, parce qu'il était toujours à côté de Moise.

Dans cette situation, dans ce contexte, Dieu vient lui rencontrer et lui parler. Il lui donna une mission de remplacer Moise et de poursuivre la mission de Dieu de conduire le peuple d'Israël jusqu'au pays promis, le Canaan. Dieu descend et parle à Josué. Dieu lui réconforta, lui donna une promesse: Je serais toujours avec toi, je ne t'abandonnerai jamais.

Dieu parla avec Josué et lui demanda d'être toujours obéissant, de ne pas s'écarter de la Parole, de la Loi et des Commandements de l'Eternel. Au verset 7, vient donc l'exhortation de l'Éternel en ces termes: »Oui, sois fort et très courageux; veille à agir selon toute la Loi que t'a prescrite Moïse, mon serviteur. Ne t'en écarte pas ni a droite ni a gauche afin de réussir partout où tu iras«. (Josué 1, 7)

La force et l'énergie spirituelle, le courage de la foi sont nécessaires pour que le cœur ait assez de confiance pour obéir et soit libre des influences, des craintes et des motifs qui agissent sur l'homme naturel et tendent à détourner le croyant du chemin de l'obéissance, et qu'il puisse faire attention à la parole de Dieu.

Comme Josué a eu la mission de conduire le peuple de Dieu jusqu'à la terre promise, tout chrétien a aussi une mission, une responsabilité à laquelle il ne peut se dérober. Dans ses enseignements sur la Montagne, Jésus lui-même dit : »Heureux les artisans de paix, car ils seront appelés fils de Dieu« (Mt 5, 9). Nous avons donc en tant que chrétiens la responsabilité de promouvoir la paix.

Aujourd'hui nous parlons de Dietrich Bonhoeffer qui a accepté l'appel de Dieu et la mission que Dieu lui a confié dans les moments les plus difficiles de l'histoire allemande. Il a préféré rejoindre l'Eglise Confessante et s'opposait activement à l'idéologie nazie. Il n'a pas eu peur de prêcher l'Evangile de la paix et d'enseigner aux gens la paix que Dieu donne. Il appela les croyants à la résistance contre le régime nazi.

Même si la paix peut être définie comme l'état de l'homme qui possède le bien-être de l'existence quotidienne et qui vit en harmonie avec la nature, avec lui-même et avec Dieu, la paix signifie également l'existence d'une bonne entente entre les individus, donc comme l'absence de la guerre et des conflits.

Dans ce sens, la paix manque parce qu'il y a le désordre et le non-respect des lois et des commandements de Dieu. C'est pourquoi, nous trouvons dans la Bible, plusieurs prophètes qui se sont donnés corps et âmes pour lutter contre les alliances internationales et les pratiques injustes faites par le peuple d'Israël et ou de ses représentants.

Le Prophète Michée a dénoncé fortement toutes les pratiques injustes (des créanciers impitoyables, des commerçants fraudeurs, des familles divisées, des prêtres et des prophètes cupides, des juges corruptibles…) qui favorisaient des riches au détriment de la masse paysanne pauvre (Michée 6, 1).

Dans ses prophéties, le prophète Amos a dénoncé les injustices sociales et la vie luxueuse des riches et des autorités royales qui occasionnaient les inégalités entre le peuple, qui agrandissaient la misère des opprimées… D'autres prophètes comme Isaïe, Jérémie et Ezéchiel ont fait des mêmes reproches.

Dieu nous recommande de vivre en paix et aussi de la promouvoir, de lutter contre tout ce qui peut m'empêcher, nous empêcher de vivre en paix et de laisser les autres vivre en paix. A l'instar des prophètes, il revient à l'Eglise et à des communautés chrétiennes de lutter contre toutes les pratiques injustes qui occasionnent les guerres, les tueries, les haines…

Face à la pauvreté grandissante, à la guerre nucléaire, à la course aux armements, au terrorisme, à des guerres et des conflits sociaux et interethniques, au chômage grandissant, au non-respect des droits humains, nous sommes appelés à réagir, à faire quelque chose, à y opposer les actes et pratiques d'amour et de paix. La justice et la paix peuvent être réalisées dans la société humaine, à laquelle nous appartenons, sur cette planète, qui est notre maison à tous (des hommes, des animaux et de leur milieu).

Chères sœurs et chers frères en Christ,

Nous sommes des Josué d'aujourd'hui. Dieu nous a appelés. Dieu nous appelle et nous confie une mission. Celle d'être des artisans de paix et de réconciliation. Nous devons être à l'écoute de la Parole de Dieu et à son Esprit qui nous assiste et nous donne courage de vaincre nos prétextes : la peur, la faiblesse physique, le manque de moyens, ….

Par l'énergie de l'Esprit, devrions-nous prendre nos responsabilités en tant que des leaders des églises en luttant contre toutes les forces négatives qui aliènent l'être humain.

La paix et la réconciliation demandent à être pratiquées, à être laborieusement mises en œuvre par des artisans de paix et de réconciliation. Elles doivent être cultivées par des hommes et des femmes réconciliés avec le Seigneur, avec et entre eux-mêmes. Ce qui nous exhorte à renoncer aux idoles du régionalisme, de l'ethnisme, du racisme, du tribalisme, de partis politiques, de la religion et de la culture. Dans le respect de la Bible, de la tradition africaine et au vécu actuel, nous pouvons y puiser l'essentiel pour construire la paix et promouvoir la réconciliation sociale.

Selon Dietrich Bonhoeffer, »L'Eglise n'est réellement Eglise, que quand elle existe pour ceux qui n'en font pas partie« – »C'est le devoir inconditionnel de l'Eglise envers les victimes de tous les systèmes sociaux même s'ils n'appartiennent pas à la communauté des chrétiens«.

Pour être des vrais artisans de paix et de réconciliation, il nous faut donc la conversion continue et sincère de nos cœurs; et à la suite de Dietrich Bonhoeffer être pas seulement à l'écoute de la Parole de Dieu, mais aussi des chrétiens engagés, dévoués et responsables pour la paix et la réconciliation. Quel défi et quel programme pour nous, pour nos familles, pour nos institutions ecclésiastiques, pour l'Eglise du Christ partout dans le monde?

Nous devrions emboîter le pas de ce pasteur qui a assumé ses responsabilités en tant que chrétien et »témoin de Jésus-Christ parmi ses frères«. Il a pris le risque de perdre sa vie pour sauver les milieux de juifs qui étaient poursuivis et persécutés par le régime nazi. Il prêcha l'Evangile de la Paix et appela les autres chrétiens à la résistance contre l'idéologie du nazisme.

Un travail sans doute immense, mais avec la force de Dieu, demandons à lui de nous transformer pour que nous soyons ses instruments et artisans de la paix et de la réconciliation partout où nous sommes. Comme Dieu a été avec Josué, Il sera également avec nous: »Sois fort et courageux? Ne tremble pas, ne t'effraie pas, car le Seigneur, ton Dieu, sera avec toi partout où tu iras«. (Josué 1, 9)

Au nom du Père, du Fils et du Saint-Esprit, Amen.

»Le sang est plus épais que l'eau«

Helmut Keiner

»Le sang est plus épais que l'eau«, c'est la traduction littérale d'un proverbe allemand. J'ai consulté Wikipedia pour trouver des correspondances ailleurs. Elles existent en anglais, aussi en quelques langues slaves. Je suis sûr qu'il existe un proverbe similaire parmi les 5.000 proverbes en Kinyarwanda que les ethnologues ont déjà répertoriés. Le sens est clair: C'est mon appartenance, ma famille, mes gènes, qui m'influencent. Ils comptent, plus que toutes les autres loyautés et obligations et relations.

»Le sang est plus épais que l'eau de baptême?« Est-ce que c'est vrai aussi? L'expérience amère des Rwandais après le génocide était: Tout ce qu'on avait appris de Jésus ne comptait plus, il y a vingt ans. Beaucoup s'interrogeaient: »Pourquoi une telle catastrophe chez nous, chez un peuple chrétien à quatre-vingt pour cent?«

C'est apparemment une expérience universelle humaine: Notre identité est formée par notre appartenance à la famille, à notre promotion de classe d'école, notre région, notre ethnie, bien sûr notre religion, notre soutien à tel ou tel club de football, et j'en passe…

En Europe ce réflexe d'appartenance est (ou semble être !) dans la plupart des cas quelque chose de folklorique. On fait des blagues là dessus. Cependant, en Afrique, sans caisse sociale, sans mutuelle de maladie, sans assurance contre le chômage et contre toutes les autres catastrophes de la vie, c'est une question de survie d'être membre d'un réseau d'entraide. La relation de sang est mon destin. Après le génocide quelques centaines de mille Rwandais se sont retrouvés seuls, sans aucun réseau social, une expérience sociale jamais connue auparavant dans une société africaine.

Dans la biographie de Bonhoeffer on peut compter deux grands tournants. Je commence par le deuxième: En été 1939 il était à New York, pour donner quelques conférences et rencontrer ses anciens amis. On pouvait déjà ressentir le début de la guerre en Europe. Ses amis suppliaient Bonhoeffer de ne plus rentrer dans l'Allemagne des Nazis: »Tu trouveras facilement une paroisse ou un poste de professeur dans une de nos facultés de théologie!« Bonhoeffer répondit: »Je dois rentrer dans ma patrie, chez moi, chez mes compatriotes et partager le destin de mon peuple.« Il rentra à Bremerhaven avec un des derniers navires, juste avant le début de la deuxième guerre mondiale, le 1er Septembre 1939.

Et le premier tournant dans sa vie, il se produisit quelques années auparavant, en 1932. Bonhoeffer avait obtenu une bourse du Conseil œcuménique, pour une année à New York dans la faculté de Théologie protestante du »Union Theological Seminary«. Là, il rencontra un jeune Français, Jean Lasserre, boursier comme lui. Tous les deux avaient perdu des membres proches de leurs familles dans la Grande Guerre. Bonhoeffer, issu d'une famille de la haute bourgeoisie allemande, avait, comme presque chaque protestant allemand, une position nationaliste: »Les vainqueurs de la Guerre Mondiale de 1914 à 1918 avaient forcé l'Allemagne à accepter le honteux et humiliant traité de Versailles.« Lasserre par contre, était pacifiste. Il avait déjà travaillé comme pasteur dans le milieu ouvrier des mines de charbon au Nord de la France. Ces deux jeunes hommes étaient obligés à habiter pour une année dans le même couloir à l'internat du Union College à New York. Malgré leurs appartenances si différentes ils sont devenus des grands amis. Ils se sont influencés, ils »se sont apprivoisés mutuellement«, comme Frédéric Rognon l'écrit dans sa biographie sur Bonhoeffer.

Quel est ce problème du besoin d'appartenance à son groupe, son réseau, son milieu social, son pays ?

Apparemment chaque groupe (ou presque chaque groupe!) développe un côté extérieur froid et hostile. Apparemment il n'existe pas de solidarité à l'intérieur sans méfiance, dénigrement, hostilité vers l'extérieur, vers les autres. »Il n'est pas de chez nous !« Ca suffit comme argument. Fin de la discussion. Arriver à la solidarité à l'intérieur du groupe, ça se fait au prix de l'hostilité, voire même la haine contre ceux de l'extérieur.

Pire encore: Ce mécanisme peut facilement être manipulé et instrumentalisé pour des objectifs sinistres. Comme le Rwanda l'a vécu il y a vingt ans. Et dans la région des Grands Lacs les exemples nous préoccupent jusqu'à aujourd'hui.

Et nous les chrétiens ? Est-ce que nous n'avons aucune chance de développer un esprit différent, un esprit de respect et d'amour du prochain, qui dépasse les limites de l'appartenance à son groupe. Est-ce que le sang est toujours plus épais, aussi plus épais que l'eau du baptême ? Que faire ?

Regardons dans l'histoire de Jésus. Curieusement on constate que Jésus a partagé les réflexes identitaires humains de son peuple juif. Deux exemples: Il dit à la femme Samaritaine (Jean 4) »Il faut adorer Dieu à Jérusalem. Car le salut vient des Juifs.« Et à la femme étrangère au-delà de la frontière au Nord d'Israël, il dit: »Il n'est pas bien de prendre le pain des enfants et de le jeter aux chiens.« »C'est vrai, Maître, dit la femme, pourtant même les chiens mangent les miettes qui tombent de la table de leurs maîtres.« Jésus est ému et touché par la foi et la persévérance de cette femme et guérit sa fille. (Matthieu 15, 21-28)

Jésus dépasse les réflexes identitaires au cours de son ministère et quand il commence son chemin vers Jérusalem, où son destin se décidera de faire la paix entre Dieu et l'humanité et entre les hommes, il a trouvé une clarté et une détermination, qu'il enseigne aussi à ces disciples. C'est une petite histoire dans les Evangiles, peu connue, qui reflète l'évolution de la pensée, le développement en lui. Nous la lisons en Luc 9, les versets 51 à 56:

Lorsque le moment approcha où Jésus devait être enlevé (au ciel), il décida fermement de se rendre à Jérusalem. Il envoya des messagers devant lui. Ceux-ci partirent et entrèrent dans un village des Samaritains pour lui préparer une auberge. Mais les habitants refusèrent de le recevoir parce qu'il se dirigeait vers Jérusalem. Quand les disciples Jacques et Jean apprirent cela, ils dirent: »Seigneur, veux-tu que nous commandions au feu de descendre du ciel et de les exterminer ?« Jésus se tourna vers eux et leur fit des reproches et dit: »Vous ne savez pas à quel esprit vous appartenez. Car le Fils de l'homme n'est pas venu pour détruire les vies des hommes, mais pour les sauver.« Et ils allèrent dans un autre village.

Quelques remarques pour mieux comprendre. Verset 51: Luc raconte tout son Évangile comme un trajet vers Jérusalem, là où se décidera son destin et le salut du Monde et de l'Humanité. Comme chaque Juif qui se respecte, il sait qu'on ne passe pas par la Samarie, pour aller à Jérusalem. On fait un grand détour par la vallée du Jourdan ou par la route le long de la Méditerranée. Versets 52 et 53: C'est un grand groupe qui est en voyage. Jésus envoie deux des ses amis, qui marchent un peu plus vite que les autres. Arrivés au premier village sur leur chemin, ils vont d'une maison à l'autre, frappent aux portes pour demander un hébergement. Partout on refuse. On se reconnaît aux dialectes, les Juifs et Samaritains. Ces deux peuples étaient des peuples-frères avec la même histoire, la même langue, la même culture et surtout la même foi en Jahvé, le dieu d'Abraham. Mais on était lié l'un à l'autre par une aversion, un mépris séculaire. Verset 54: Les disciples veulent même manipuler Dieu pour leur vengeance.

On peut observer deux décisions de Jésus qui aident ses disciples à dépasser cette attitude, on pourrait dire »baptiser« le réflexe identitaire.

La première décision: Il était impossible de traverser la Samarie dans une journée de marche à pied. On devait nécessairement passer une nuit quelque part dans les habitations des Samaritains. En choisissant le chemin à travers la région des Samaritains, il se fait volontairement dépendant de la bonne volonté et l'aide des »autres«. Dans une relation conflictuelle, se montrer dans une position de faiblesse, faire appel à leur aide, à leur générosité est une méthode bien délibérée, que nous découvrons ici.

La deuxième décision: Verset 56 »Et ils allèrent dans un autre village.« Jésus n'entre pas en conflit, il ne riposte pas. Et cela n'est pas de la lâcheté. Il met fin au cercle vicieux éternel: l'action méchante, riposte, vengeance. Luc ne raconte pas, s'ils ont été mieux reçus dans un autre village.

Il est vrai: Les méthodes de Jésus comportent des risques. Elles exigent un grand courage et une grande détermination. Jésus pose la question à ces disciples et il la pose aussi à nous: »Qu'est-ce que vous avez appris de moi en suivant mes traces. De quel esprit êtes-vous animés ?«

Je connais un pasteur rwandais, un grand ami, qui m'a dit en 1994, il y a quelques mois après le génocide: »J'ai honte de chanter dans nos cultes et prières le chant connu et aimé par les chrétiens Rwandais 'Jye nd'Umukristo', 'Je suis un chrétien'. On devrait chanter plutôt 'Jye nd'Umuhutu' – 'Je suis Hutu' ou 'Jye nd'Umututsi' – 'Je suis Tutsi'« Je rêve du moment où nous pourrons chanter avec joie et d'un cœur soulagé:

»Jye nd'Umukristo, nzahora ndi we. Mu bintu byose ngeze ku gupfa?« – »Je suis un chrétien. Je le resterai toujours, dans toutes les circonstances, jusqu'a la mort.«

The Church Response on the issue of justice

Thérèse Mukamakuza

The Text: Matthew 5:13-16

In simple words Justice is to give everyone his due, justice is God's nature whereby he is carried to the doing of which is righteous and equal. Justice is one of the essences of God, he revealed himself to us as God of justice.

With the fact that God's nature is justice, it is our responsibility also as a Church and Christians to carry out God's mission to practice justice to the world. Therefore *justice should be the heart of the Church*; the Church mission is to reverse alienation, oppression and injustice in exercising love, enabling forgiveness and seeking justice.

The Church may be in the world with all implies but as Paul insisted, it is not meant to conform to values and strategies that conflict the Gospel (Rom 12, 1-2), in Jesus words, the Church is called *to be salt and the light of the world, and it cannot really make a difference to the world if it lose its taste*.

Of course, the church is not an entity separate from the world but deeply embedded in its life. It is a community within a wider society. As such, the church is part of the world, an institution comprised of men and women who are in the world, the church shares its sin and suffering, its struggles and its hopes with the world. It cannot be otherwise. This explains in part the ambiguities that surround its witnesses.

Nevertheless the church of God is holy, it has the holy mission, it is committed to a particular mission of the world. It should speak out on the general goals that a society should pursue.

In his essay »the church and the Jewish question« Bonhoeffer views the Church as »compelled (obliged) to speak« to the state, when there is *either too much law or order and too little law and order*. He goes on explaining that too little law and order permits lawlessness, means that the »state develops its power to such an extent that it denies Christian preaching and Christian faith or their rights.« For Bonhoeffer, *preaching is essential to the state's well-being because the state receives its authority from God and must not »enthrone itself«*. Since the state's origin is divine, Bonhoeffer asserts that the church knows better than the state what the state's legitimate actions are. As strange as it sounds to us here, Bonhoeffer looks at the Jewish Question from the perspective that the church knows better than the state how to apply justice, and it is in the state's interest not to limit the church's freedom to preach and practice Christianity.

The gospel is the state's life blood and if the state cuts this off, then the state dies and becomes ludicrous. *The state needs the church to correct it when it practices injustice.*

The conclusions that Bonhoeffer reaches from this is that there are three ways in which the church can act toward the state when the church finds that the state is acting unjustly:

- First, the church can ask the state to examine its actions in light of justice. In so doing, the church simply reminds the state of its moral responsibility to provide justice for those living within its boarder.
- If the state continues to act unjustly, then secondly, the church must aid the victims of injustice because Christians have »an unconditional obligation to the victims, even if they do not belong to the Christian community«. Here the church places itself in harm's way by demonstrating love in action (justice toward the neighbor).
- But if the injustice continues, then the third and final step for the church is »not just to bandage the victims under the wheel, but to jam a spoke in the wheel itself«.

The church then becomes a political actor and enters the struggle for justice in a confrontational manner. This, says Bonhoeffer, can happen when there is too little law and order so that a group of citizens has its rights destroyed and when there is too much law and order so that the state interferes with the church's proclamation of the gospel.

Thus it is in the best interest of the state for the Christian faith to be proclaimed radically and for Christians to act on behalf of the victims of state persecution.

But what happens, when church fails its mission, when it loses prophetical voice, as we have seen in genocide of Jewish and Rwandans, in apartheid system where the church serves as social domination and its power is used by the politicians to oppress the powerless? In Karios document, South African theologians call it *State Theology* defined as a *theological justification* of the status quo with its racism, capitalism and totalitarianism. It does this by misusing theological concepts and biblical texts for its own political purposes.

Rwanda is an example of power used for evil during genocide. That time Rwanda was regarded as one of the most Christian countries in Africa and even in the whole world. Statistically speaking 80 to 90% of the population regarded themselves as Christians. However this big number of Christians and their power as people of God did not stop genocide to happen. Rather it became a tool of evil – church members participated in genocide tragedy.

According to some estimates, more people were killed in the church compounds than somewhere else. Numerous Tutsi priests, Pastors brothers and sisters were killed by their own parishioners and fellow Christians. During genocide some people were coming to mass or worship services each day to pray and after mass went out to work (kill). Some pastors, priests and evangelist went far to say that *God let Tutsi die*, so there is no sin to kill them. They found theological justification for killing their fellow Christians.

For sure, when injustice and oppression emerged even in the church structures, God's people don't see any sign of the Kingdom of God. Their hope and faith only refer to afterworld. This is seen through songs sung in the church and sermon preached where Christians are in hurry going to heaven, where they believe that there will be no injustice.

However, as Christians we have to remember that the Kingdom of God starts here and we were given the responsibilities *to bring the light and be the salt of the world*, to transform the world into justice so that we can enjoy it while we prepare for the future fulfillment.

As individuals, Christians are called to be responsible for justice, peace and reconciliation and the church should work with the state for the wellbeing of the society, however should not accept to be used as a tool of injustice, oppression and any other kind of evil. Rather the church needs to take a distance and a critical approach of solidarity. It needs to keep a distance with a prophetical voice in order to challenge any kind of injustice and appreciation that can occur.

Dietrich Bonhoeffer states that the Christians should take *a stronger stand in favour of the weak rather than considering first the possible right of the strong*.

Moreover he adds that the followers of Christ have been called to love, to do justice and to be peace makers. And to that end they renounce all violence and war and hatred even if it can cost one's life. After all there are some things for which it pays to engage you without compromise.

The Bonhoeffer left this world with these words to a fellow prisoner:

»This is the end. For me the beginning of life«

Let us stand for peace and justice which is why we are called to be Christians and followers of Christ.

Amen

Meditation

Jan Habinshuti van Schaardenburgh

0. We sung »Morning has broken« 3 verses, in english and also in german.

1. *»Bavandimwe, – tuv'inda imwe«*: In the Rwandese church we address each other with *one* word: bavandimwe, that indicates both, brothers *and* sisters, as it indicates that we all are *»originating from the same womb«*! In fact using this term is like a confession of faith: all that separates human-beings is overcome in Christ.

2. Let us pray the so-called »prayer of Franciscus of Assisi«, that has been formulated, as it seems, during the Great War (WorldWar I), »Lord, make me an instrument of Thy peace...«

Mwami, - umpindure igikoresho cy'amahoro yawe, - reka mbe uwo kubiba urukundo ahari urwango, - imbabazi aho abantu bakomeretsanya, - kwizera ahari ugushidikanya, - ibyiringiro ahari ugushoberwa, - umucyo ahari icuraburindi, - umunezero ahari umubabaro. - Data buja Mana yanjye, - reka nite ku guhumuriza aho guhumurizwa, - kumva kurusha kumvwa, - gukunda aho gukundwa. – Kuko mu gutanga turahabwa, - mu kubabarira twakira imbabazi, - mu gupfa tuzavukira ubuzima bw'iteka ryose. – Amen.

3. Dietrich Bonhoeffer's life is marked by his basic confidence and trust in God. We are no Bonhoeffers but also each one of us has received gifts of the Holy Spirit. How will we endure? With all the problems and challenges that surround us? Or that we perceive in our own live's history? Let us read *Psalm 131* – where David expresses his basic confidence in God:

Uhoraho, sindi umwirasi, - nta n'ubwo nishyira hejuru. – Sinivanga mu bitandeba, - nta n'ubwo nivanga mu bindenze. – Ahubwo ndatuza nkicecekera, - meze nk'incuke yigwanditse kuri nyina, - koko ntuje nk'umwana w'incuke. – Mwa Bisiraeli mwe, nimwiringire Uhoraho, - nimumwiringire kuva ubu kugeza iteka ryose.

Tube abanyamahoro, that are basically inspired by confidence in Gods motherly and fatherly love. Simplicity, Quietness and Confidence, as a little child with its mother. On such basis it is possible to take repons-ability for the world that surrounds us.

4. *»Salt«***.** For Bonhoeffer the sermon on the mountain is our guideline. Pastor Therese has meditated this week on our qualification to be 'salt' in the world (Matt. 5). It reminded me a proverbe cited by Pastor Byangamvuga Gabriel at a retreat for pastors in 1984:

»Uwo umwami asiza umunyu, bamurigata bose.« (»if somebody is overloaded with salt by the king, all will come to lick him«). If we are impregnated by Gods love, it makes us attractive. Bonhoeffer has expressed his thoughts about the world not as an opposite to the church, but as the place where God is to be discovered, especially among the vulnerable. He is already present. And we are called upon to follow Him.

If we live a life of confidence (Ps 131) people will experience the presence of His love.

5. *»Urukundo rumar'ubwoba«* The sermon on the mountain is to do and to be done. '*Love overcomes fear*'. Love your neighbour – (s)he is as you are! Love your enemy – (s)he is as you are! Overcoming our fears opens a path to peace in our personal life and in society, it gives the ability to respond (reponsability). Let us read again Ps. 131, and now in english.

6. *»Friendship«.* We know so much about Dietrich Bonhoeffer thanks to Eberhard Bethge. Bonhoeffer's letters in »Widerstand und Ergebung« were written in prison, in the cellar in Tegel, Berlin. Eberhard served in the German army in Italy. Their correspondence kept on, notwithstanding distance and time. Bonhoeffer writes about his (new) intuitions and the thoroughly felt lack of a partner nearby to discuss his »rude« thoughts that need still to be developed properly. But then he expresses also his great gratitude that their friendship exists already more than 10 years. And that he is glad that Eberhard takes note of his questions and reflections, even if they are not yet »ripe«. And he continues to say that even if he might not survive the war, the Holy Spirit will be there to take care that what is useful and fruitful in his thinking will be developed and achieved. A friend, trustful and full of understanding is a big treasure in life!

7. Let us pray – partly in silence. The Lord's prayer will be sung in kinyarwanda, and then we will have some minutes of silence, where everybody can meditate and pray in her/his own way. Softly we will then start to sing »Kumbaya my Lord«, to expand slowly more and more our voices.

Data wa twese uri mu ijuru – izina ryawe ryubahwe ku isi yose – ubwami bwawe buze hose – icyo ushaka bibeho ku isi nkuko bibaho mu ijuru – uduhe none ibyokurya byacu bya uyu munsi – utubabarira ibyaha byacu, nkuko natwe tubabarira abatugiriye nabi – ntuduhane mu bitwoshya, ahubwo udukiz'Umubi. Kuko ubwami, n'ububasha, n'icyubahiro ari ibyawe, none n'iteka ryose. Amina (2x) bitinze bizaza Amina (2x) Urukundo rumar ubwoba, none n'iteka ryose! Amina (3x)

8. Imana iduhe twese umugisha wayo! God may bless us all!

Méditation

Jörg Zimmermann

Quand on est prié de diriger une prière, il se pose toujours une question: quel texte biblique faut-il choisir comme base du message? En tant que chrétiens, nous nous nourrissons par la Parole Divine! Mais ce n'est pas toujours facile de savoir quel texte biblique est adéquat dans quelle situation.

En Allemagne, nous avons une habitude de nous tirer d'affaire devant cette tâche: nous aimons prendre des versets qu'on a obtenus à travers un tirage au sort: pour chaque jour, une commission de la Communauté Morave de Herrnhut tire au hasard un verset de l'Ancien Testament, et puis on choisit un verset du Nouveau Testament qui va bien avec celui de l'Ancien Testament qu'on a obtenu par le tirage au sort. J'aimerais mettre en pratique cette méthode aujourd'hui, tout en faisant confiance à l'Esprit-Saint qu'Il nous fasse parvenir le message dont nous avons besoin ici et maintenant! Et qu'est-ce qu'on nous propose pour aujourd'hui? D'abord, c'est *Ésaie 43,11* où Dieu dit à son peuple d'Israël:

»C'est moi, moi, qui suis l'Éternel, et hors de moi, il n'y a point de Sauveur.«

Au premier moment après avoir lu ce verset, j'ai hésité: c'est un message très sévère qui semble ne pas vraiment correspondre à notre époque actuelle dont je dirais qu'elle est plutôt une époque de dialogue et de tolérance! Ce verset provoque parce qu'il nous présente un Dieu qui réclame être le seul Dieu qui mérite ce nom et ce titre. Comment pouvons-nous entrer en débat avec d'autres gens en leur présentant notre Dieu d'une façon si intolérante?

Néanmoins, je trouve que la Bible mérite toujours une méditation plus profonde. Notre impression spontanée n'est pas toujours justifiée quand nous nous donnons la peine de regarder de près. Et c'est juste ça que j'aimerais faire avec nous maintenant:

Posons-nous la question suivante: Qu'est-ce qui pousse Dieu à se réclamer le seul Dieu? Est-ce que c'est l'orgueil? L'égomanie? Ou ne serait-ce pas plutôt l'annonce du salut qu'Il apporte à son peuple?!

Pour mieux comprendre ce qui pousse Dieu à cette mise en scène sûre de soi, il vaut bien expliquer le contexte du verset: le peuple d'Israël a été terriblement battu par les Babyloniens. Ceux-ci ont détruit Jérusalem, y compris le temple, et ils ont déporté l'élite des Israëlites chez eux, en Babylonie. Humainement parlé, le people d'Israël était achevé. À la destruction s'était ajouté la déportation, donc la dispersion. Il n'y avait plus de raison d'espérer que ce peuple pouvait un jour avoir un avenir. Aux yeux de tous, c'était la fin!

Aux yeux de tous – sauf quelques prophètes parmi lesquels nous comptons le

»deuxième Ésaie« qui est supposé être l'auteur des chapitres 40-55 de ce livre biblique d'Ésaie. C'est à lui que Dieu a confié un message de réconfort et de consolation pour son peuple qui a tant souffert. Un message qui ne paraît presque plus crédible mais qui se révélera vrai dans l'avenir:

Aujourd'hui, nous pouvons nous poser la question: Qu'est-ce qu'est devenue la puissante Babylonie? On ne la trouve plus que dans les livres historiques! Comme les autres puissances de l'histoire: l'Assyrie, la Perse, voire même Rome! (Et soyez sûrs que tous ceux qui se réclament très puissants actuellement, ils trouveront le même destin!)

Par contre: sans vouloir entrer en profondeur dans la situation très difficile et compliquée d'Israël dans nos jours, nous voyons que la Bible nous présente un Dieu qui s'adonne aux peuples qui souffrent, aux gens en détresse qui ne voient devant eux que la mort! Le peuple d'Israël en a toujours été le grand témoin! Il a – malgré des épreuves presqu'indicibles! – survécu là où personne n'y aurait plus cru du tout, alors que les soi-disant »grands« du monde ont péri plus vite qu'ils ne le pensaient!

Et ceci nous amène à Dietrich Bonhoeffer: les national-socialistes, qui, eux-aussi, se croyaient tout-puissants à leur époque, voulaient le faire disparaître violemment. Et en le tuant, ils ont réussi – aux yeux du monde. Mais après sa mort, Les écrits de Bonhoeffer ont produit des effets incroyables, sa théologie a trouvé d'énormes répercussions jusqu'à nous rassembler ici au cœur de l'Afrique pour étudier ses réflexions théologiques! Dieu ne lui a pas épargné son sort brutal et déplorable, mais il lui a donné un »au-delà«, si je peux dire ainsi, dont ceux qui l'ont tué n'avaient pas la moindre idée!

Encore une fois sans entrer en profondeur: Ne serait-ce pas aussi un message consolateur et fortifiant pour le Rwanda après toutes les souffrances qui ont frappé ce pays? Ces jours-ci, nous en parlerons certainement encore…

Si nous regardons l'histoire du peuple d'Israël, l'histoire de Dietrich Bonhoeffer et aussi la tragédie rwandaise dans la lumière de la parole divine, nous arrivons à nous poser une question inévitable: N'est-ce pas très difficile de comprendre un tel Dieu? Oui, c'est difficile, avec nos moyens humains c'est même impossible! Mais regardons encore une fois cette parole de l'Ancien Testament qui nous a été donnée pour ce jour-ci: *»C'est moi, moi, qui suis l'Éternel, et hors de moi, il n'y a point de Sauveur.« (Esaie 43,11)* Et écoutons maintenant aussi la parole du Nouveau Testament qui a été choisie pour compléter et interpréter cette première parole:

»Que le Dieu de notre Seigneur Jésus-Christ, le Père de gloire, vous donne un esprit de sagesse et de révélation qui vous fasse le connaître.« (Ephésiens 1,17)

Certes, nous ne disposons pas d'une méthode pour »déchiffrer« ce Dieu dont nous parle la Bible, mais elle-même nous encourage à faire confiance afin que ce Dieu Lui-même nous guide par son Esprit-Saint à sa connaissance en profondeur!

Amen.

Mot de clôture de la conférence sur la réconciliation et la paix durable à la lumière de la théologie de Dietrich Bonhoeffer

Elisée Musemakweli

La théologie et l'exemple de Dietrich Bonhoeffer ont été une des bases solides de la reconstruction des églises en Allemagne après leur déconstruction et la destruction de la société allemande causées par le régime nazi et la deuxième guerre mondiale. Aujourd'hui, nous voulons nous inspirer de cette théologie pour reconstruire la société rwandaise et notre sous-région des grands lacs mises à mal par le génocide de 1994 contre les Tutsi et les guerres à répétition.

Mais la reconstruction ne peut être entreprise si on n'a pas fait une analyse approfondie des causes qui sont à l'origine de la destruction. Le génocide qui s'est passé au Rwanda tout comme les guerres dans la sous-région ne sont pas des accidents de l'histoire, mais des faits préparés à l'avance et mis en exécution au vue et au su de tous. La reconstruction de la paix doit alors commencer par mettre en évidence les causes qui sont à la base de ces situations extrêmes. L'analyse des soubassements de ces drames est un passage obligé pour la reconstruction d'une paix durable pour notre sous-région.

Permettez-moi juste d'évoquer une de ces causes:

Une des causes du drame rwandais est la perte du sens de la communauté. Je dis bien »perte« parce que dans le Rwanda ancien, la »communauté« était le pilier de la vie individuelle et de la société tout entière. C'est lorsque le sens communautaire est devenu caduque et la dimension spirituelle superficielle que la société rwandaise a basculée dans la folie et la tragédie sans nom. Il n'y avait plus de communauté puisqu'il n'y avait plus rien en commun (cf. P. Tillich, *Theology of Peace*, p.65). Chacun est alors devenu l'ennemi de l'autre. Toutes les valeurs humaines, sociales et culturelles qu'on avait jusque là partagées et qui constituaient le socle de la vie des Rwandais ont alors volé en éclats.

Paradoxalement, la foi chrétienne, considérée depuis longtemps comme rempart de notre vie dans le monde du péché, n'a été d'aucun secours, l'ethnicisme et la haine de l'autre ont remporté sur l'amour fraternel et nos convictions chrétiennes. Les églises et toute la société rwandaise avaient perdu le sens de la communauté et de la solidarité humaine. Le Rwanda post-génocide est donc malade.

Mais comme le dit bien Paul Tillich, »il y a dans chaque nation les éléments porteurs de salut. S'il n'y avait pas de puissance de salut dans ces nations, elles disparaîtraient toutes«. (cité par Elisée Musemakweli, *Dynamique de la prédication en Afrique*, p. 247).

C'est pourquoi le Rwanda existe encore et cherche des voies et moyens pour rétablir sa cohésion, grâce à certains de ses éléments culturels qui avaient été simplement ignorés et mis sous l'éteignoir.

Mais pour les chrétiens et les églises, nous pouvons aussi redécouvrir le sens de la communauté en nous inspirant de l'enseignement et de la théologie de Dietrich Bonhoeffer, lui, qui avait le sens aigu de la communauté. Pour lui, la vraie communauté est celle des frères et sœurs dont le Christ est le centre. Cette communauté est irriguée et vit par la prière. Nous ne pouvons pas nous mettre au service de la réconciliation et construire une paix durable, si nous n'avons pas encore redécouvert le sens de la solidarité humaine et de la vie communautaire.

Quel doit être notre réponse à cette tragédie humaine et à la situation de précarité que vivent nos peuples? Il y en beaucoup, mais permettez-moi d'évoquer deux d'entre elles:

La première réponse est bien entendu notre engagement dans la lutte contre le mal en suivant l'exemple de D. Bonhoeffer. Comme le dit bien Frédéric Rognon, dans son livre consacré à la vie et à la pensée de Dietrich Bonhoeffer, »nous n'avons peut-être pas besoin d'un nouveau Bonhoeffer, mais les questions qu'il posait aux chrétiens et à l'Église, il y a 70 ans restent de mise pour aujourd'hui.«[1]. Nous devons leur trouver des réponses. Pourquoi y a-t-il tant de mal et d'injustice dans notre monde? Quel est le rapport entre notre foi et notre vie? Si la vie chrétienne est une affaire de conviction, pourquoi alors agissons-nous contre notre propre conviction? Telles sont certaines de ces questions paraphrasées. Le génocide de 1994 au Rwanda a mis au défi notre foi et nos convictions les plus profondes. Il a ébranlé tous nos fondements spirituels et culturels et mis en lambeaux toutes nos valeurs. Comment redevenir chrétien et parler encore de Dieu dans un tel contexte? Comment interpréter le silence de Dieu face à la haine déchaînée de l'homme? Tous ceux qui s'engagent contre le mal et l'injustice doivent-ils finir comme D. Bonhoeffer assassinés, tués de façon si atroce? Telles sont les questions auxquelles nous devons trouver des réponses aujourd'hui.

La deuxième réponse est le refus de la vengeance. L'évocation de la mémoire ne signifie pas faire revivre la violence à travers la vengeance. Théologiquement et anthropologiquement parlant, dans l'évocation de la mémoire, nous puisons une force morale et spirituelle qui nous aide à reconstruire notre présent et le futur de nos enfants. De telles occasions sont des occasions de »kairos«, c'est-à-dire des occasions propices pour le changement, pour la renaissance. Nous devons donc les saisir sans hésiter et les utiliser pour la reconstruction des sociétés où chacun trouve son compte.

Je voudrais conclure en citant Julius Nyerere, le premier président tanzanien qui

[1] Frédéric Rognon: Dietrich Bonhoeffer, Olivetan 2011, 144.

a dit: »A moins que l'Eglise participe activement dans la lutte contre toutes ces structures et organisations qui condamnent les gens à la pauvreté et à la dégradation, l'Église sera sans aucune importance«.

De même une telle conférence sera sans effet, si les chrétiens et les églises ne fassent pas leur propre introspection et ne s'engagent pas résolument dans la lutte pour la paix durable au Rwanda et dans le reste de l'Afrique.

Final Statement[1]

As theologians, church leaders, students and other engaged Christians from various countries of Africa and Europe we have assembled in Karongi/Rwanda on Feb 25-28 2014 for an International Conference to discuss the legacy of German Theologian Dietrich Bonhoeffer for Peace and Reconciliation in the European and African context and beyond.

We have heard stories about suffering of people in Germany under the Nazi regime, in Rwanda during the keep a raisonnablegenocide and in Congo today – stories of victims of grave violence. We have listened to the witness of Dietrich Bonhoeffer in his plea for peace and justice in the time of the Nazi regime. We have been touched by the culpability confessions of churches in Germany and in Rwanda and by Bonhoeffer himself. We have gladly learned about examples of forgiveness and reconciliation between former enemies.

We have learned from Dietrich Bonhoeffer that it is the obligation of the churches to stand up for the victims and be a strong voice in the public when injustice happens. We pledge to encourage our churches to become public churches which witness to the gospel not only in our personal lives but also in politics and society.

Churches should not shy away from politics but at the same time should not to be swallowed by it. In relation to politics, the church should keep a reasonable and critical distance. We need a Public Theology which teaches us to bear witness in the public square.

We are worried about the ongoing war in the region in which we have come together. Many people in Kivu provinces in Congo are indirectly victims of the genocide in Rwanda against the Tutsi in 1994 even today.

Various militias destabilize the region and commit crimes against humanity. A lasting, just peace is the necessary prerequisite to make a life in dignity possible for every person in this region.

Bonhoeffer has taught us that violence cannot create peace. Only trust can make peace possible. We pray to God to stand by those who are victims of violence. We appeal to political leaders in Great Lakes region to make every possible effort to move towards a peaceful development of the region. The international community has the task to support such developments. As churches we must contribute to peace building with all our resources and bring people together to build up trust. We pledge to continue to come together in brotherhood and sis-

[1] For a german translation see also: Schlusserklärung der internationalen Konferenz »Versöhnung und nachhaltiger Frieden – Impulse der Theologie Dietrich Bonhoeffers für den europäischen und afrikanischen Kontext« in Kibuye/Ruanda vom 25. – 28. Februar 2014, in: Ökumenische Rundschau 63/2 (2014), 284-285.

terhood to exchange our experiences and reflections from our different cultural and geographical contexts and thus witness as the community of the church as a sign for a common humanity. We will follow the idea of establishing a Dietrich Bonhoeffer Research Center for Public Theology for Central Africa in Kigali/Rwanda.

In the midst of the challenges to peace and justice we face today, we express our will to the future with the words of Dietrich Bonhoeffer: »It may be that the day of judgment will dawn tomorrow; in that case we will gladly stop working for a better future. But not before.«

Karongi, the 28th of February 2014

Déclaration finale[1]

Nous, théologiens, dirigeants de l'église, étudiants et autres chrétiens engagés en provenance de différents pays d'Afrique et d'Europe, nous sommes réunis à Karongi / Rwanda du 25 au 28 février 2014 lors d'une conférence internationale: nous avons discuté de l'héritage laissé par le théologien allemand Dietrich Bonhoeffer concernant la paix et la réconciliation en Europe, en Afrique et ailleurs dans le monde.

Des personnes en Allemagne sous le régime nazi, au Rwanda pendant le génocide et au Congo aujourd'hui nous ont parlé des douleurs endurées et des violences horribles subies. Nous avons écouté le témoignage de Dietrich Bonhoeffer dans son plaidoyer pour la paix et la justice pendant le régime nazi. Nous avons été touchés par les aveux de culpabilité des églises d'Allemagne et du Rwanda et par Bonhoeffer lui-même. Nous avons entendu avec soulagement et joie les exemples de pardon et de réconciliation entre les anciens ennemis.

Dietrich Bonhoeffer nous a appris que les églises doivent défendre les victimes et dénoncer publiquement à haute voix les injustices. Nous nous engageons à encourager nos églises pour qu'elles deviennent des églises publiques qui témoignent publiquement de l'Évangile, non seulement dans nos vies personnelles, mais aussi dans la vie politique et de la société.

Les églises ne doivent pas fuir la politique, mais elles ne doivent pas non plus se laisser »avaler« par elle. En ce qui concerne la politique l'Eglise doit garder une distance raisonnable et critique. Nous avons besoin d'une théologie publique qui nous apprend à témoigner en public.

La guerre en cours dans la région, où nous nous sommes réunis, nous inquiète beaucoup. Beaucoup de gens des provinces du Kivu au Congo sont devenus indirectement les victimes du génocide perpétré contre les Tutsis en 1994 jusqu'à nos jours.

Plusieurs groupes de miliciens déstabilisent la région et commettent encore des crimes contre l'humanité. Enfin, une paix juste et durable est la pré-condition nécessaire pour que chaque personne puisse vivre dans la dignité dans cette région.

Bonhoeffer nous a enseigné que la violence ne peut pas créer la paix. Seule la confiance peut rendre la paix possible. Nous prions Dieu pour qu'il soutienne les victimes des violences. Nous en appelons aux leaders politiques de la région des grands lacs pour que tous les efforts possibles soient déployés pour établir

---

[1] Pour une traduction en allemande voir aussi: Schlusserklärung der internationalen Konferenz »Versöhnung und nachhaltiger Frieden – Impulse der Theologie Dietrich Bonhoeffers für den europäischen und afrikanischen Kontext« in Kibuye/Ruanda vom 25. – 28. Februar 2014, in: Ökumenische Rundschau 63/2 (2014), 284-285.

une paix durable et la réalisation d'un développement pacifique dans la région. La communauté internationale a le devoir de soutenir ce développement. En tant qu'églises nous devons contribuer à la restauration de la paix avec tous les moyens à notre disposition dans le but d'unir les peuples et de rebâtir la confiance. Nous nous engageons à organiser des réunions dans un esprit de fraternité pour échanger nos expériences et réfléchir chacun à partir de son contexte culturel et géographique et pour délivrer le message que nous sommes une communauté de l'Église et que nous faisons partie de l'humanité commune. Nous poursuivrons l'idée de créer un centre de recherche Dietrich Bonhoeffer sur la théologie publique en Afrique centrale à Kigali au Rwanda.

Devant les défis actuels à l'encontre de la paix et de la justice auxquels nous faisons face, nous réitérons notre volonté de bâtir un avenir inspiré des mots de Dietrich Bonhoeffer: »il peut être possible que le jour du jugement soit demain; dans ce cas nous cesserons avec joie de travailler pour un meilleur avenir, mais pas avant cela.«

Fait à Karongi (Bethanie) le 28 Février 2014

Dictionary of Authors

Prof. Dr. Byaruhanga Rukooko Archangel, Associate Professor at the Department of Philosophy, Makerere University, Kampala (Uganda), formerly Deputy Dean and subsequently Dean at the Faculty of Arts, Makerere University (2004-2014).

Dr. Vincent Muderwa Barhatulirwa, Rev. of the Baptist Church in Democratic Republic of Congo (CBCA), Professor at Université Libre des Pays des Grands Lacs (ULPGL).

Dr. Pascal Bataringaya, President of the Presbyterian Church in Rwanda (EPR) since 2015, who holds a German doctoral degree in Bonhoeffer's ethics.

Prof. Dr. Heinrich Bedford-Strohm, President of the EKD Council (Evangelical Church in Germany), Bishop of the Evangelical Lutheran Church in Bavaria

Jannika Haupt, Assistant Professor at the Chair of Systematic Theology at Ruhr-University Bochum (2009-2015), current Phd-Student at the faculty of Protestant Theology.

Albert Henz, Theological Member of the Governing Church Board of the Evangelical Church of Westphalia and Theological Vice-President of the Evangelical Church of Westphalia (Germany).

PD Dr. Kai Horstmann, Associate Professor for Practical Theology at the University of Saarbrücken, Pastor in Cologne/Bonn (Germany).

Prof. Dr. Traugott Jähnichen, Professor for Christian Social Ethics at Ruhr-University Bochum.

Christine Jürgens, student of protestant theology at the Westfälische Wilhelms-University Münster.

Dr. Jered Kalimba, Bishop of Shyogwe diocese, Anglican Church of Rwanda (EAR).

Helmut Keiner, Pastor of the Evangelical Church in the Rhineland (Neukirchen-Vluyn, Germany), from 1983 to 1991 Pastor of the Presbyterian Church of Rwanda.

Dr. Abednego Keshomshahara, Bishop of North-Western diocese, Evangelical-Lutheran Church of Tanzania (ELCT), Bukoba (Tanzania).

Dr. Ulrich Möller, Member of the Governing Church Board of the Evangelical Church of Westphalia and Head of its Department for Mission, Ecumenism and Global Responsibility.

Thérèse Mukamakuza, Rev., President of Zinga Presbytery, Presbyterian Church of Rwanda (EPR).

Prof. Dr. Elisée Musemakweli, Rev., President of Presbyterian Church in Rwanda (EPR) until 2015, Director (Rector) of PIASS, Protestant Institut of Arts and Social Science, Huye/Rwanda.

Samuel Mutabazi, Rev. of Anglican Church in Rwanda (EAR), Coordinator of BNEP/ Bureau National d'Enseignement Protestant du Conseil Protestant au Rwanda (CPR).

Dr. Katharina Peetz, Assistant Professor at the Chair of Systematic Theology at the University of Saarland.

Jan van Schaardenburgh, Rev of Protestant Protestant Church of the Netherlands, Haaksberg, from 1978 to 1985 Pastor of the Presbyterian Church of Rwanda.

Maximilian Schell, student of protestant theology and psychology at Ruhr-University Bochum, student assistant at the Chair of Christian Social Ethics.

Dr. Christine Schliesser, Assistant Professor at the Center for Ethics at Zurich University.

Dr. Clemens Wustmans, Assistant Professor at the Chair of Christian Social Ethics at Ruhr-University Bochum.

Jörg Zimmermann, Pastor of the Evangelical Church in the Rhineland / Bonn, Germany, from 1991 to 1994 Pastor of the Presbyterian Church of Rwanda.